DIANE ROSSEN WORTHINGTON

The Cuisine of California

CHRONICLE BOOKS

SAN FRANCISCO

Library of Congress
Cataloging-in-Publication Data:

Worthington, Diane Rossen.
     The Cuisine of California / Diane Rossen Worthington
          p.   cm.
     Originally published: 1st ed. Los Angeles : J.P. Tarcher, c1983.
     Includes index.
     I S B N   0 - 8 1 1 8 - 1 6 5 1 - 6   (p b)
     1. Cookery, American—California style.   I. Title.
TX715.2.c34W6723   1997
641.59794—dc21   96-51124
                                                               CIP

Printed in the United States of America.

Recipe Editor: Faye Levy
Wine Consultant: Phillip Reich
Designed by Deborah Bowman
Composition by Deborah Bowman
Cover photograph by Jonelle Weaver

Distributed in Canada by Raincoast Books
8680 Cambie Street
Vancouver, British Columbia V6P 6M9

10 9 8 7 6 5 4 3 2

Chronicle Books
85 Second Street
San Francisco, California
9 4 1 0 5

Web Site: www.chronbooks.com

To Michael, My Husband, with Love and Gratitude.

acknowledgments

TO **MITZI COSTIN**, FOR HER WILLINGNESS TO HELP AT A MOMENT'S NOTICE AND FOR HER SKILLFUL RECIPE TESTING. **ANNE HAFNER**, FOR HER UNENDING PATIENCE IN ORGANIZING AND DECIPHERING MY RECIPES AND FOR HER SUSTAINED PARTICIPATION. **JANICE GALLAGHER**, MY EDITOR, FOR HER GUIDANCE AND BELIEF IN MY IDEA. **CHRONICLE BOOKS**, AND ESPECIALLY **BILL LE BLOND**, **LESLIE JONATH**, AND **SARAH PUTMAN**, FOR BELIEVING IN AND PUBLISHING THIS BOOK TO INSPIRE A NEW GENERATION OF READERS. **DOMINICK ABEL**, FOR ACTING ON MY PROPOSAL AND SMOOTHING THE WAY FOR ITS COMPLETION. **FAYE LEVY**, FOR HER THOROUGH UNDERSTANDING OF CLASSICAL TECHNIQUES AND FOR HER EXCELLENT RECIPE EDITING AND DEVELOPMENT. **PHILLIP REICH**, FOR HIS EXCEPTIONAL KNOWLEDGE OF CALIFORNIA WINES. **BERNARD JACOUPY**, ESPECIALLY, FOR HIS KNOWLEDGE AND CHALLENGING OPINIONS. **BARBARA WINDOM**, FOR SHARING HER STYLE AND FOR TESTING RECIPES EVEN WHEN SHE HAD LITTLE TIME. **CHUCK POLLOCK**, FOR CONTRIBUTING CREATIVE IDEAS. **DENNY LURIA**, FOR HER UNIQUE QUALITY IN ALWAYS GIVING OF HERSELF GENEROUSLY AND FOR HER VALUED INPUT AT EVERY PHASE OF THE PROJECT. **MARY ROSE**, FOR HELPING ME TO CLARIFY THE CONCEPT AND FOR HER CONTINUAL SUPPORT. **LAURIE BURROWS GRAD**, FOR BEING BOTH A FRIEND AND A COLLEAGUE AND FOR PROVING THAT THE TWO CAN WORK TOGETHER. **NANCY HAFFNER**, **LESLIE MARGOLIS**, AND **JOAN FRIEDMAN**, FOR THEIR ONGOING ENCOURAGEMENT. **KAREN** AND **FRIEDA CAPLAN**, LOS ANGELES'S SPECIALTY PRODUCE DISTRIBUTORS, FOR ANSWERING ALL OF MY QUESTIONS AND FOR INFORMING CONSUMERS ABOUT THE NEW VARIETIES OF SPECIALTY PRODUCE BECOMING AVAILABLE ACROSS THE NATION. **CARL SONTHEIMER**, FOR HIS ASSISTANCE. MY PARENTS, **RUTH** AND **ALLAN ROSSEN**, MY SISTER, **MARCINE**, AND MY BROTHERS, **RICHARD** AND **BOB**, FOR THEIR ENCOURAGEMENT. **MICHAEL**, MY HUSBAND, FOR HIS UNWAVERING SUPPORT, PATIENCE, AND WILLINGNESS TO PROVIDE THE WORD PROCESSOR WHENEVER NEEDED! SPECIAL THANKS TO THOSE WHO GAVE THEIR TIME TO TALK TO ME ABOUT CALIFORNIA FOOD: **LAURIE CHENEL**, **MARION CUNNINGHAM**, **JOHN DOWNEY**, **VAL FELICE**, **ROLAND GIBERT**, **MARK HANCOCK**, **MARGARET MALLORY**, **BRUCE MARDER**, **ALICE MEDRICH**, **MARK MILLER**, **JIM PHALAND**, **JUDY RODGERS**, **VERNON** AND **CHARLENE ROLLINS**, **CARYL SAUNDERS**, **JEREMIAH TOWER**, **JANET TREFETHEN**, **PATRICIA UNTERMAN**, AND **JONATHAN WAXMAN**. I ALSO WISH TO THANK **ALICE WATERS** AND **WOLFGANG PUCK**, TWO CALIFORNIA CHEFS WHOSE INNOVATIVE COOKING CONTINUES TO INSPIRE OTHERS IN FURTHERING THIS STYLE OF COOKING.

CONTENTS

INTRODUCTION

Years before I wrote this cookbook in 1983, I began observing certain trends in California cooking. California chefs were venturing down new trails, led by youthful, inquisitive minds. They were moving away from classical rules and rich sauces and toward original combinations and lighter cuisine. Simple techniques such as grilling were growing in popularity as chefs began experimenting with flavors and textures. We began to see California wines appear as both ingredients and accompaniments, along with an astounding array of ethnic and indigenous ingredients.

Underlying this evolution was a growing appreciation for the availability of fresh local produce, herbs, fish, and dairy products. California's unique geographic location and climate allows for seasonal items to be purchased at optimum freshness year-round, giving us a colorful palette from which to choose. Marketing became an integral part of the movement. New specialty items were fast becoming available in California markets, such as scientifically cultivated fresh mushrooms, arugula, and sugar snap peas. But, as we would soon witness, there was much more on the horizon since California cuisine was still in its formative stages.

Over a decade later, the recipes in this book have stood up to the test of time. Some of the restaurants mentioned may have changed names, and some of the chefs may have left the kitchens in which they were working; but their imprint remains and the food they inspired in these recipes is still as fresh as the day I wrote them. There may be a little more butter in these pâtés than some may like, but good-quality olive oil makes a fine substitute without any loss of integrity to the original dish. One thing that has changed is the immense popularity of this California-based style of cooking and the twists and turns it has taken as it has moved across America.

Daring California chefs began experimenting with different combinations, based upon ingredients drawn from Thai, Mexican, Chinese, Middle Eastern, Japanese, French, and Italian cuisines. We were quickly becoming educated on our growing international pantry. Items that once seemed mysterious to Americans have become commonplace in supermarkets, such as shiitake mushrooms, lemongrass, and fresh poblano chiles.

As California's cuisine has matured, so too have the cuisines of areas across the nation. Different regions have developed and refined their own styles of cooking, creating a new modern American cuisine. Ours is a collective journey which takes pride in locally grown foods and embraces the ideas of others. This book offered the first definition of modern California cuisine at a time when California was defining its own regional style and making important ingredient and technique discoveries.

These discoveries proved exciting for both professional and home cooks, and I have been fortunate to have shared in this growth. Through my professional work, I have met people across the country who have cooked out of this book and formed lasting relationships with their favorite recipes. While on vacation in Steamboat Springs, Colorado, in 1990, I met an experienced cook from Ohio who, upon learning I was the author of this book, proceeded to recite all the page numbers of her favorite recipes. Another time, during a radio show in 1995, I mentioned this book and several days later a business associate sent me her original copy, tattered, stained, and worn after years of use. It was the ultimate compliment. To me, these experiences illustrate the widespread appeal of quick, simple recipes that leave lasting impressions.

When I began writing *The Cuisine of California*, there was a true sense of excitement surrounding the food discoveries taking place, and the energy was contagious. An extraordinary cooking movement followed. Today, it is a strong force dedicated to the foundation on which it grew: freshness, simplicity, and creativity. Although the culinary adventure continues, the simplicity of these recipes makes them timeless. So, as you expand your own culinary horizons, have fun with these recipes. Toss in different fresh herbs and spices. Add ingredients indigenous to your area to create variations on a theme. Let your creative juices flow and have fun. After all, that's the spirit of California cuisine.

AUTHOR'S NOTE

In the pages that follow, recipes are organized by course in the order in which they are customarily served. Advance preparation time is provided when possible for the cook's convenience. Wine recommendations are offered in selected chapters and are written in standard wine terminology. A wine glossary is provided.

APPETIZERS AND FIRST COURSES

*I*N CALIFORNIA, APPETIZERS ARE SERVED IN AN INFORMAL MANNER, USUALLY WITH COCKTAILS OR WINE. First courses are more elaborate and are served individually at a table in small portions. Some appetizers can also be served as first courses. Many of the first courses may be served as luncheon entrées in larger portions. Other possibilities for first courses are found in the chapters on Soups; Pasta, Pizza, and Frittatas; and Salads.

Baby Red Potatoes with Caviar

Garden Vegetable Basket

Spicy Lemon Shrimp

Salmon Tartare

Chicken Liver Mousse

Smoked Whitefish Mousse

Smoked Tongue Pâté

Guacamole

Marinated Golden and Red Peppers

Celery Root Terrine

Spinach-Carrot Terrine

Veal and Pork Pâté with Pistachios and Prunes

Carpaccio, California Style

Fresh Tuna with Avocado and Cucumber

Tomatoes with Fresh Mozzarella and Basil

Baked Sonoma Goat Cheese with Emerald Sauce

Olive Oil–Pine Nut Bread

BABY RED POTATOES WITH CAVIAR

Serves 6 to 8

Baby red potatoes are available much of the year in California. Baking them results in a crusty, crunchy skin and a fluffy interior. In this dish the caviar garnish adds an elegant touch. For a truly memorable meal, follow with Beet and Walnut Salad with Blue Cheese, Tenderloin of Beef with Roasted Shallots and Tarragon, and Sauté of Julienned Garden Vegetables. For a light dessert, serve your favorite sorbet in Tulip Cookie Cups.

RECOMMENDED CALIFORNIA WINE:

Serve a dry (brut) California Blanc de Blancs or the subtler Blanc de Noirs. Or serve one of the richer Napa Valley Chardonnays to match the rich flavor of the caviar.

1½ pounds baby red potatoes
   (approximately 12 to 16)
2 tablespoons oil
½ cup sour cream

1 teaspoon finely chopped chives
¼ teaspoon salt
Pinch of coarsely cracked black pepper

FOR GARNISH:

¼ cup sour cream
2 ounces any variety caviar or fish roe
1 tablespoon fresh dill sprigs (optional)

1 Preheat oven to 475°F. Place potatoes on a baking sheet and bake for 45 to 50 minutes, depending on size. Prick with a knife or skewer to test for doneness. They should be cooked through and slightly crisp.

2 Remove from oven and let cool. Cut in half and scoop out potato pulp, leaving a thin layer of pulp attached to skins. Brush potato skins with oil and place skin-side down on baking sheet. Bake for 10 to 15 minutes, or until crisp.

3 Mix together potato pulp, sour cream, chives, salt, and pepper. With a pastry bag fitted with the medium star tip, pipe potato pulp back into crisp shells.

4 Reduce oven temperature to 425°F. Place potatoes in oven for 10 to 15 minutes, or until heated through. Transfer to serving dish and garnish each with a dollop of sour cream, spoonful of caviar, and sprig of dill, if desired.

May be prepared up to 4 hours ahead through Step 3. Cover and keep at room temperature.

❧

GARDEN VEGETABLE BASKET

Serves as many as desired

Picture a basket filled with the freshest of garden vegetables: bright red baby tomatoes, crunchy white jicama, pale green asparagus, yellow bell peppers—availability should be the only limit to your selection. Make sure to vary the colors, tastes, and textures of the vegetables you choose. Allow ⅛ to ¼ pound of each vegetable per person, and arrange them in a dish, basket, or tray. I like to serve big bowls of Spinach-Watercress Sauce or Cucumber-Mustard Dill Sauce as accompanying dips.

One of the lighter Chardonnays works well (for example, Napa or Santa Barbara County), or try a crisp, fresh Fumé Blanc. The fresh, light wine flavors bring out the vegetables' freshness.

Baby asparagus spears, whole stalk
   removed if tough
French green beans, cleaned,
   ends removed, left whole
Broccoli, cut into florets
Green, yellow, or red bell peppers,
   seeded and cut into strips
Carrots, peeled and cut into sticks
Cauliflower, cut into small florets

Celery, peeled and cut into sticks
Chinese long string beans, cleaned, ends
   removed, cut into 3-inch lengths
Chinese snow peas, cleaned, string
   removed, left whole
European cucumber, cut into sticks
Belgian endive, wiped clean, leaves
   separated
Fennel bulb, cut into sticks or slices

Whole red cabbage
Red leaf lettuce
Parsley sprigs

Spicy Red Salsa (page 282)

Spinach-Watercress Sauce (page 291)

Fennel Sauce (page 292)

Fresh Garlic Mayonnaise (page 288)

Spicy Garlic Mayonnaise (page 289)

Cucumber-Mustard Dill Sauce (page 292)

1 Prepare vegetables as desired. A serrated cutter makes an attractive edge for the vegetable sticks.

2 Cook green beans, Chinese long string beans, and sugar snap peas, if desired, in separate pans of boiling water for 1 minute. Cool quickly by running cold water over each vegetable.

3 Slice the top off red cabbage. Use a grapefruit knife to cut out center portion, then scoop out with a spoon. Fill with desired dipping sauce. If preparing more than one sauce, spoon remaining sauces into bowls.

4 Line a basket with red leaf lettuce, allowing leaves to extend over the edge. Arrange cabbage in center. Arrange each type of vegetable in mounds in a concentric, geometric, or other decorative pattern and separate with parsley sprigs.

ADVANCE PREPARATION:

The basket may be kept up to 4 hours in refrigerator. Wet paper towels should be placed on top to prevent dryness. If vegetables are left at room temperature, they should be sprayed periodically with a fine mist of water.

SPICY LEMON SHRIMP

Serves 4 to 6

This spicy shrimp works equally well as an appetizer or as a first course. While a traditional shrimp cocktail relies on heavy tomato sauce, this California variation combines dry white wine and lemon to enhance rather than disguise the natural sweetness of the shrimp. The red pepper, onion, and black olives not only add to the taste but provide color and texture as well. Serve with cocktails or wine, or as a first course.

A crisp Fumé Blanc plays up the lemony tang of this dish. You can also serve a medium-bodied Chardonnay.

1 pound large or medium raw
   shrimp (approximately 14-16 large
   or 30 medium)
1 cup water
1 cup dry white wine
1 bay leaf

1 small red bell pepper, seeded and
   thinly sliced
1 small red onion, thinly sliced
½ cup pitted black olives, halved
1 medium lemon, peeled and thinly sliced

FOR MARINADE

½ cup freshly squeezed lemon juice
½ cup olive oil
1 tablespoon red wine vinegar
1 clove garlic, minced
1 tablespoon dry mustard

¼ teaspoon cayenne pepper
½ teaspoon salt
⅛ teaspoon coarsely cracked black pepper
1 tablespoon finely chopped fresh parsley

FOR GARNISH:

Red leaf lettuce

1 Shell and devein shrimp, but leave tips of tail shells on.

2 Combine water, wine, and bay leaf in a 2-quart saucepan and bring to a boil. Add shrimp. Reduce heat and cook for 3 to 5 minutes, or until shrimp are pink on the outside and just cooked in the center. Remove with a slotted spoon to a bowl.

3 Immerse red pepper in shrimp-cooking liquid and simmer for 1 minute over medium heat. Remove with slotted spoon and drain. Add to bowl of shrimp. Add onion, olives, and sliced lemon.

4 In a separate bowl, combine marinade ingredients and pour over shrimp mixture.

5 Refrigerate for at least 4 hours. Remove shrimp from marinade, drain, and serve on red leaf lettuce. Pour some marinade over shrimp.

ADVANCE PREPARATION:

May be kept up to 1 day in refrigerator. Place shrimp on bed of lettuce just before serving.

SALMON TARTARE

Serves 4 to 6

Because fresh salmon is available six months out of the year in California, I like to experiment and use it in a variety of dishes. One of my favorite methods takes advantage of the delicate flavor of raw salmon, highlighting it subtly with the piquancy of cornichons (French baby pickles), mustard, and capers. This is a light dish, an ideal starter when your main course is more substantial. Serve it in a crock or ramekin set in a large basket filled with an assortment of crackers or lightly toasted French bread.

RECOMMENDED CALIFORNIA WINE:

Any Chardonnay. A second, more exotic choice would be a dry Gewürztraminer, whose unique spicy flavor complements the salmon.

1 pound fresh salmon fillet, cut into
   3-inch pieces

¼ cup coarsely chopped cornichons

¼ cup plus 1 teaspoon freshly
   squeezed lemon juice

2 teaspoons mayonnaise

2 tablespoons grainy mustard

2 tablespoons finely chopped fresh parsley

1 tablespoon plus 1 teaspoon capers,
   drained and rinsed

⅛ teaspoon Tabasco sauce

⅛ teaspoon finely ground white pepper

Salt to taste

1 Chop salmon in coarse pieces in a food processor fitted with the steel blade or with a sharp knife. Transfer to a medium bowl.

2 Add cornichons, lemon juice, mayonnaise, mustard, and parsley and mix well. Gently add capers, Tabasco, and pepper and taste for seasoning. Spoon into a crock or ramekin. Refrigerate for at least 2 hours to intensify flavor.

ADVANCE PREPARATION:

May be kept up to 6 hours in refrigerator.

VARIATION SUBSTITUTE:

½ pound fresh halibut for half of the salmon

CHICKEN LIVER MOUSSE

Serves 8 to 12

When I first got a food processor, I began experimenting with liver pâtés. This mousse was the crowning success of all my early efforts. The pork sausage and California walnuts provide a flavorfully coarse texture, yet the cream cheese makes it lighter than the traditional French mousse. It is easy to make and tastes best spread on thin crackers or sliced toast. You will find this mousse versatile as an informal cocktail accompaniment.

RECOMMENDED CALIFORNIA WINE:

A big Chardonnay with plenty of fruit and oak (try one from Sonoma County) goes well with the rich spicy-apple flavors.

1 cup walnuts	½ pound pork sausage
3 tablespoons unsalted butter	½ pound chicken livers
2 tablespoons oil	¼ cup apple brandy
1 onion, coarsely chopped	½ teaspoon dried tarragon
2 shallots, finely chopped	⅛ teaspoon dried thyme
1 pippin or other tart apple,	⅛ teaspoon allspice
coarsely chopped	1½ teaspoons salt
1 clove garlic, minced	¼ teaspoon finely ground white pepper
2 (8-ounce) packages cream cheese	½ teaspoon crushed red pepper

FOR GARNISH:

Walnut halves

1 Preheat oven to 350°F. Toast walnuts on a baking sheet in oven for 7 to 10 minutes, or until lightly browned. Coarsely chop and reserve.

2 In a 10-inch skillet, melt butter and 1 tablespoon of the oil over medium-high heat. Add onion, shallots, and apple and sauté, stirring occasionally, until mixture is soft and transparent, about 10 minutes. Add garlic and continue to cook for 1 minute.

3 Transfer to a food processor fitted with the steel blade and puree. Add cream cheese and process until well blended.

4 Heat remaining tablespoon oil in a skillet. Add sausage and chicken livers and sauté over medium-high heat for about 10 minutes. Sausage should be cooked through, and chicken livers should be slightly pink. Drain off excess drippings from skillet.

5 In the same skillet heat brandy and ignite it with long match, averting your face and making sure overhead fan is not on.

6 Add liver mixture to apple mixture in food processor and process for about 30 seconds. Add all the seasonings and process until smooth. Add toasted walnuts and process just until combined, so that walnuts retain their texture. Taste for seasoning.

7 Pour into a 4-cup crock or mold. Decorate with walnut halves. Chill for at least 2 hours before serving.

ADVANCE PREPARATION:

May be kept tightly covered up to 5 days in refrigerator.

SMOKED WHITEFISH MOUSSE

Serves 4 to 6

This is another easy dish for an informal gathering with cocktails or wine. It has a unique flavor—light and slightly smoky. The dash of cream gives it a smooth texture, perfect for spreading on thin crackers or fresh French bread. Be sure to have enough on hand, as some guests find it addictive.

RECOMMENDED CALIFORNIA WINE:

Ask your wine merchant for one of the better dry Sauvignon Blancs or Chardonnays that have been aged in oak. The oak flavors accentuate the smokiness of the whitefish. Sauvignon Blanc brings out the lemony flavor, Chardonnay reduces it.

1 pound smoked whitefish,
    skin and bones removed
¼ cup mayonnaise

¼ cup whipping cream
¼ cup freshly squeezed lemon juice
⅛ teaspoon cayenne pepper

1 tablespoon finely chopped fresh parsley

1 In a food processor fitted with the steel blade, process fish until fine. Add remaining ingredients, except parsley, and process for 30 seconds. Taste for seasoning.

2 Spoon into a 2-cup ramekin. Garnish with parsley. Serve cold.

ADVANCE PREPARATION:

May be kept up to 1 day in refrigerator. Remove from refrigerator ½ hour before serving.

SMOKED TONGUE PÂTÉ

Yields 1 nine-by-five-inch terrine

Try this unusual mousse-style pâté for a refreshing change. Dill, mustard, and sour cream enhance the smoked tongue while creating a delicate flavor. Creamy yet light, it makes a delicious appetizer spread on plain crackers or French bread.

RECOMMENDED CALIFORNIA WINE:

A big, oaky Chardonnay should be the first choice with the robust meat, smoke, and dill flavors, but any dry white wine can be served.

1¾ pounds smoked tongue

1 envelope unflavored gelatin

2 tablespoons freshly squeezed
    lemon juice

1 cup veal or beef stock (page 274),
    heated

1 cup sour cream

½ cup mayonnaise

2 tablespoons finely chopped chives

¼ cup finely chopped fresh parsley

2½ tablespoons Dijon mustard

3 tablespoons chopped fresh dill,
    or 1 tablespoon dried dill

FOR GARNISH:

Fresh watercress

1. Place tongue in a 6-quart stockpot, cover with water, and bring to boil. Lower heat so liquid simmers, and cook tongue 2 hours, uncovered, or until soft when pierced with a two-pronged fork. Remove from pot and cool. Remove skin and clean tongue well, cutting away all fat with a sharp knife. Cut cleaned tongue into 3-inch pieces.

2. Chop tongue in a food processor fitted with the steel blade, turning machine on and off until meat is finely chopped but not completely pureed. Transfer to a large mixing bowl.

3. Dissolve gelatin in lemon juice in a small saucepan over low heat until no crystals show. Pour into hot stock and mix well.

4. Add stock and remaining ingredients except watercress to tongue. Mix thoroughly.

5. Pour into an ungreased 9-by-5-inch terrine or loaf pan and refrigerate until set, about 2 hours.

6. To serve, loosen pâté by running a knife around edge. Unmold onto a medium rectangular platter. Surround with fresh watercress.

ADVANCE PREPARATION:

May be kept up to 4 days covered in refrigerator.

GUACAMOLE

Serves 4 to 6

California avocados account for eighty percent of the total crop grown in the United States. Available in many varieties year-round, they are often put to good use in guacamole, the quintessential California dip. There are as many recipes for its preparation as there are California chefs. The traditional Mexican guacamole tends toward a simple, chunky mixture of avocado, cilantro, and a dash of lemon or lime. This more adventuresome variation also blends in tomatoes, onions, mild chiles, and cumin. It provides a spicy introduction to a meal of Mexican Chicken with Raisins and Almonds or Pork Tacos, California Style.

Although beer or margaritas are a first choice with guacamole, it is also possible to serve wine. A big Chardonnay works well, as does a Blanc de Noirs (a pale pink dry wine made from Pinot Noir).

1 California chile (see Note)	¼ teaspoon ground cumin
2 very ripe avocados	1 teaspoon salt
1½ tablespoons freshly squeezed lemon juice	2 tomatoes, peeled, seeded, and coarsely chopped
2 tablespoons finely chopped red onion	2 teaspoons finely chopped cilantro

FOR GARNISH:

Red lettuce leaves (optional)
Hot crisp tortilla chips

1 To peel chile, place on broiler pan and broil approximately 6 inches from heat until blackened on all sides. Use tongs to turn chile.

2 Put chile in a plastic bag and close tightly. Let rest for 10 minutes.

3 Remove chile from bag, drain, and peel off skin. Make a slit in chile and open it up. Core, cut off stem, scrape off seeds and ribs, and coarsely chop.

4 In a medium bowl, mash avocado flesh with fork until soft and pureed.

5 Add lemon juice, onion, chile, cumin, and salt and mix to combine. Gently mix in tomatoes and cilantro. Taste for seasoning.

6 Place in a small crock or on red lettuce leaves. Surround with fresh hot tortilla chips.

ADVANCE PREPARATION:

May be prepared up to 4 hours ahead. Place avocado pit in center of guacamole to keep mixture from darkening and cover with plastic wrap. Refrigerate until serving.

VARIATION:

Decorate with sour cream, tomatoes, and olives, if desired. Place a large dollop of sour cream in center. Surround with rings of tomatoes and olives.

NOTE:

When working with chiles always wear rubber gloves. Wash cutting surface and knife immediately afterward.

MARINATED GOLDEN AND RED PEPPERS

Serves 6

Colorful golden peppers are grown in San Martin, California, and in the surrounding Central and Northern California areas. In this autumn dish, both golden and red peppers are overlapped in strips and garnished with tiny black olives and freshly chopped basil. The anchovy-laced dressing complements the sweet taste of the freshly skinned peppers. When serving as a prelude to an Italian-inspired menu, follow with Pasta and Fresh Mushroom Sauce or Green Fettucine with Goat Cheese, Broccoli, and Cauliflower. For an entrée try Chicken with Tomatoes and Sausages or Grilled Veal Chops with Rosemary. Finish with fresh fruit. The peppers may also be served as a part of a salad buffet.

RECOMMENDED CALIFORNIA WINE:

Although this dish is not ideal for wine, it will not cross any dry wine that is used for other courses in the meal.

FOR DRESSING:

2 teaspoons freshly squeezed lemon juice

3 tablespoons red wine vinegar

1 clove garlic, minced

1 teaspoon anchovy paste

⅛ teaspoon salt

Pinch of finely ground pepper

6 tablespoons olive oil

3 red bell peppers (see Note)

3 yellow bell peppers

FOR GARNISH:

2 tablespoons finely chopped fresh basil

2 tablespoons small black niçoise olives

1 For dressing: Combine all ingredients except olive oil and mix well. Whisk in oil slowly. Set aside.

2 To peel peppers, place on broiler pan and broil approximately 5 inches from heat until blackened on all sides. Use tongs to turn peppers.

3 Put peppers in a plastic bag and close tightly. Let rest for 10 minutes.

4 Remove from bag. Drain peppers and peel off skin. Make a slit in each pepper and open it up. Core and cut off stem. Scrape off seeds and ribs from peppers.

5 With a sharp knife or pizza wheel, cut peppers in ½-inch-wide strips. Place in a serving dish and pour dressing over. Sprinkle with chopped basil and decorate with olives. Serve at room temperature or slightly chilled.

ADVANCE PREPARATION:

May be kept up to 5 days in refrigerator. Remove from refrigerator 2 hours prior to serving so that dressing is clear and just slightly chilled. Add garnish just before serving.

NOTE:

You can use all red, yellow, or green bell peppers, or any combination desired.

CELERY ROOT TERRINE

Serves 6 to 8

Acclaimed for its subtle flavor and contrasting layers of green beans, carrots, and green peas, this terrine makes for a colorful presentation. Unlike those made in French charcuteries, it does not have a meat base. Instead, it gets its nutty, slightly sharp taste from the combination of Gruyère, shallots, and celery root (celeriac). For a first course, slice and serve with Raw Tomato-Basil Sauce (page 278). It is also excellent as a light summertime lunch.

RECOMMENDED CALIFORNIA WINE:

As with other all-vegetable dishes, dry white or red wine will work well.

3 pounds celery root, peeled

2 quarts water

2 tablespoons all-purpose flour

1 tablespoon freshly squeezed
    lemon juice

1¾ teaspoons salt

3 shallots, finely chopped

3½ cups shredded Gruyère cheese
    (about 14 ounces)

3 tablespoons whipping cream

2 eggs

½ teaspoon finely ground white pepper

1 carrot, cut in half, peeled,
    and julienned

2 ounces French green beans
    (haricots verts) (see Note)

¼ cup shelled fresh baby peas
    (¼ pound unshelled)

    1 tablespoon unsalted butter, softened

    1 tablespoon grated Gruyère cheese

    Raw Tomato-Basil Sauce (page 278)

1 Cut peeled celery root into 3-inch chunks.

2 Make a solution by combining water, flour, lemon juice, and ¼ teaspoon of the salt in a medium saucepan. Bring to a boil, stirring, and boil for 2 minutes. Add celery root to boiling solution and reduce heat to a simmer. Partially cover and cook 15 to 20 minutes, or until tender. Drain thoroughly.

3 Puree celery root in a food processor fitted with the steel blade and place in a mixing bowl. Add shallots, cheese, cream, eggs, remaining salt, and pepper. Taste for seasoning. Set aside.

4 Preheat oven to 350°F. Heavily butter an 8-by-4-inch loaf pan. Sprinkle Gruyère into mold and tap sides of mold to distribute cheese evenly over base and sides. Turn upside down and tap pan to remove excess cheese.

5 Immerse carrot pieces in a pan of boiling water and boil for 2 minutes. Drain and pour cold water over carrot to stop the cooking process. Drain thoroughly.

6 Immerse green beans in a pan of boiling water and boil for 3 minutes. Drain and pour cold water over green beans. Drain thoroughly.

7 Immerse peas in a pan of boiling water and boil for 5 minutes, or until tender. Drain and pour cold water over peas. Drain thoroughly.

8 Spoon one-third of the celery puree into the mold, making sure layer is even. Use a spatula to smooth it. Place a row of carrots, then a row of peas, then a row of green beans along length of pan. Repeat, alternating vegetables until puree is covered.

9 Spoon another third of puree on top of vegetables and add another layer of vegetables, as described above. Cover with remaining puree.

10 Bake for 50 to 60 minutes, or until slightly puffed. Remove from oven and let cool. Refrigerate at least 2 hours.

11 Turn out onto a rectangular serving platter. Slice and serve with Raw Tomato-Basil Sauce.

May be kept up to 2 days in refrigerator. It is best served slightly cool but almost at room temperature. Remove from refrigerator 1 hour before serving.

Make sure that the green beans are cut very thin in the French style. Otherwise, green beans must be sliced in half lengthwise so that they are the same size as carrots.

SPINACH-CARROT TERRINE

Serves 6 to 8

Brightly colored layers hint at a variety of flavors and textures. Created by my interior designer friend and colleague Barbara Windom, this terrine is composed of readily available ingredients. Sliced and served at room temperature with cocktails, Spinach-Carrot Terrine is also an elegant vegetable accompaniment to Grilled Lemon-Mustard Chicken (see Note). Also try it with other vegetable salads for a lunchtime buffet.

RECOMMENDED CALIFORNIA WINE:

Although any dry wine, red or white, will work well, the ginger and cheese in the terrine work best with Chardonnay or Pinot Noir.

FOR PREPARING MOLD:

2 tablespoons unsalted butter, softened

1 ½ tablespoons freshly grated Parmesan cheese

FOR SPINACH MIXTURE:

2 bunches fresh spinach (about 1 pound)	1 ½ tablespoons all-purpose flour
½ cup (4 ounces) cream cheese	1 shallot, finely chopped
½ cup (4 ounces) cottage cheese	½ teaspoon salt
3 eggs	⅛ teaspoon finely ground white pepper
	½ cup shredded Cheddar cheese

1 cup shredded peeled carrot

2 eggs

1 shallot, finely chopped

1/2 teaspoon ground ginger

1/4 teaspoon salt

1/8 teaspoon finely ground white pepper

2 tablespoons all-purpose flour

1/4 cup shredded Monterey jack cheese

2 teaspoons whipping cream

Parsley sprigs or watercress leaves

1 Preheat oven to 350°F. Heavily butter a 9-by-5-inch loaf pan. Sprinkle Parmesan into mold and tap sides of mold to distribute cheese evenly over base and sides. Turn upside down and tap to remove excess cheese.

2 For spinach mixture: Remove spinach stems and rinse leaves thoroughly. Coarsely chop leaves. Immerse spinach in a large pan of boiling water and boil for 1 minute. Drain and wring out excess moisture. Reserve.

3 Using mixer or a food processor fitted with the plastic blade, blend cream cheese and cottage cheese together, making sure there are no lumps in cream cheese.

4 Add eggs, flour, shallot, salt, pepper, Cheddar cheese, and spinach. Mix well, taste for seasoning, and reserve.

5 For carrot mixture: Immerse carrots in a pan of boiling water and boil for 3 minutes. Drain well. Reserve.

6 Using the mixer or food processor fitted with the plastic blade, blend eggs, shallot, ginger, salt, and pepper.

7 Slowly add flour, jack cheese, and cream and blend well.

8 Add carrots and stir so that ingredients are well combined. Taste for seasoning.

9 To assemble, spoon half of spinach mixture into pan, then spoon the carrot mixture carefully over spinach. Finish with rest of spinach. You will have three distinct layers. Use a spatula to smooth top, making sure it is perfectly even before placing in oven.

10 Bake for 50 to 60 minutes, or until puffed but not browned on top.

11 Let cool at least 1 hour and turn out onto a rectangular platter. Refrigerate for 2 hours.

12 To serve, slice 1-inch pieces and overlap on serving platter. Garnish with parsley or watercress leaves. Serve at room temperature.

ADVANCE PREPARATION:

May be kept up to 3 days in refrigerator.

NOTE:

As an accompaniment to a main course, the terrine may be served warm by slicing and heating in 350˚ F oven for 15 minutes.

⌒

VEAL AND PORK PÂTÉ
WITH PISTACHIOS AND PRUNES

Serves 8 to 12

When sliced, this pâté is a study in contrasts. The pink ham and green pistachio filling are set off by a center of black prunes. California is now the world's leading supplier of prunes, which impart a light sweetness to the dish. I suggest Veal and Pork Pâté with sourdough bread as a mellow, fruity first course for a picnic. You may omit the layer of prunes and serve with mustard and tiny cornichons for variation. Plan ahead, because the pâté should be chilled 2 days for maximum flavor.

RECOMMENDED CALIFORNIA WINE:

This dish is made for California's best big, fruity, oaky Chardonnays.

½ cup California brandy

8 pitted prunes

1 pound veal stew meat, ground

1 pound pork stew meat, ground

½ pound pork fat, ground

1 cup cooked ham, cut into small dice

4 shallots, finely chopped

2 cloves garlic, minced

¼ cup all-purpose flour

2 eggs

⅓ cup whipping cream

½ cup finely chopped fresh parsley

¼ pound chicken livers, ground

1 tablespoon salt

½ teaspoon finely ground pepper

¾ teaspoon chopped fresh savory,
    or ¼ teaspoon dried savory

¾ teaspoon chopped fresh oregano,
    or ¼ teaspoon dried oregano

1½ teaspoons chopped fresh thyme, or ½ teaspoon dried thyme

¾ teaspoon allspice

¾ teaspoon ground cinnamon

¾ teaspoon freshly grated nutmeg

¼ cup pistachios

½ pound caul or back fat, thinly sliced

1 bay leaf

FOR GARNISH:

Parsley sprigs

1 Heat brandy in small saucepan over medium heat. Pour brandy over prunes and soften for ½ hour.

2 Preheat oven to 300°F. Remove prunes from brandy and reserve prunes and brandy. Mix reserved brandy, stew meats, pork fat, ham, shallots, garlic, and flour together. Add eggs, cream, parsley, and ground chicken livers. Add all seasonings and mix so that ingredients are well combined. Add pistachios and mix again to incorporate.

3 Line a large (11½-by-5½-inch) terrine or loaf pan with the caul or back fat, making sure pan is completely covered and fat hangs over the edge. Put half of meat mixture in pan. Arrange prunes along center of meat mixture and top with remaining meat mixture, carefully patting down so there are no air bubbles. To enclose pâté, cover with overhanging caul or back fat and place bay leaf in center. Cover with aluminum foil.

4 Place terrine in a larger pan and add enough warm water to come halfway up terrine. Bake for 3½ hours.

5 Remove from oven and let cool. When cool, remove from pan and invert onto a board or platter to drain off fat. Blot off all additional fat. Wrap in aluminum foil and refrigerate until serving. It can be served when completely cool, but for best results, refrigerate 2 days before serving.

6 To serve: Cut ½-inch slices and present on plates garnished with parsley sprigs.

VARIATION:

The prunes may be omitted for a more classic pâté. If desired, after cooking invert pâté on a baking sheet or pan. Place a brick or other weight on top so that pâté will be pressed down. This will give pâté a much denser texture and will make it easier to slice.

ADVANCE PREPARATION:

May be kept up to 1 week in refrigerator.

CARPACCIO, CALIFORNIA STYLE

Serves 6

This dish demonstrates the melting pot of ethnic influences in California cooking. Originally an Italian favorite made with paper-thin raw beef, it introduces a Japanese twist with the addition of enoki mushrooms. Follow this dish with Sautéed Chicken Breasts with Mustard and Tarragon and steamed zucchini and carrots.

RECOMMENDED CALIFORNIA WINE:

Although a Cabernet Sauvignon or Pinot Noir would be expected choices, this dish is surprisingly good with a big oaky Chardonnay, which works well with the flavor of uncooked beef.

1 pound very fresh top sirloin, top round,
   or strip steak, cut into ⅛-inch slices
4 ounces fresh enoki mushrooms

¼ cup olive oil
½ cup freshly grated Parmesan cheese
Coarsely cracked black pepper to taste

1 Pound beef between 2 sheets of waxed paper until beef is paper-thin, being careful not to tear meat. Cut into pieces that can be draped over one another.

2 Carefully transfer 2 large pieces of meat to each of 6 individual serving plates.

3 Evenly sprinkle mushrooms over carpaccio.

4 Pour or spoon olive oil in a circle around mushrooms and sprinkle with Parmesan cheese. Grind pepper on top and serve immediately.

ADVANCE PREPARATION:

May be prepared up to 4 hours ahead through Step 2, covered tightly with plastic wrap, and kept in refrigerator.

FRESH TUNA WITH AVOCADO AND CUCUMBER

Serves 6

Here is a flavor combination popularized by Japanese sushi bars, whose popularity has grown rapidly in California. Wasabi, the predominant taste in the dressing, is a dried root from the horseradish family, available in the Asian foods section of your market. Avocado, cucumber, and toasted sesame seeds give a textural balance between creamy and crunchy. For late suppers, try it as a main course, or, if you prefer, use it as a light first course followed by Grilled Lemon-Mustard Chicken and Autumn Rice with Red Peppers and Pine Nuts. Be sure to prepare it just before serving with the freshest tuna available.

RECOMMENDED CALIFORNIA WINE:

This dish is ideal for a big, buttery, oaky Chardonnay.

1 pound raw tuna fillet, skin and
    dark part removed
1 cucumber, peeled
1 cup water
½ teaspoon salt

½ avocado
1 teaspoon freshly squeezed lemon juice
2 tablespoons finely chopped green onion,
    white and green parts

FOR DRESSING:

2 tablespoons soy sauce
2 teaspoons wasabi powder

1 tablespoon rice vinegar
1 tablespoon freshly squeezed lemon juice

FOR GARNISH:

2 tablespoons sesame seeds, toasted
Red leaf lettuce

1 Cut tuna into ¾-inch slices, then cut into ¾-inch chunks. Reserve.

2 Cut cucumber in half and scoop out seeds. Cut into ¾-inch-wide slices, then cut into ¾-inch chunks.

3 Combine water and salt in a bowl and soak cucumber pieces in water for 15 minutes to remove bitterness.

4 Drain cucumber in colander, rinse off salt, and pat dry. Place in a bowl. Add tuna.

5 For dressing: Mix together all dressing ingredients in a medium bowl. Set aside.

6 Peel avocado and cut into ¾-inch pieces. Sprinkle with 1 teaspoon lemon juice and reserve.

7 To toast sesame seeds for garnish, place in a skillet over high heat. Shake until light brown, about 2 minutes. Remove immediately from skillet. Reserve.

8 Add dressing to tuna and cucumber and stir. Add green onion and avocado and mix gently.

9 Spoon onto red leaf lettuce and garnish with sesame seeds. Serve immediately.

VARIATION:

Slice tuna and avocado and alternate on a serving plate lined with red leaf lettuce. Finely dice cucumber and arrange in a circle around tuna and avocado. Pour dressing evenly over tuna and sprinkle with sesame seeds.

TOMATOES WITH FRESH MOZZARELLA AND BASIL

Serves 6

Fresh buffalo or whole cow's milk mozzarella has a silken, creamy texture. Overlapped with ripe red tomatoes and garnished with fragrant basil, it emphasizes California's light and refreshing combinations. Select the ripest tomatoes and use only whole milk mozzarella, found in Italian specialty stores. Serve on individual plates or on a single large platter for a buffet. Follow with Pasta with Santa Barbara Calamari or Pasta with Fresh Mushroom Sauce.

RECOMMENDED CALIFORNIA WINE:

This dish can be served with white or red wine. Among whites, Chardonnay and Fumé Blanc work best; among reds, Pinot Noir and Zinfandel.

4 large tomatoes, peeled and sliced
¼ inch thick

½ pound fresh buffalo mozzarella cheese,
drained, patted dry, and sliced
¼ inch thick

¼ cup coarsely chopped fresh basil

FOR GARNISH:

Fresh basil leaves

2 tablespoons balsamic vinegar

1 On 6 large salad plates, overlap tomato slices and mozzarella cheese in an attractive pattern. Sprinkle with chopped basil leaves; garnish with whole basil leaves.

2 Pour balsamic vinegar over tomatoes and serve.

VARIATIONS:

1. *Use ¼ cup Pesto Sauce (page 290) instead of fresh basil leaves and vinegar.*
2. *Use peeled Italian plum tomatoes, cherry tomatoes, or yellow tomatoes instead of large red tomatoes.*
3. *Use ¼ cup Balsamic Vinaigrette (page 282) instead of vinegar.*
4. *Eliminate mozzarella and overlap fresh tomatoes garnished with basil and ¼ cup Balsamic Vinaigrette.*

ADVANCE PREPARATION:

May be made through Step 1 and kept up to 4 hours in refrigerator. Add vinegar and basil just before serving.

BAKED SONOMA GOAT CHEESE
WITH EMERALD SAUCE

Serves 4

California goat cheese comes in various forms, either in small wheels or in logs, and is often flavored with a variety of fresh herbs or garlic. If Sonoma goat cheese is unavailable, French goat cheese may be substituted. This particular treatment is a study in contrasts. A crunchy, golden brown coating surrounds the soft goat cheese wedge. Blanched watercress and spinach are incorporated into a cool vinaigrette, which offsets the warmth of the goat cheese. The cheese is placed in the center of the plate and surrounded by fresh watercress leaves. This well-balanced appetizer is highly adaptable to many California menus. I recommend it with Sword-fish in Lemon-Ginger Marinade and Sautéed Swiss Chard.

RECOMMENDED CALIFORNIA WINE:

This dish is made for California's big, high-alcohol, oak wines, which can be successfully served with a vinaigrette sauce because of their low acidity. Choose a big Chardonnay, Cabernet, Pinot Noir, or Zinfandel with intense flavor for a truly arresting food-wine combination.

2 tablespoons olive oil	8 ounces Sonoma goat cheese or
¼ cup French bread or whole-wheat	French goat cheese
bread crumbs	

FOR EMERALD SAUCE:

1 bunch fresh spinach (about ½ pound)	½ cup olive oil
1 cup watercress leaves	¼ cup red wine vinegar
¼ cup vegetable oil	Salt and freshly ground pepper to taste

FOR GARNISH:

Fresh watercress leaves

1. Preheat oven to 475°F.

2. Spoon olive oil into one bowl and bread crumbs into another.

3. Cut cheese into 4 wedges. Dip cheese into olive oil and roll in bread crumbs; place in shallow baking dish. Refrigerate uncovered for 1 hour.

④ For sauce: Remove spinach stems and rinse leaves thoroughly. Immerse watercress in a saucepan of boiling water and boil for 20 seconds. Rinse with cold running water. Wring out watercress in a kitchen towel until all liquid is extracted. Repeat boiling, rinsing, and wringing with spinach.

⑤ Combine watercress, spinach, and remaining sauce ingredients in a blender or a food processor fitted with the steel blade and blend for 30 seconds. Set aside.

⑥ Bake goat cheese for 10 minutes, or until brown on the outside and soft on the inside.

⑦ Pour enough Emerald Sauce to cover base of small serving plates. Place a wedge of goat cheese in center of each plate. Encircle cheese with fresh watercress leaves and serve.

ADVANCE PREPARATION:

Sauce may be kept up to 1 day in refrigerator. Cheese may be breaded up to 6 hours ahead and refrigerated before cooking.

OLIVE OIL–PINE NUT BREAD

Yields 1 loaf

Although pine nuts are not indigenous to California, they grow well in the Southwest, and Californians have taken advantage of their proximity. The pairing of dry white wine with fruity olive oil gives this unusual bread its distinctive rich flavor. Rolling the loaf in chopped pine nuts adds a nutritious sweetness and a slightly crunchy crust. I was introduced to this version at Green's restaurant, in San Francisco, where it was served with wine before the meal. It also makes an excellent companion to Corn, Red Pepper, and Leek Soup or to a Lamb Stew with Rosemary.

2 (¼-ounce) envelopes active dry yeast
or 2 (⅗-ounce) cakes fresh yeast
½ cup lukewarm water
½ cup dry white wine
¼ cup virgin olive oil

1½ cups whole-wheat flour
1¼ cups unbleached all-purpose flour
¼ cup rye flour
2 teaspoons salt

FOR GLAZE:

1 egg yolk
1 tablespoon whipping cream
½ cup pine nuts, coarsely chopped

1 Sprinkle dry yeast or crumble fresh yeast over lukewarm water in a cup or small bowl. Let stand for 10 minutes and stir to dissolve yeast. Add wine and oil.

2 In a bowl, mix all 3 types of flour together with the salt. Place all except 1 cup of the flour mixture in the large bowl of an electric mixer. Pour in the liquid yeast mixture slowly while mixer is on low; mix, using dough hook.

3 Gradually stir in remaining 1 cup combined flours. Wait until each batch of flour is absorbed before adding more. Knead in mixer on low speed about 8 minutes, or until dough is smooth and elastic.

4 Turn dough out on a lightly floured board and knead by hand a few minutes. If dough is dry, knead in 1 tablespoon water; if dough is very sticky, knead in 1 to 2 tablespoons flour. Transfer dough to an oiled bowl and turn dough over to oil its entire surface. Cover with a damp cloth and let rise in a warm place overnight, or at least 3 hours.

5 Punch down dough and knead again on lightly floured surface. Shape with hands into smooth, round loaf about 6 inches in diameter.

6 For glaze: Beat egg yolk with cream and brush all over loaf. Roll loaf in chopped pine nuts spread on a flat surface. Grease a baking sheet and set loaf on center of it. Cover with a damp cloth and let rise in a warm place about 1½ hours, or until nearly doubled in volume.

7 Preheat oven to 350°F. Place a pan of water on bottom rack of oven while preheating, to provide steam.

8 With a very sharp knife, slash an X across top of loaf. Bake for about 45 minutes. When you tap bottom of loaf with your fist, loaf should sound hollow. Let cool on rack. Serve lukewarm or at room temperature.

1. *Follow recipe through Step 4. Roll dough into flat disk about 14 inches in diameter by ¼ inch thick. For smaller breads, roll dough about 7 inches in diameter and ½ inch thick. Preheat oven to 400°F.*

2. *Poke holes in dough with tip of a sharp knife or with your fingertips and insert either of the following for different loaves: (A) One small yellow onion, sliced thinly, then cut in half, inserted into holes. Press lightly into dough, brush with 3 tablespoons olive oil, and sprinkle with ½ teaspoon coarse salt. (B) Two cloves garlic, thinly sliced, and sprigs of fresh rosemary, inserted into slashes in dough. Brush with 3 tablespoons olive oil and sprinkle with ½ teaspoon coarse salt and ¼ teaspoon coarsely cracked pepper.*

3. *Let rise 20 minutes. If disk is ¼ inch thick, bake for 15 minutes; if ½ inch thick, bake for 30 minutes. Let cool on rack. Serve lukewarm or at room temperature.*

Do not freeze or refrigerate dough before baking.

SOUPS

*T*RADITIONALLY, SOUPS HAVE BEEN MADE FROM LEFTOVERS TOSSED INTO THE STOCKPOT. In California the accent is on fresh produce, herbs, and homemade stocks. Soups may be slowly simmered, or chilled, depending on the season and the menu. They are usually served in small portions, but heartier portions accompanied by chunks of bread and a simple salad can transform the soup course into an entire meal.

Corn, Red Pepper, and Leek Soup

Garlic-Vegetable Soup

Three-Onion Soup

Zucchini-Fresh Oregano Soup

Dilled Carrot Soup

Herbed Butternut Squash-Apple Soup

Fresh Tomato-Basil Soup

Mushroom Soup with Fresh and Dried Mushrooms

Fennel, Potato, and Leek Soup

White Bean Soup with Red Swiss Chard

Twelve-Vegetable Soup with Pasta
and Garlic Mayonnaise

Garden Vegetable-Beef Soup

Santa Monica Fish Soup Laced with
Chardonnay and Saffron

Winter Fish Essence with Spicy Garlic Mayonnaise

Chilled Cucumber-Avocado Soup

Cold Curried Eggplant Soup

Chilled Cantaloupe Soup

CORN, RED PEPPER, AND LEEK SOUP

Serves 6

This bold union of ingredients creates a new taste experience typical of California cooking and reminiscent of Mexico. The sweetness of the corn and red pepper is tempered by the mild leek. A touch of cayenne adds a piquant hotness. Enjoy with warm buttered corn tortillas. Follow with Sautéed Lamb Chops with Madeira, Carrots, and Green Beans.

5 ears of corn

2 tablespoons unsalted butter

3 tablespoons oil

3 leeks, cleaned and coarsely chopped

1 large red bell pepper, seeded and
    coarsely chopped

1 ½ quarts chicken stock (page 276)

½ cup whipping cream

½ teaspoon salt

⅛ teaspoon coarsely cracked
    white pepper

Pinch of cayenne pepper

FOR GARNISH:

2 tablespoons chopped fresh parsley

① Scrape kernels off corn cobs using a sharp knife. Reserve ¼ cup for garnish.

② Heat butter and oil in a large saucepan. Add leeks and sauté over medium heat, stirring occasionally, until soft, about 5 minutes. Add red pepper and continue sautéing for 5 more minutes. Peppers should be slightly soft. Add corn and cook 3 minutes.

③ Add chicken stock and bring to boil. Reduce heat and simmer slowly, uncovered, for 30 minutes.

④ Pour into a blender or a food processor fitted with the steel blade and process for 1 minute.

⑤ Put through a food mill or fine strainer, then return to saucepan (see Note).

⑥ Add cream, salt, pepper, and cayenne. Reheat over low heat. Taste for seasoning.

⑦ Immerse corn reserved for garnish in a pan of boiling water and boil 2 minutes. Drain.

⑧ Pour soup into bowls; garnish with corn and fresh parsley.

May be prepared up to 3 days ahead through Step 6 and kept in refrigerator. Taste for seasoning when reheating.

Step 5 may be omitted; the texture of the soup will be much coarser, however.

GARLIC-VEGETABLE SOUP

Serves 6 to 8

This soup is an unfamiliar mix of ethnic flavors. The stock, redolent of mellow sweet garlic, is combined with Parmesan, parsley, julienned carrots, and eggs in a California version of the Chinese egg drop soup. This light soup makes an excellent first course followed by Roast Chicken Stuffed Under the Skin with Goat Cheese-Leek Filling and Sautéed Sugar Snap Peas and Red Peppers.

3 cups chicken stock (page 276)

3 cups water

30 cloves garlic, peeled

2 sprigs fresh thyme

½ teaspoon salt

¼ teaspoon finely ground white pepper

2 tablespoons freshly grated Parmesan cheese

3 tablespoons finely chopped fresh parsley

1 small carrot, peeled and julienned

2 eggs

1 In a medium saucepan, combine stock, water, garlic, thyme, salt, and pepper. Bring to boil. Cover and simmer 20 minutes. Discard thyme. Remove from heat.

2 With a slotted spoon, transfer garlic to a food processor fitted with the steel blade or to a blender. Puree until smooth. It may be necessary to add ¼ cup stock mixture to pureed garlic.

3 Return garlic puree to saucepan and blend with soup. Reheat to a simmer.

4 Add cheese, parsley, and carrot to soup and simmer 1 minute. Remove from heat.

5 Lightly beat eggs with a fork and pour into soup. Stir with a fork until threads appear. Taste for seasoning and serve immediately.

ADVANCE PREPARATION:

May be prepared up to 1 day ahead through Step 3 and kept in refrigerator. Bring to a simmer before continuing.

❧

THREE-ONION SOUP

Serves 6 to 8

A bountiful variation on basic onion soup, this recipe calls for lots of yellow and sweet Bermuda onions and fresh leeks. Patience is the chief requirement for cooking, as it takes up to 1 hour just to brown the onions. Since this full-flavored soup is served with toasted French bread and melted cheese, it is a meal all by itself. The addition of Ventura Limestone Lettuce with Toasted Pine Nuts and Raspberry Vinaigrette makes for an especially satisfying meal.

¼ cup (½ stick) unsalted butter

2 tablespoons vegetable oil

4 Bermuda onions, thinly sliced

4 yellow onions, thinly sliced

½ teaspoon sugar

4 leeks, white part only, cleaned and
    thinly sliced

2½ quarts veal stock (page 274),
    chicken stock (page 276), or mixture
    of the two

3 cloves garlic, minced

1 bay leaf

1 cup dry white wine

¼ cup California brandy

1 teaspoon salt

¼ teaspoon finely ground pepper

1 teaspoon chopped fresh thyme, or
    ½ teaspoon dried thyme

18 slices French bread, lightly toasted

1 cup shredded Gruyère cheese (¼ pound)

1 In a large enamel or stainless-steel casserole, heat butter and oil.

2 Add Bermuda and yellow onions and sauté until wilted. Add sugar and continue cooking over medium heat, stirring frequently, until onions begin to turn light brown, 45 minutes to 1 hour.

3 Add leeks and cook, stirring frequently, until leeks are light brown and onions are caramel colored, about 30 minutes.

4 Add stock, garlic, bay leaf, white wine, and brandy. Partially cover, and simmer for an additional 30 minutes. Add salt, pepper, and thyme and taste for seasoning. Discard bay leaf.

5 Preheat broiler if necessary. Pour soup into individual ovenproof soup bowls. Place 2 or 3 slices French bread on top of each bowl and sprinkle bread with cheese. Broil until browned. Serve immediately.

VARIATION:

For a lighter soup, serve without the bread and cheese.

ADVANCE PREPARATION:

May be prepared up to 3 days ahead through Step 4 and kept in refrigerator.

ZUCCHINI-FRESH OREGANO SOUP

Serves 4 to 6

This aromatic soup is equally good hot or cold. Served steaming hot with fresh cream, it is a wonderful opener for Gratin of Vegetables on a vegetarian menu. Chilled and served with a dollop of plain yogurt in the center, it can precede Cold Poached Salmon with Tomato-Basil Vinaigrette and fresh sliced cucumbers. Fresh oregano accentuates the flavor of the zucchini.

2 tablespoons unsalted butter

1 tablespoon olive oil

1 yellow onion, finely chopped

1¾ pounds zucchini, sliced

3½ cups chicken stock (page 276)

2 tablespoons finely chopped fresh
    oregano

½ teaspoon salt

¼ teaspoon finely ground pepper

½ cup whipping cream or plain yogurt

1 tablespoon finely chopped fresh oregano

1 In a 3-quart saucepan, heat butter and oil. Add onion and sauté over low heat, stirring occasionally, until translucent. Add zucchini and continue sautéing for 2 minutes.

2 Add stock and 2 tablespoons oregano and bring to simmer. Cover and cook for 30 minutes, or until tender.

3 For a coarse texture, puree soup in a food processor fitted with the steel blade. For a finer texture, puree in a blender.

4 Return to saucepan. Add salt and pepper. Add cream if serving hot. If serving cold, bring soup to room temperature and whisk in yogurt. Taste for seasoning. Garnish with remaining oregano.

ADVANCE PREPARATION:

May be kept up to 1 day in refrigerator, but oregano flavor will diminish.

DILLED CARROT SOUP

Serves 6

Carrots are a member of the parsley family, which also includes caraway, coriander, celery, parsnip, and dill. The addition of dill in this recipe yields another California variation on classic carrot soup. Fresh dill is available most of the year and is easily grown in a home herb garden. This is an elegant first course when followed by Sea Bass with Garlic Mayonnaise and Sautéed Swiss Chard.

2 tablespoons unsalted butter

1 tablespoon oil

2 leeks, white part only, cleaned and
   thinly sliced

4 large carrots (1½ pounds), peeled
   and finely diced

2 large baking potatoes (1½ pounds),
   peeled and finely diced

5 cups chicken stock (page 276)

2½ teaspoons finely chopped fresh
   thyme, or 1¼ teaspoons dried thyme

1 bay leaf

1 pint half-and-half

1½ teaspoons salt

Pinch of finely ground white pepper

½ teaspoon freshly grated nutmeg

3 tablespoons finely chopped fresh dill,
   or 1 tablespoon dried dill

2 tablespoons freshly squeezed lemon juice

¼ teaspoon Tabasco sauce

1 tablespoon finely chopped fresh dill,
   or 1 teaspoon dried dill

1 Heat butter and oil in a large saucepan. Add leeks and sauté, stirring occasionally, until soft.

2 Add carrots and potatoes. Sauté 5 minutes.

3 Add chicken stock and bring to simmer. Add thyme and bay leaf and simmer, covered, for 30 to 40 minutes, or until carrots and potatoes are tender. Remove bay leaf.

4 Puree in a food processor fitted with the steel blade or in a blender, and add remaining ingredients. Bring mixture to boil and taste for seasoning. Serve hot or very cold. Garnish with dill just before serving.

ADVANCE PREPARATION:

May be kept up to 2 days in refrigerator.

HERBED BUTTERNUT SQUASH-APPLE SOUP

Serves 6 to 8

Try butternut squash and apples together in this mild, sweet soup, and see for yourself how very delicious the combination can be. Fresh pungent herbs offset the mild sweetness. For a hearty meal, accompany with French or sourdough bread.

1½ quarts chicken stock (page 276)

2 pounds butternut squash, peeled, seeded, and cut into 2-inch pieces

2 green pippin, Granny Smith, or other tart apples, peeled, cored, and cut into 2-inch pieces

1 large onion, finely chopped

2 shallots, finely chopped

1 teaspoon finely chopped fresh rosemary, or ½ teaspoon dried rosemary

2 teaspoons finely chopped fresh thyme, or 1 teaspoon dried thyme

½ cup half-and-half

½ teaspoon salt

¼ teaspoon finely ground pepper

FOR GARNISH:

½ cup sour cream

Fresh rosemary and thyme leaves

1 In a 6-quart enamel or stainless-steel casserole, heat chicken stock until simmering.

2 Add squash, apples, onion, shallots, and herbs. Simmer, covered, for 30 minutes, or until vegetables are soft and tender.

3 Puree in a food processor fitted with the steel blade or in a blender.

4 Return mixture to pan and add half-and-half. Add salt and pepper and simmer 5 minutes. Taste for seasoning.

5 Ladle into soup bowls and garnish with spoonfuls of sour cream and rosemary and thyme leaves.

ADVANCE PREPARATION:

May be prepared up to 2 days ahead through Step 3 and kept in refrigerator. Add half-and-half just before serving.

FRESH TOMATO-BASIL SOUP

Serves 4

With its rich and heady fragrance of fresh tomatoes and basil, this soup captures the spirit of warm-weather months. A special red hue accented by green flecks of basil creates a most appealing color combination. It can be enjoyed with only a light salad, or try it as an appetite-awakening first course before Sautéed Lamb Chops with Madeira, Carrots, and Green Beans. Serve the soup hot or cold.

3 tablespoons unsalted butter	2 tablespoons chopped fresh basil, or
1 tablespoon oil	2 teaspoons dried basil
1 onion, sliced or chopped	4 ripe tomatoes, coarsely chopped
1 leek, cleaned and finely chopped	3 tablespoons tomato paste
1 carrot, peeled and finely chopped	2 tablespoons all-purpose flour
1 stalk celery, finely chopped	2½ cups chicken stock (page 276)
Bouquet garni (see Note)	½ cup half-and-half or whipping cream
	Salt and finely ground black pepper to taste

FOR GARNISH:

Fresh basil leaves or chopped fresh parsley

1 Heat butter and oil in a 2-quart saucepan. Add onion, leek, carrot, celery, bouquet garni, and basil and sauté 5 minutes over low heat, stirring occasionally.

2 Add tomatoes and tomato paste and cook about 5 minutes. Sprinkle with flour and mix well. Add chicken stock, cover, and simmer about 20 minutes. Remove bouquet garni.

3 Pour into a food processor fitted with the steel blade or into a blender, and puree. Pass through a fine strainer.

4 Return to saucepan and add half-and-half or cream. Bring to boil. Reduce heat and simmer 2 to 3 minutes. Add salt and pepper to taste. Serve hot, garnished with fresh basil leaves or chopped fresh parsley.

VARIATION:

Omit basil and add ¼ to ½ teaspoon curry powder for a completely different taste. May be refrigerated for up to 1 day and served chilled.

May be prepared up to 2 days ahead through Step 3 and kept in refrigerator.

To make a bouquet garni, wrap a parsley stem, bay leaf, and a sprig of fresh thyme in cheesecloth and tie with string.

MUSHROOM SOUP WITH FRESH AND DRIED MUSHROOMS

Serves 4 to 6

With a smoky, earthy flavor, this mix of fresh and dried mushrooms is an excellent beginning to a meal featuring Fresh Tuna with Sautéed Peppers and Garlic in Parchment. Olive Oil–Pine Nut Bread is a good choice to serve alongside. I suggest the use of a food processor rather than a blender to control texture and consistency.

2 ounces dried mushrooms
   (shiitake or porcini)
2 tablespoons unsalted butter
1 tablespoon oil
1 onion, finely chopped
1 pound fresh button mushrooms,
   thinly sliced
¼ cup all-purpose flour

1 teaspoon salt
¼ teaspoon finely ground black pepper
1 cup veal or beef stock (page 274)
1 cup chicken stock (page 276)
1¼ cups half-and-half
5 tablespoons dry sherry
2 tablespoons freshly squeezed lemon juice

FOR GARNISH:

½ cup sour cream
2 tablespoons finely chopped fresh parsley

1. Place dried mushrooms in a medium bowl and cover with boiling water. Let stand for at least 1 hour.

2. Heat butter and oil in a medium saucepan and add onion. Sauté over

low heat, stirring occasionally, for 3 to 5 minutes, or until soft. Add fresh mushrooms, stir, and cook until softened.

3 Sprinkle mushrooms with flour, salt, and pepper. Stir for 1 minute to coat mushrooms, then add veal or beef stock and chicken stock.

4 Drain dry mushrooms, reserving soaking liquid. Strain liquid through cheesecloth to remove grit. Add enough water to make 2 cups and add to saucepan. Add dried mushrooms and simmer 15 minutes.

5 Puree half of soup mixture in a food processor fitted with the steel blade. Remove, set aside, and repeat with other half. Return mixture to saucepan, bring almost to a boil, and add half-and-half, sherry, and lemon juice. Taste for seasoning.

6 To serve, garnish with a dollop of sour cream and the chopped parsley. Serve cold or piping hot.

VARIATION:

Try substituting other local fresh mushrooms for the white mushrooms. Chicken stock may be substituted for beef or veal stock.

ADVANCE PREPARATION:

May be kept up to 2 days in refrigerator.

FENNEL, POTATO, AND LEEK SOUP

Serves 6 to 8

Fennel, with its delicate anise flavor, adds an unexpected surprise to the classic leek and potato soup. Fresh fennel is available in most supermarket produce sections from October to March, and it reaches its peak around the holiday season. This soup is hearty enough to serve alone. You may also enjoy a small bowl of it followed by Swordfish Brochette and Saffron Rice.

2 fennel bulbs with 2 inches stalk (about 1 pound)	2 leeks, white part only, cleaned and coarsely chopped
3 tablespoons unsalted butter	2 quarts chicken stock (page 276)
1 tablespoon vegetable oil	1 teaspoon salt
2 baking potatoes (about 1 pound), peeled and coarsely chopped	½ teaspoon finely ground white pepper
	2 teaspoons Pernod (optional)

1 Remove core from fennel and slice; reserve some sprigs for garnish.

2 In a medium soup pot, heat butter and oil over low heat. Add leeks and sauté, stirring occasionally, until soft. Add fennel and potatoes and continue sautéing for 10 more minutes, or until softened.

3 Add chicken stock and bring to simmer. Partially cover and cook 30 minutes.

4 Puree soup in a food processor fitted with the steel blade, in a blender, or in a food mill and return to pot. Add salt, pepper, and Pernod, if desired. Taste for seasoning.

5 Pour into soup bowls and decorate with fennel sprigs.

ADVANCE PREPARATION:

May be kept up to 3 days in refrigerator.

WHITE BEAN SOUP WITH RED SWISS CHARD

Serves 6 to 8

One of my favorites, this soup balances an exceptional lightness with the sturdy flavor of white beans. Red Swiss chard adds color and subtle texture to this savory soup. I enjoy it with Three-Lettuce Salad, which adds its own distinctive toast flavor. For a complete meal, accompany with chunks of warm sourdough or French bread and fresh butter.

1 cup Great Northern beans	5 cups chicken stock
3 tablespoons olive oil	2 cups bean-soaking water
2 large onions, coarsely chopped	3 cloves garlic, minced
2 carrots, peeled and coarsely chopped	1 bay leaf
1 bunch (½ pound) red Swiss chard,	1½ teaspoons salt
ribs and leaves, coarsely chopped	½ teaspoon finely ground pepper
(see Note)	3 tablespoons finely chopped parsley

FOR GARNISH:

¼ cup finely chopped parsley
¼ cup freshly grated Parmesan cheese

1 Soak beans overnight in cold water to generously cover; or do a quick soak by bringing beans to boil in water to cover, boiling 2 minutes, covering, and letting stand 1 hour. Drain beans, reserving 2 cups soaking liquid.

2 In a 6-quart soup pot, heat oil, add onions, and sauté over low heat about 5 minutes, stirring occasionally. Add carrots and sauté another 3 minutes. Reserve 2 tablespoons of chopped Swiss chard ribs and add remaining Swiss chard to soup pot. Cook about 3 minutes, or until wilted.

3 Add chicken stock, reserved bean-soaking liquid, beans, garlic, and bay leaf. Partially cover, and simmer about 1 hour, until beans are tender. Remove bay leaf.

4 Steam reserved Swiss chard ribs for 2 minutes in a pan of boiling water fitted with a steamer rack, or in a steamer. Remove and rinse with cold water to stop cooking process. Reserve for garnish.

5 Puree half the soup through a food mill or a food processor fitted with the steel blade; return pureed soup to pot containing remainder of soup. Stir in salt, pepper, and parsley. Taste for seasoning.

6 Serve soup garnished with Swiss chard ribs, parsley, and Parmesan cheese.

VARIATION:

Add ½ cup coarsely chopped cooked chestnuts for a hearty and interesting taste.

ADVANCE PREPARATION:

May be kept up to 3 days in refrigerator.

NOTE:

If red Swiss chard is unavailable, use spinach or white Swiss chard.

TWELVE-VEGETABLE SOUP
WITH PASTA AND GARLIC MAYONNAISE

Serves 6 to 8 as main course

The addition of tangy garlic mayonnaise and thin pasta gives this fresh soup a fragrance all its own. For a pleasing meal, serve with whole-wheat bread.

1 cup fresh baby lima beans, or
  ⅓ cup dried
1 cup cooked garbanzo beans
  (chickpeas), or ⅓ cup dried
¼ cup olive oil
2 yellow onions, thinly sliced
2 carrots, peeled and diced
2 stalks celery, diced
3 small zucchini, diced
1 turnip, peeled and diced
¼ pound Jerusalem artichokes,
  peeled and diced
¼ pound green beans, cut in
  1-inch lengths

¼ pound yellow beans, cut in
  1-inch lengths
3 ripe tomatoes, peeled and diced
1 quart chicken stock (page 276)
2 cups water
1 teaspoon salt
¼ teaspoon finely ground pepper
½ small cauliflower, divided into
  medium florets
½ cup very thin pasta such as vermicelli
1 cup Fresh Garlic Mayonnaise (page 288)

1. To prepare dried beans, pour boiling water over beans and soak separately overnight, or do a quick soak by bringing beans to boil in water to cover, boiling 2 minutes, covering, and letting stand 1 hour. Put lima beans and garbanzo beans in separate saucepans with water to cover generously. On medium-low heat, simmer lima beans for 1½ hours and garbanzo beans for 2 hours, or until tender. Reserve.

2. Heat oil in a large saucepan. Add onions, carrots, and celery and cook over low heat, stirring often, until soft but not brown. Stir in zucchini, turnip, Jerusalem artichokes, and green and yellow beans and cook about 3 minutes, stirring, until softened.

3. Add tomatoes, stock, water, salt, pepper, cauliflower, cooked lima beans, and cooked garbanzo beans and bring to boil. Cover and cook over low heat 1 hour, or until vegetables are very tender.

4 When soup is ready, add pasta and continue to simmer, uncovered, 5 minutes, or until pasta is just tender. Season to taste. Ladle into soup bowls and top with Fresh Garlic Mayonnaise.

ADVANCE PREPARATION:

May be prepared up to 1 day ahead through Step 2 and kept in refrigerator.

GARDEN VEGETABLE-BEEF SOUP

Serves 8 to 10

While most seasons are marked by changes in weather and in availability of seasonal fruits and vegetables, there is a year-round abundance of fresh produce in California. Thus, it is possible to enjoy this hearty soup, a typical winter meal, at any time of year. The vegetables can be varied, depending on what is locally available. Spaghetti squash, which can always be found, adds the texture of pasta without the calories. Sourdough bread is an excellent accompaniment.

½ cup dried cannellini beans, or	2½ quarts chicken stock (page 276)
1 cup cooked	or water
6 tablespoons olive oil	1 bay leaf
2 onions, finely chopped	1 tablespoon chopped fresh basil
1 pound stewing beef, partially frozen	1½ teaspoons salt
¼ pound salt pork, cut into small dice	½ teaspoon finely ground pepper
2 beef soup bones	1 teaspoon finely chopped fresh thyme,
2 pounds tomatoes, peeled, seeded,	or ½ teaspoon dried thyme
and coarsely chopped	4 zucchini, sliced ½ inch thick
6 carrots, peeled and cut in 3-inch lengths	6 mushrooms, cleaned and sliced
½ to ¾ head cabbage, shredded	½ inch thick
6 stalks celery, sliced ½ inch thick	2 tablespoons chopped fresh parsley

FOR SERVING:
Freshly grated Parmesan cheese (optional)

1 To prepare dried beans, pour boiling water over and soak overnight, or do a quick soak by bringing beans to boil in water to cover, boiling 2 minutes, covering, and letting stand 1 hour. Over medium-low heat, simmer in water to generously cover for 1½ hours, or until tender. Drain and reserve.

2 Heat 4 tablespoons of the olive oil in a large pot. Add onions and sauté 5 minutes, stirring occasionally, until soft. Remove and set aside.

3 In a food processor fitted with the slicer blade, put partially frozen meat into feed tube and slice.

4 Heat remaining oil in pot and add beef, salt, pork, and bones. Sauté until brown. Drain drippings. Add tomatoes and return onion mixture to pot. Cover and simmer 20 minutes.

5 Add carrots, cabbage, and celery to meat mixture and cook 20 minutes longer. Then add stock, bay leaf, basil, salt, pepper, and thyme and simmer, covered, for about 1 hour.

6 Add zucchini, mushrooms, and cooked cannellini beans and simmer 15 minutes longer. Add parsley and taste for seasoning. Remove bay leaf. Serve with freshly grated Parmesan cheese, if desired.

VARIATION:

Add ½ cup cooked spaghetti squash to finished soup and heat through. It will add texture.

ADVANCE PREPARATION:

May be kept up to 3 days in refrigerator.

SANTA MONICA FISH SOUP
LACED WITH CHARDONNAY AND SAFFRON

Serves 6

This hearty but elegant soup is as distinctive in appearance as it is in taste. Pacific Coast swordfish is one of the more delicate tastes in seafood, and while there's plenty of it here, it never overpowers the other ingredients. Fresh mushrooms, red pepper, saffron, and wine blend easily with the swordfish and fresh sea bass to provide a filling, flavorful soup. A meal in itself, this fish soup can be enjoyed alone or with a simple salad and sourdough bread.

3 tablespoons unsalted butter

3 leeks, cleaned and finely chopped

1 red bell pepper, seeded and thinly julienned

1 quart fish stock (page 277)

1 cup Chardonnay or other dry white wine

1 cup whipping cream

½ teaspoon salt

¼ teaspoon finely ground white pepper

Generous pinch of saffron threads

¼ pound mushrooms, sliced

¾ pound swordfish steaks, cut into bite-sized chunks

¾ pound sea bass fillets, cut into bite-sized chunks (see Note)

FOR GARNISH:

2 tablespoons finely chopped fresh parsley

1 In a medium skillet, heat 2 tablespoons of the butter over low heat. Add leeks and sauté, stirring occasionally, for 5 minutes, or until soft. Add red bell pepper and sauté another 2 minutes. Set aside.

2 In a 4-quart nonreactive saucepan, combine fish stock and wine and boil about 10 minutes, or until reduced to about 1 quart. Add cream and boil again for 10 minutes. Add salt, white pepper, and saffron and taste for seasoning. Add leeks and red bell pepper.

3 In a medium skillet, heat the remaining 1 tablespoon butter over medium heat. Add mushrooms and sauté briefly, stirring, until cooked but not browned. Reserve.

4 Heat soup base and add swordfish. Simmer 3 minutes, and add sea bass. Simmer another 3 minutes, or until just tender and moist but not overdone. Add mushrooms and heat through.

5 Ladle into soup bowls and garnish with chopped parsley.

VARIATION:

Use ¾ pound bay scallops in place of sea bass.

ADVANCE PREPARATION:

May be kept up to 4 hours in refrigerator. To reheat, strain soup base and heat separately, then add fish and vegetables and heat through. Be careful not to overcook the fish. May be prepared up to 8 hours ahead through Step 3 and kept in refrigerator. Reheat before continuing.

NOTE:

If sea bass is unavailable, any local fish may be used as long as it is fresh and firm.

WINTER FISH ESSENCE
WITH SPICY GARLIC MAYONNAISE

Serves 6 to 8

Local fresh fish is cooked, pureed, and strained to obtain its vital essence. For a further enhancement, toasted bread is placed on top with grated cheese and the spicy garlic-flavored topping. For a complete meal, follow with Grilled Lemon-Mustard Chicken and Sauté of Julienned Garden Vegetables.

¼ cup olive oil

2 onions, thinly sliced

3 pounds red snapper, bones
 removed, skin on

4 whole cloves garlic

2 pounds ripe tomatoes,
 coarsely chopped

Generous pinch of saffron threads

1 tablespoon chopped fresh thyme,
 or 1 teaspoon dried thyme

1 teaspoon minced fennel sprigs,
 or ½ teaspoon fennel seed

2½ quarts cold water

1 teaspoon salt

¼ teaspoon finely ground black pepper

FOR GARNISH:

12 slices French bread, toasted

½ cup Spicy Garlic Mayonnaise (page 289)

1 cup shredded Gruyère cheese (¼ pound)

1 Heat olive oil in a 6-quart nonreactive Dutch oven or stockpot over low heat. Add onions and sauté 10 minutes, stirring frequently, until soft and translucent.

2 Add fish, garlic, tomatoes, saffron, thyme, and fennel. Simmer vegetables and fish, stirring frequently, until slightly soft.

3 Add cold water and bring to boil. Reduce heat, partially cover, and simmer 20 minutes.

4 Place ingredients in batches in a blender or a food processor fitted with the steel blade, and puree. Strain through a fine strainer or through a food mill into stockpot. Add salt and pepper; taste for seasoning.

5 Bring soup to boil, lower heat, and simmer, uncovered, until slightly thickened. Ladle into soup bowls. Spread toast with Spicy Garlic Mayonnaise and top soup with toast. Sprinkle shredded Gruyère on top. Serve immediately.

ADVANCE PREPARATION:

May be prepared up to 8 hours ahead through Step 4 and kept in refrigerator. Reheat before serving.

CHILLED CUCUMBER-AVOCADO SOUP

Serves 4 to 6

This cool, refreshing soup is amazingly simple to prepare. I first developed it while experimenting with my food processor and have enjoyed it frequently ever since, served with a dollop of sour cream and a sprinkling of chives or green onions, or garnished with a cucumber flower adorned with caviar. I recommend serving it with Saturday Salad for an easy meal that will keep you out of a hot kitchen on an August afternoon.

1 large ripe avocado
1 European cucumber, unpeeled and
   cut into pieces
1½ cups chicken stock (page 276)
2 tablespoons finely chopped chives

2 tablespoons freshly squeezed
   lemon juice
¾ cup sour cream
Salt and finely ground white pepper to taste

FOR GARNISH:
¼ cup sour cream
¼ cup finely chopped chives

1 Peel avocado and cut into pieces. Puree in a food processor fitted with the steel blade or in a blender. Add cucumber. Process until smooth.

2 Add chicken stock and then chives; blend.

3 Add lemon juice and sour cream and blend until smooth. Season to taste with salt and white pepper.

4 Chill and serve in glass bowls. Garnish with sour cream and chives.

VARIATION:

With a citrus stripper, peel strips of cucumber peel lengthwise ½-inch apart all the way around, then slice. Slices should resemble flowers. Place 1 cucumber slice on each portion of soup. Top with a dollop of sour cream and with fish roe or caviar of your choice.

ADVANCE PREPARATION:

May be kept up to 4 hours in refrigerator. Add lemon juice no more than 1 hour before serving.

COLD CURRIED EGGPLANT SOUP

Serves 4 to 6

Aromatic curry adds an exotic bite to the delicate eggplant here. Try to find an Indian curry powder for the best flavor. Serve chilled and follow with Seafood Pasta Salad with Lemon-Dill Dressing. Finish with refreshing Kiwi Sorbet for an informal lunch or dinner.

¼ cup (½ stick) unsalted butter

1 onion, chopped

1 tablespoon curry powder

1 ¼ pounds eggplant, peeled and cut into ½-inch cubes

1 quart chicken stock (page 276)

½ cup half-and-half

½ teaspoon salt

¼ teaspoon finely ground white pepper

FOR GARNISH:

2 tablespoons finely chopped fresh parsley

1 In a 3-quart saucepan, melt butter over medium heat and add onion. Sauté, stirring occasionally, until soft. Add curry powder and cook over low heat for 2 minutes.

2 Add eggplant and chicken stock and bring to boil. Reduce heat, cover, and simmer for 45 minutes, or until eggplant is soft.

3 Transfer mixture to a food processor fitted with the steel blade or to a blender, and puree.

4 Return mixture to saucepan and add half-and-half, salt, and pepper. Taste for seasoning. Let soup cool. Chill for at least 4 hours. Serve garnished with parsley.

ADVANCE PREPARATION:

May be kept up to 1 day in refrigerator.

CHILLED CANTALOUPE SOUP

Serves 4 to 6

Chilled melon soups are another Oriental contribution to California Cuisine. Here again, local ingredients are combined in a completely new way. Sweet vermouth, ginger, and basil are added to a cantaloupe base in this lighter version of Santa Barbara chef John Downey's original recipe. This pale orange refresher is an excellent first course with Three-Lettuce Salad. For an original California menu, follow with Skewered Shrimp with Cilantro and Green Salsa, and Lemon Rice with Capers and Parsley.

2 cantaloupes (about 4 pounds)

Grated zest of 1 orange

Juice of 1 orange

1 teaspoon grated fresh ginger

1 tablespoon finely chopped fresh basil

2 tablespoons sweet white vermouth

¼ teaspoon salt

¼ teaspoon finely ground black pepper

½ cup sour cream or crème fraîche (page 280)

2 tablespoons sour cream

6 fresh basil leaves

1. Cut melons in half and remove seeds. Scoop out 6 tiny balls from 1 melon half for garnish.

2. Remove skin from melons and cut flesh into small chunks.

3. Combine cantaloupe, orange zest, orange juice, ginger, and basil with vermouth, salt, and pepper in a blender or a food processor fitted with the steel blade. Puree until fine. Add sour cream and blend.

4. Strain soup into a large bowl and taste for seasoning. Refrigerate 4 hours before serving.

5. Serve in chilled bowls and garnish with sour cream, cantaloupe balls, and basil leaves.

ADVANCE PREPARATION:

May be kept up to 8 hours in refrigerator. Serve cold.

PASTA, PIZZA, AND FRITTATAS

$\mathcal{F}$ROM THE APPEARANCE OF SPECIALIZED PASTA "BOUTIQUES" TO THE REGULAR ADDITION OF A PASTA COURSE ON THE MENU, CALIFORNIA IS CREATING A NEW EMPHASIS ON THIS ITALIAN TRADITION; IN FACT, RESTAURANTS OFTEN FEATURE A PASTA OF THE DAY. Pasta, pizza, and frittatas are flexible in menu planning and may be equally suitable as first courses, luncheon main courses, or dinner entrées. Pizza and frittatas may also be split up into pieces for a colorful appetizer.

In California, innovation with pizzas began several years ago. Canned tomatoes were discarded for fresh seeded tomatoes, and bland mozzarella cheese was replaced with buffalo mozzarella, Italian Fontina, or other distinctive varieties. Naturally, only the freshest ingredients are used, resulting in marvelous flavor in both pasta and pizza.

The frittata, which is a type of flat omelet, is a lighter version of pizza. The influence is distinctly Italian, the form is similar, and it is often served in wedges like a pizza.

Fresh Pasta

Pasta with Fresh Mushroom Sauce

Fresh Pasta with Smoked Salmon, Dill, and Golden Caviar

Penne with Chicken, Tomato, and Leek Sauce

Springtime Vegetable Pasta

Pasta with Pesto

Green Fettucine with Goat Cheese, Broccoli, and Cauliflower

Spicy Chinese Noodles with Vegetables

Pasta with Santa Barbara Calamari

Fresh Pasta Roll Filled with Spinach

Pasta Soufflé

Basic Pizza Dough

Pizza with Shrimp, Tomatoes, and Garlic

Pizza with Leeks, Tomatoes, and Pancetta

Eggplant Pizza

Mexican Pizza

Calzone with Prosciutto and Sonoma Goat Cheese

Vegetable Frittata

Frittata with Zucchini, Spicy Sausage, and Red Peppers

Corn and Shrimp Frittata

FRESH PASTA

Yields ¾ pound; serves 2 to 3 as main course; 4 to 6 as first course

This basic egg pasta recipe was devised after much experimentation with the proportions of flour and semolina. Semolina is a coarsely milled wheat flour available at most Italian specialty markets. It gives the pasta the necessary body without sacrificing delicate texture. As in pastry making, water proportions can vary with the humidity. Feel free to double this recipe and to vary it with different vegetables or herbs for color. The taste changes are subtle, but the visual presentation will change markedly.

1 cup unbleached all-purpose flour
½ cup semolina

2 large eggs
2 tablespoons water

FOR TOSSING:

2 tablespoons oil or softened unsalted butter

FOR COOKING:

1 tablespoon oil
1 teaspoon salt

1 To prepare dough by hand, combine flour and semolina and place on table or work surface. Form a well in center with a knife or your fingers. Add eggs and water to the well. Beat eggs and water with a fork, gradually stirring in flour. When mixture is pasty, use your hands to work remaining flour into eggs by bringing flour from outside of well into center. Form mixture into a ball, flouring hands and work surface often.

2 Knead about 10 minutes by pushing and folding with the heel of your hand. Dough should feel smooth and elastic without being tough. Divide dough into 4 equal parts. Cover 3 of the portions with a damp cloth. Continue with Step 4.

3 To prepare dough in a food processor, combine flour, semolina, and eggs in a food processor fitted with the steel blade. Process until dough begins to come together. Add water if necessary; dough should be pliable enough to pat down for rolling but not so sticky that it sticks to rollers of pasta machine. Divide dough into 4 equal parts. Cover 3 of the portions with a damp cloth.

4 To finish in pasta machine, set pasta machine rollers at widest setting. Knead by feeding each of 4 pieces through pasta machine. (Keep pieces of dough that are not being kneaded covered with damp cloth.) Fold each piece in thirds and press down firmly to form a neat, compact package. Repeat kneading in machine 8 times for each piece of dough. The dough will begin to flatten out. Hang dough on chair or wooden laundry rack after each piece has been kneaded.

5 Readjust pasta machine to next thinnest setting and pass each of 4 pieces of dough through machine. Repeat, readjusting pasta machine and passing dough through until dough reaches second-thinnest setting. While feeding dough through rollers, dust dough with flour if it becomes sticky.

6 Hang pasta sheets and let dry for 10 to 15 minutes; do not let dough become brittle.

7 Set pasta machine to desired setting: fettucine (⅛-inch-wide noodles), or tagliarini (1/16-inch-wide noodles). Feed sheets of dough through cutters. While dough is being cut, hold one hand under machine to catch noodles. (This way they will not stick to each other and will be easy to hang and dry.)

8 Hang noodles for at least 10 to 15 minutes more, or up to 1 hour before cooking.

9 To cook pasta add oil and salt to a large pot of boiling water. Cook fresh pasta over high heat for 20 to 30 seconds, then test for doneness by biting a piece of pasta. It should be just slightly resistant to teeth (al dente) (see Note). Test every 15 seconds thereafter.

10 Drain and place immediately into a large bowl. Toss with oil or soft butter to prevent pasta from sticking together. Add desired sauce and toss.

VARIATION:

To vary the color and only slightly alter the taste, substitute 2 tablespoons toma-to paste, carrot puree, beet puree, or spinach puree for the water.

ADVANCE PREPARATION:

Pasta may be prepared up to 2 days ahead and refrigerated up to 2 days in plastic bags. Cook just before serving.

NOTE:

Some sauces may be finished in the pan with the pasta tossed right in. In this case, undercook the pasta slightly to compensate for its additional cooking in the heated sauce.

PASTA WITH FRESH MUSHROOM SAUCE

Serves 2 to 3 as main course or 4 to 6 as first course

The growth of the California mushroom industry in recent years has been truly striking. We now have varieties of all of the world's great fungi, from Japan's shiitake and shimeji oyster mushrooms, to the famous French varieties: cèpes, morels, and chanterelles. Here is an adaptation of creative chef Wolfgang Puck's recipe. Use whatever seasonal mush-rooms you can obtain, since the real excitement in this recipe comes from the mixture of fresh mushrooms.

RECOMMENDED CALIFORNIA WINE:

If made with cream, serve a Chardonnay or Pinot Noir; if made without cream, serve a Cabernet Sauvignon or Zinfandel.

FOR SAUCE:

2 tablespoons unsalted butter

1 tablespoon olive oil

3 shallots, finely minced

¼ pound fresh oyster mushrooms, sliced

¼ pound fresh chanterelle mushrooms, sliced

¼ pound fresh shiitake mushrooms, sliced

¼ pound button mushrooms, sliced

2 tablespoons tawny port

½ cup chicken stock (page 276) or veal stock (page 274)

½ cup whipping cream (optional; see Note)

1 teaspoon salt

½ teaspoon finely ground pepper

1 tablespoon oil

1 teaspoon salt

¾ pound fresh pasta, cut into tagliatelle, linguine, or angel hair pasta

FOR GARNISH:

½ cup freshly grated Parmesan cheese

1 For sauce: In a 2-quart saucepan, heat butter and oil until foaming. Add shallots and all mushrooms and sauté, stirring occasionally, for 3 to 5 minutes, or until slightly brown.

2 Add port, stock, and cream, if desired. Simmer until slightly thickened, about 3 to 5 minutes. Add salt and pepper. Taste for seasoning.

3 Add oil and salt to a large pot of boiling water. Add pasta and cook over high heat until al dente. Drain well.

4 Toss hot pasta with mushroom sauce in a medium serving bowl and serve immediately. Pass Parmesan cheese separately.

NOTE:

Cream gives a richer consistency and taste but is not necessary.

FRESH PASTA WITH SMOKED SALMON, DILL, AND GOLDEN CAVIAR

Serves 4 as first course

The ingredients in this warm pasta dish are luxurious, as is its taste. The sauce is kept light so that the flavor of the salmon and golden caviar can predominate. Golden caviar is the roe of the whitefish and gets its name from its golden apricot color. It is processed without preservatives or additives. The fish is caught in the Great Lakes, but the process is a California invention. Use a high-quality natural smoked salmon that is not too salty. When combining the ingredients, be sure to toss gently so that the caviar doesn't break apart. Serve as a first course.

RECOMMENDED CALIFORNIA WINE:

Serve with a full-bodied Chardonnay or a sparkling Blanc de Noirs brut.

FOR SAUCE:

1 cup whipping cream

2 tablespoons cream cheese, softened

1 tablespoon butter

¼ teaspoon salt

Pinch of finely ground white pepper

1 tablespoon oil

1 teaspoon salt

¾ pound fresh pasta, cut into tagliarini or fettucine

¼ pound smoked salmon, cut into small pieces

2 tablespoons finely chopped fresh dill

3 ounces golden caviar

FOR GARNISH:

Dill sprigs

1 For sauce: In a 1-quart saucepan, heat cream over moderately high heat until reduced to ¾ cup. Add cream cheese and whisk until slightly thickened. Add butter and continue cooking for 1 minute. Add salt and pepper. Set aside.

2 To cook pasta, add oil and salt to a large pot of boiling water. Add pasta and cook over high heat until al dente. Drain well. Place in a medium bowl.

3 To finish sauce add reduced cream mixture to pasta. Sprinkle smoked salmon, dill, and one-third of caviar over pasta and mix gently but thoroughly. Taste for seasoning.

4 Divide among 4 plates and garnish with remaining caviar and dill sprigs. Serve immediately.

PENNE WITH CHICKEN, TOMATO, AND LEEK SAUCE

Serves 4 to 6 as main course

Crisp pancetta, poached chicken, and sautéed leeks mingle in a fresh thyme-infused marinara sauce. Just prior to serving, the sauce is poured over the pasta. I prefer using the short, tubular penne so that the pieces of chicken, pancetta, and pasta are all roughly the same size and easy to balance on a fork. Serve as a main course with Sliced Vegetable Salad with Fennel and Gorgonzola.

RECOMMENDED CALIFORNIA

Wine: Serve with a dry Sauvignon Blanc or Zinfandel.

3 cups chicken stock (page 276) or water
with ½ teaspoon salt added

1 pound or 2 whole small chicken breasts,
skinned and boned

¼ pound pancetta, thinly sliced

2 small leeks, cleaned and finely chopped

1 quart Marinara Sauce (page 278)

½ cup whipping cream

2 teaspoons finely chopped fresh thyme,
or 1 teaspoon dried thyme

Pinch of crushed red pepper

½ to 1 teaspoon salt

1 tablespoon oil

1 teaspoon salt for boiling water

1 pound penne or other short (3-inch)
tubular pasta

FOR GARNISH:

½ cup freshly grated Parmesan cheese

1 For sauce: In a medium skillet with high sides or a medium saucepan, bring chicken stock or enough water to cover chicken to simmer. If stock doesn't cover chicken, add water to cover. If using water only, add ½ teaspoon salt. Add chicken breasts and simmer for 10 to 12 minutes, depending on size, or until just tender.

2 Remove pan from heat and cool chicken in liquid. Drain chicken and cut into ½-inch slices. Reserve.

3 Cook pancetta in a large skillet over medium-low heat until crisp and slightly brown. Remove from pan with a slotted spoon and drain on paper towels. Crumble and reserve. Discard all but 2 tablespoons drippings.

4 Add leeks and sauté over medium heat, stirring occasionally, until soft but not brown, about 5 to 7 minutes.

5 Add Marinara Sauce, cream, thyme, red pepper, and ½ teaspoon salt or more, to taste. Bring to boil and cook for 3 to 5 minutes.

6 Just before serving add pancetta and sliced chicken to sauce and heat briefly. Taste for seasoning.

7 Add oil and salt to a large pot of boiling water. Add pasta and cook over high heat until al dente. Drain well. Transfer to a medium serving bowl.

8 Pour sauce over pasta and toss. Serve immediately. Pass Parmesan cheese separately.

ADVANCE PREPARATION:

May be prepared up to 4 hours ahead through Step 5 and kept in refrigerator. Do not add chicken and pancetta until just before serving.

SPRINGTIME VEGETABLE PASTA

Serves 4 as main course or 6 as appetizer

Spring is a year-round phenomenon in California when it comes to the availability of produce. This pasta dish, flavored with a sauce of Gorgonzola, Parmesan, and prosciutto, is a satisfying luncheon or light dinner entrée. Serve with Jerusalem Artichoke–Spinach Salad.

RECOMMENDED CALIFORNIA WINE:

This can be served with an oaky version of dry Sauvignon Blanc or Chardonnay, a Blanc de Pinot Noir, or a lightly chilled Gamay.

FOR VEGETABLES AND SAUCE:

1 cup fresh shelled peas (about 1 pound unshelled)

½ cup (1 stick) unsalted butter

4 shallots, finely chopped

2 zucchini, thinly sliced

2 carrots, peeled and thinly sliced

½ small cauliflower, broken into small florets

½ pound mushrooms, thinly sliced

¼ red bell pepper, seeded and cut into small dice

½ cups chicken stock (page 276)

1 cup whipping cream

2 tablespoons finely chopped fresh basil, or 1 tablespoon dried basil

¼ pound imported Gorgonzola cheese, cut into small pieces

3 ounces prosciutto, cut into 1/8-inch slices and coarsely chopped

½ teaspoon salt

¼ teaspoon finely ground white pepper

1 tablespoon oil

1 teaspoon salt

1 pound fresh pasta, cut into fettucine or linguine

FOR GARNISH:

2 tablespoons chopped fresh parsley

½ cup freshly grated Parmesan cheese

1 For vegetables and sauce: Cook peas in a medium saucepan of boiling water over high heat for 5 minutes, or until just tender. Pour cold water over peas to stop the cooking process. Drain thoroughly.

2 Heat butter in a large skillet over medium heat. Add shallots and sauté, stirring occasionally, until softened. Add zucchini, carrots, cauliflower, mushrooms, and red pepper and stir-fry about 3 minutes. They should be cooked but still crisp. Set aside ¼ cup vegetables for garnish.

3 Add chicken stock, cream, and basil to skillet. Simmer for about 3 minutes. Stir in Gorgonzola and let melt in sauce.

4 Add peas and prosciutto and cook 1 more minute. Add salt and pepper. Taste for seasoning.

5 Add oil and salt to a large pot of boiling water. Add pasta and cook over high heat until al dente. Drain well.

6 Pour vegetable-sauce mixture over pasta and toss. Top with reserved vegetables and chopped parsley. Pass Parmesan cheese separately.

ADVANCE PREPARATION:

May be prepared through Step 3 up to 2 hours ahead. Cover and keep at room temperature.

PASTA WITH PESTO

Serves 2 to 3 as main course or 4 to 6 as first course

This classic Italian sauce intensifies pasta's fine flavor. Substitute walnuts for pine nuts in the pesto for a different result. Combined here with cream for additional smoothness, pesto, peas, and pancetta go together brilliantly. I like this dish hot or cold. With the addition of a small amount of Basic Vinaigrette, it becomes a fragrant pasta salad. If serving hot, serve with Three-Lettuce Salad and sliced tomatoes.

RECOMMENDED CALIFORNIA WINE:

Serve with a big, fruity Chardonnay.

½ pound pancetta, thinly sliced

1 cup fresh shelled baby peas

   (about 1 pound unshelled)

1⅓ cups Pesto Sauce (page 290)

½ cup whipping cream

¼ teaspoon finely ground pepper

1 tablespoon olive oil

1 teaspoon salt

¾ pound fresh pasta, cut into tagliarini or fettucine

½ cup freshly grated Parmesan cheese

1 For sauce: In a 9-inch skillet, cook pancetta over medium heat, turning occasionally, until crisp and brown. Drain on paper towels and crumble. Reserve.

2 Cook peas in a small saucepan of boiling water for 5 minutes, or until just tender. Drain thoroughly.

3 In a medium skillet, combine Pesto Sauce and cream over medium heat. Bring to simmer. Remove from heat and cover skillet to keep sauce warm.

4 Add oil and salt to a large pot of boiling water. Add pasta and cook over high heat until al dente. Drain well.

5 Add pasta to sauce in skillet and toss. Add peas, pancetta, and pepper and toss again. Taste for seasoning and serve immediately. Pass Parmesan cheese separately.

VARIATION:

Use ⅓ pound prosciutto cut in ⅛-inch slices and coarsely chopped.

ADVANCE PREPARATION:

May be kept up to 4 hours in refrigerator. Mix with ½ cup Basic Vinaigrette (page 281) and serve cold.

GREEN FETTUCINE WITH GOAT CHEESE, BROCCOLI, AND CAULIFLOWER

Serves 2 to 3 as main course or 4 to 6 as appetizer

A common partner to fettucine is a rich cream and Parmesan cheese sauce. This adaptation uses local goat cheese and chicken stock rather than cream to create a dish that is anything but common. Fresh thyme, an important ingredient here, adds its cool and biting bouquet. The broccoli and cauliflower are arranged around the edge of the dish for an interesting contrast. Excellent as a first course, followed by a simple grilled chicken or Grilled Veal Chops with Rosemary.

RECOMMENDED CALIFORNIA WINE:
This works well with a big, oaky Chardonnay, or a full-bodied Zinfandel.

2 cups broccoli florets

2 cups cauliflower florets

1½ cups chicken stock (page 276)

8 ounces Sonoma goat cheese or French
    goat cheese, such as Montrachet

2 teaspoons chopped fresh thyme,
    or 1 teaspoon dried thyme

½ teaspoon salt

¼ teaspoon finely ground white pepper

1 tablespoon oil

1 teaspoon salt

¾ pound fresh pasta, made with
    spinach and cut into fettucine

FOR GARNISH:

1 tablespoon finely chopped fresh parsley

1 Immerse broccoli and cauliflower in a large pan of boiling water and boil about 5 minutes or until cooked but slightly crunchy. Drain and pour cold water over vegetables to stop the cooking process. Drain thoroughly.

2 In a 9-inch skillet, boil chicken stock until reduced to 1 cup.

3 Scrape rind off goat cheese with a serrated knife, removing as thin a layer as possible. Cut cheese into small pieces. Whisk goat cheese into stock. Add thyme, salt, and pepper and simmer about 5 minutes, or until slightly thickened. Taste for seasoning. Add broccoli and cauliflower, reserving 6 florets of each.

4 Add oil and salt to a large pot of boiling water. Add pasta and cook over high heat until al dente, about 30 seconds. Drain well. Place in skillet with sauce and toss until well combined.

5 Put in serving bowl or on plates and arrange reserved vegetables around pasta for garnish. Sprinkle with parsley and serve immediately.

ADVANCE PREPARATION:
May be prepared up to 2 hours ahead through Step 1 and kept covered at room temperature.

SPICY CHINESE NOODLES WITH VEGETABLES

Serves 6 as side dish

Thin French green beans (haricot verts), which now grow in Southern California, are used instead of Chinese long beans in this spicy Chinese-style recipe. Serve with Shrimp and Leek Stir-Fry with Toasted Pine Nuts.

RECOMMENDED CALIFORNIA WINE:
This is delicious with a Blanc de Pinot Noir or Sauvignon Blanc.

½ pound Chinese wheat and egg noodles

5 tablespoons peanut oil

4 carrots, peeled and julienned

½ pound green beans, julienned,
    or thin French-style green beans

½ cup fresh shiitake or oyster mushrooms,
    sliced (see Notes)

¼ cup chopped green onions

1 to 2 teaspoons chili paste with garlic
    (see Notes)

¼ cup soy sauce

¼ cup dry white wine

2 tablespoons chopped cilantro

1 Cook Chinese noodles in a large pot of boiling water over medium heat for 4 minutes. Drain well and put in bowl with 1 tablespoon of the peanut oil. Toss so that noodles don't stick together.

2 Immerse carrots and beans separately in a small pan of boiling water and boil each for 2 minutes. Drain and pour cold water over vegetables to stop the cooking process. Drain well.

3 In a large skillet or wok, heat the remaining peanut oil over high heat until very hot. Add carrots, beans, and mushrooms, and stir-fry, stirring often, for about 1 minute. Add green onions and continue to stir-fry.

4 Add chili paste, soy sauce, and wine and bring to a boil. Taste for seasoning.

5 Combine noodles with vegetable mixture and heat through. Sprinkle cilantro on top, mix quickly, and serve immediately.

ADVANCE PREPARATION:

May be prepared up to 4 hours ahead through Step 2. Cover noodles and vegetables separately and keep at room temperature.

NOTES:

(1) *Cultivated white mushrooms can be substituted.*
(2) *Chili paste with garlic can be found in Chinese markets or in the Asian section of your market. Amount used depends on spiciness desired.*

❧

PASTA WITH SANTA BARBARA CALAMARI

Serves 4 to 6

Calamari (Italian for "squid") are caught in great quantities year-round in the Monterey Bay region of California. When purchased fresh from a market, they should already be cleaned. If not, ask your fish vendor to clean them for you. Serve this dish when your time is limited, since it is simple and easy to prepare. Accompany with Three-Lettuce Salad or Caesar Salad.

RECOMMENDED CALIFORNIA WINE:

The natural lightness of a Santa Barbara or San Luis Obispo Chardonnay or Fumé Blanc makes a refreshing foil for this dish.

3 pounds squid, cleaned and rinsed

4 shallots, finely chopped

Coarse salt

¼ cup dry white wine

6 tablespoons (¾ stick) unsalted butter

½ teaspoon salt

3 cloves garlic, minced

¼ teaspoon finely ground white pepper

1 tablespoon oil

1 teaspoon salt

1 pound fresh pasta, cut into fettucine
   or spaghetti

1 For squid and sauce: To clean squid, cut off tentacles and reserve. Pull out large white bone from body and discard. Rinse squid in cold water. Remove head (where eyes are) and pull; this should remove most of the innards, which should be discarded, along with the head. Scrape out any remaining material. Carefully remove and discard ink sac.

2 Rub coarse salt on squid to help remove skin, then pull off skin. Rinse squid once more.

3 Cut squid bodies crosswise in ½-inch slices. Cut tentacles into 2-inch pieces.

4 Melt butter in a 10-inch skillet. Add squid pieces and sauté until their color changes to pink, about 10 to 12 minutes. Add garlic, shallots, and wine and bring to a boil. Add salt and pepper and taste for seasoning. Do not overcook or squid will become rubbery.

5 Add oil and remaining salt to a large pot of boiling water. Add pasta and cook over high heat until al dente. Drain well. Divide pasta among 4 individual plates for serving. Pour squid sauce over pasta. Serve immediately.

FRESH PASTA ROLL FILLED WITH SPINACH

Serves 4 to 6 as main course or 8 to 10 as side dish

An exciting alternative to lasagna, this also works well at a buffet, since it seals in both flavor and warmth. It can be prepared ahead of time and baked just prior to serving. Serve sliced with Grilled Lemon-Mustard Chicken, Turkey Sauté with Lemons, Mushrooms, and Capers, or Leg of Lamb, California Style.

RECOMMENDED CALIFORNIA WINE:

This will accompany any main course wine or can be served as a separate course with a dry Sauvignon Blanc or a coastal-country Zinfandel.

FOR SAUCE:

¼ cup (½ stick) unsalted butter

3 tablespoons all-purpose flour

2 cups milk

6 tablespoons Marinara Sauce (page 278)

FOR FILLING:

8 bunches spinach (about 4 pounds)

3 tablespoons olive oil

1 onion, finely chopped

½ pound mushrooms, finely chopped

¼ pound mortadella (Italian pork
    sausage), finely chopped

2 cups ricotta cheese

2 whole eggs

2 egg yolks

1¼ cups freshly grated Parmesan cheese

¼ teaspoon freshly grated nutmeg

Salt and freshly ground pepper to taste

FOR PASTA ROLL:

1 cup unbleached all-purpose flour

½ cup semolina

2 eggs

1 to 2 tablespoons water

2 tablespoons milk (for brushing)

2 tablespoons olive oil

1 teaspoon salt

FOR TOPPING:

½ cup freshly grated Parmesan cheese

1 For sauce: Melt butter in a medium saucepan over low heat until foamy. Add flour and cook, whisking, for 2 minutes. The mixture should bubble but not change color.

2 Add milk and whisk over medium heat until thickened, about 5 minutes. Add Marinara Sauce and continue to stir until blended. Remove from heat and cover with plastic wrap or dab with a small piece of butter to prevent skin from forming. Set aside.

3 For filling: Remove spinach stems and rinse leaves thoroughly. Steam spinach in a 6-quart pot over medium heat until cooked, about 2 minutes. Pour cold water over spinach to stop the cooking process. Wring out spinach in a kitchen towel to remove all excess moisture. Coarsely chop spinach with a sharp knife or in a food processor fitted with the steel blade.

4 Heat olive oil in a medium skillet over medium heat. Add onion and sauté, stirring occasionally, for 3 minutes. Add mushrooms and continue to cook until soft. Remove to a medium bowl.

5 Add mortadella, spinach, and remaining filling ingredients and blend well. Season to taste with salt and pepper and set aside.

6 For pasta roll: Make pasta dough, divide in half, and proceed as directed for using pasta machine (page 62). Roll out each sheet on second-thinnest setting. Lay across a pasta rack or a chair and dry for 5 to 10 minutes.

7 Place both pasta sheets, one beside the other, on work surface and seal by brushing the touching edges with milk. Using a rolling pin, roll dough out so that the 2 pieces stick together and roll becomes a bit larger.

8 Let pasta sheet rest for 10 minutes to partially dry.

9 Boil a generous amount of water in a spaghetti pot with insert (it is best to use pot with insert to avoid extra handling of dough). Add 1 tablespoon of the olive oil and the salt.

10 Prepare a large bowl of ice water and add remaining 1 tablespoon olive oil.

11 Place the pasta sheet in the boiling water and boil for 30 seconds. Do not fold the sheet over when immersing it in boiling water. Remove insert with pasta sheet inside it and plunge into ice water. Let cool in ice water 10 minutes.

12 Preheat oven to 350°F. Wet a large kitchen towel and spread it out on a board. Place pasta sheet on cloth and let rest 10 minutes. Even out end and edges with a sharp knife or pizza cutter. The width should be about 12 inches.

13 Spread filling evenly over sheet of pasta, leaving a ¾-inch border on all 4 sides.

14 Carefully and gently roll up the sheet with the aid of the cloth.

15 Place the roll in a buttered baking dish. Spoon enough sauce over roll to cover and sprinkle with Parmesan cheese.

16 Bake for 25 to 30 minutes, or until top is lightly golden. Remove from oven and allow to cool 10 minutes in pan.

17 To serve: Slice and place on a serving plate. Additional sauce may be served on the side.

ADVANCE PREPARATION:

May be prepared up to 1 day ahead through Step 15 and kept in refrigerator. Bake for 40 minutes at 350°F if cold.

❧

PASTA SOUFFLÉ

Serves 4 to 6

This recipe is a favorite of mine. A layer of thin pasta forms the base, followed by layers of carrots, red peppers, and green leeks. The Parmesan-flavored soufflé mixture is added and the entire dish cooked until it is a crusty golden brown. Use an ovenproof clear glass soufflé dish to show off its colorful layers. Serve with Chicken with Tomato and Sausages or Grilled Veal Chops with Rosemary. It can also be served as the main course for a luncheon; begin with Ventura Limestone Lettuce Salad with Toasted Pine Nuts and Raspberry Vinaigrette and finish with assorted sorbets.

RECOMMENDED CALIFORNIA WINE:

This can be served with any already-selected main-course wine; if served as a separate course it can be accompanied by a light, fruity, coastal-county Zinfandel.

FOR PREPARING SOUFFLÉ:

2 tablespoons unsalted butter

2 tablespoons freshly grated Parmesan cheese

5 tablespoons unsalted butter

2 leeks, cleaned and finely chopped

2 small carrots, peeled and cut into
small dice

1/4 small red bell pepper, seeded and
cut into small dice

2 tablespoons oil

1 1/2 teaspoons salt

1/2 pound very thin pasta
(such as vermicelli)

3 tablespoons all-purpose flour

1 1/2 cups half-and-half

1 teaspoon Dijon mustard

1 1/2 teaspoons finely chopped fresh
basil, or 1/2 teaspoon dried basil

Pinch of finely ground white pepper

Pinch of freshly grated nutmeg

1 cup freshly grated Parmesan cheese

3 egg yolks

5 egg whites

Pinch of salt

1 Preheat oven to 350°F. Heavily butter a 1½-quart soufflé dish. Sprinkle Parmesan cheese into dish and tap sides of dish to distribute cheese evenly over base and sides. Turn upside down and tap to remove excess cheese.

2 In medium skillet, melt 2 tablespoons of the butter over medium heat. Add leeks, carrots, and bell pepper and sauté, stirring occasionally, until beginning to soften, about 3 to 5 minutes.

3 Add 1 tablespoon of the oil and 1 teaspoon of the salt to a medium pot of boiling water. Add pasta and cook over high heat until al dente. Drain well. Pour cold water over noodles and drain well. Place in a medium bowl. Add the remaining 1 tablespoon oil to prevent noodles from sticking together, and toss.

4 Melt the remaining 3 tablespoons butter over low heat in a medium saucepan. Add flour and whisk for about 2 minutes over medium heat. Mixture should start to bubble but not change color. Add half-and-half and whisk over heat until thickened.

5 Add mustard, basil, the remaining ½ teaspoon salt, the pepper, nutmeg, and ½ cup plus 2 tablespoons of the Parmesan cheese.

6 Allow mixture to cook and then whisk in egg yolks one at a time.

7 Beat egg whites with pinch of salt until stiff. Fold whites into the cooled cheese mixture.

8 Spoon noodles on bottom of soufflé dish and sprinkle with 2 tablespoons Parmesan. Spread the sautéed vegetables over the noodles and sprinkle with 2 more tablespoons cheese.

9 Pour soufflé mixture over vegetables and sprinkle with remaining cheese. Bake for 35 to 45 minutes, or until puffed and brown. Serve immediately.

VARIATION:

Cook ¼ pound pancetta until crisp. Drain and crumble into small pieces. Add to mixture in Step 5.

ADVANCE PREPARATION:

May be prepared up to 4 hours ahead through Step 5 and refrigerated. Bring to room temperature before continuing.

BASIC PIZZA DOUGH

Yields 2 pizzas

Here is a basic pizza dough with instructions for making it by hand.

3 cups all-purpose flour	1 cup lukewarm water
2 (¼-ounce) envelopes active dry yeast	2 tablespoons olive oil
or 2 (⅗-ounce) cakes fresh yeast	1½ teaspoons salt

1 Sift flour into a large bowl and make a well in center. Sprinkle dry yeast or crumble fresh yeast into well. Pour ½ cup of the lukewarm water over yeast and leave for 10 minutes. Stir to dissolve yeast. Add remaining water, the oil, and salt to well and mix with ingredients in middle of well.

2 Stir in flour and mix thoroughly to obtain a fairly soft dough. If dough is dry, knead in 1 tablespoon water; if dough is very sticky, knead in 1 to 2 tablespoons flour.

3 Knead dough by slapping it vigorously on a lightly floured work surface until dough is very smooth and elastic. Flour work surface occasionally if dough sticks.

4 Transfer dough to a clean bowl and sprinkle it with a little flour. Cover with a damp cloth and let rise in a warm place about 1 hour, or until doubled in volume.

5 Punch dough down and knead again briefly on a floured surface until smooth. Return to bowl and cover.

6 Return to warm place and let rise 30 to 45 minutes, or until doubled in volume.

7 Shape according to individual recipe.

ADVANCE PREPARATION:

May be prepared up to 8 hours ahead through Step 5 and refrigerated. To continue, remove from refrigerator and let rise 20 to 30 minutes, then shape according to individual recipe.

PIZZA WITH SHRIMP, TOMATOES, AND GARLIC

Yields 2 pizzas; serves 4 as main course

Fresh tomatoes and garlic make all the difference in a pizza. With the addition of sweet local shrimp arranged in a circular pattern, the effect is visually exciting. Unlike the pizza Americans are used to, this pizza recalls old-world style with our own local quality ingredients.

FOR TOPPING:

1 pound small or medium raw shrimp, shelled and deveined

½ cup olive oil

6 large cloves garlic, minced

3½ pounds ripe tomatoes, peeled, seeded, and chopped

½ teaspoon salt

⅛ teaspoon finely ground pepper

½ teaspoon dried thyme

1 recipe Basic Pizza Dough (page 78)

1 For topping: Put shrimp in a shallow bowl. Add 2 tablespoons of the olive oil and ⅓ of the minced garlic. Cover and leave to marinate for 1 to 2 hours in refrigerator.

2 In a large skillet or sauté pan, heat ¼ cup of the olive oil over medium heat. Add the remaining garlic and cook, stirring, for 30 seconds. Stir in tomatoes and add salt, pepper, and thyme. Cook stirring occasionally, about 20 minutes or until mixture is dry. Taste for seasoning. Reserve.

3 Oil 2 baking sheets. Knead dough again briefly, divide in 2 equal parts, and put each on a baking sheet. With oiled hands, pat each piece of dough out to a 9- to 10-inch circle with the rim slightly higher than rest of circle. Alternatively, use a rolling pin to roll out dough on a floured surface and transfer to baking sheets.

4 Spread tomato mixture over dough, leaving a ¾-inch border of dough. Arrange shrimp, tails facing inward, in a ring at edge of tomato mixture. Arrange any remaining shrimp in a ring near center of pizza. Sprinkle shrimp lightly with salt and pepper, then with any garlic and oil remaining in bowl in which they were marinated. Generously brush rim of pizza with oil. Sprinkle any remaining oil over topping.

5 Let rise about 15 minutes. Preheat oven to 400°F.

6 Bake for about 30 minutes, or until the dough is golden brown and firm but not too hard. Serve immediately.

ADVANCE PREPARATION:

Topping may be prepared 4 hours ahead through Step 2 and kept in refrigerator.

❧

PIZZA WITH LEEKS, TOMATOES, AND PANCETTA

Yields 2 pizzas; serves 4 as main course

Leeks are a standard ingredient in French cooking. In this recipe they impart a fragrant taste that is less imposing than that of the yellow onion traditionally found on pizza. Pancetta, an Italian bacon, is cured rather than smoked, which results in a milder, more delicate flavor. Here it imbues the fresh tomatoes, mild leeks, and aromatic basil with a distinctive character. This pizza makes a great main course with Tricolor Vegetable Salad with Mustard Vinaigrette.

RECOMMENDED CALIFORNIA WINE:

Serve with a dry Sauvignon Blanc or a fresh young Zinfandel.

FOR TOPPING:

3 tablespoons unsalted butter	1 pound ripe tomatoes, peeled, seeded,
2 pounds leeks, white and light green	and chopped
parts cleaned and cut into thin slices	1 tablespoon chopped fresh basil,
1/4 teaspoon salt	or 1 teaspoon dried basil
1/8 teaspoon finely ground pepper	1 tablespoon oil
1/4 pound pancetta, thinly sliced	

1 recipe Basic Pizza Dough (page 78)

1 For topping: Heat butter in a deep skillet or sauté pan over low heat. Add leeks, salt, and pepper and mix thoroughly. Cover and cook over low heat, stirring often, about 20 minutes, or until very tender. If liquid remains in pan, uncover and continue cooking, stirring often, until it evaporates. Taste for seasoning.

2 In a medium skillet, cook pancetta lightly over medium-low heat until crisp and slightly brown. Remove pancetta to paper towels and drain. Crumble into small pieces. Remove drippings from skillet.

3 Add tomatoes to skillet in which pancetta was cooked. Cook over medium heat, stirring often, about 15 minutes, or until mixture is dry. Add pancetta and basil and taste for seasoning.

4 Oil 2 baking sheets. Knead dough again briefly and divide in 2 equal parts. Put each on baking sheet. With oiled hands, pat each piece of dough out to a 9- to 10-inch circle with the rim slightly higher than rest of circle. Alternatively, use a rolling pin to roll out dough on a floured surface and transfer to baking sheets.

5 Spread half of leek mixture over outer edge of each circle of dough. Spread tomato mixture over center of circle, leaving leek mixture showing near rim.

6 Brush rim of pizzas with oil. Sprinkle any remaining oil over topping.

7 Let rise about 15 minutes. Preheat oven to 400°F.

8 Bake for about 30 minutes, or until the dough is golden brown and firm but not hard. Serve immediately.

Topping may be prepared up to 4 hours ahead through Step 3 and kept in refrigerator. Bring to room temperature before cooking.

EGGPLANT PIZZA

Yields 2 pizzas; serves 4 as main course

Rather than using a tomato sauce, this pizza uses chunks of fresh tomato to highlight the eggplant's purple skin. Use only tender young eggplants so that the skin is as soft as the inner flesh. Serve with Three-Lettuce Salad or use as a first course and follow with Swordfish Brochette.

RECOMMENDED CALIFORNIA WINE:

Serve with a dry Sauvignon Blanc or a young Zinfandel.

FOR TOPPING:

½ pound ripe plum tomatoes, peeled

1 pound small eggplants, unpeeled

½ cup olive oil

3 tablespoons freshly grated
    Parmesan cheese

½ teaspoon salt

⅛ teaspoon finely ground pepper

1½ teaspoons chopped fresh thyme,
    or ½ teaspoon dried thyme

1 recipe Basic Pizza Dough (page 78)

1 For topping: Slice tomatoes crosswise. Put slices in a colander and leave to drain for 1 hour; this will remove excess liquid.

2 Meanwhile, cut eggplants in thin slices crosswise. Heat half the oil in a large skillet over medium-high heat. Add enough eggplant slices to make one layer. Fry for about 4 minutes on each side, or until brown and very tender. Remove to a plate with a slotted spoon. Continue frying remaining slices, adding oil to pan as necessary and heating pan before adding more slices. When all eggplant is cooked, set aside.

3 Oil 2 baking sheets. Knead dough again briefly, divide into 2 equal parts, and put each on a baking sheet. With oiled hands, pat each piece of dough out to a 9- to 10-inch circle with the rim slightly higher than rest of circle. Alternatively, use rolling pin to roll out dough on floured surface and transfer to baking sheets.

4 Sprinkle Parmesan cheese on dough and arrange tomato slices, overlapping slightly, in a ring near rim of each pizza. Cover rest of pizza with one layer of eggplant slices, overlapping slightly. Sprinkle tomatoes and eggplant with salt, pepper, and thyme. Generously brush rim of pizzas with oil. Sprinkle any remaining oil over topping.

5 Let rise about 15 minutes. Preheat oven to 400°F.

6 Bake for about 30 minutes, or until crust is golden brown and firm but not hard. Serve immediately.

MEXICAN PIZZA

Yields 2 pizzas; serves 4 as main course

Mexican Pizza is perhaps the most familiar first-course pizza in California. Unlike with other pizzas, Cheddar cheese flavors the tomato topping, along with chiles and cilantro. Finally, the baked pizza is garnished with avocado and sour cream. Serve as a first course, cut into small pieces and accompanied with beer or margaritas, and follow with Grilled Chicken with Salsa and Mustard Butter, or serve as a main dish with a simple green salad.

RECOMMENDED CALIFORNIA WINE:

Although beer or margaritas are a first choice, this could be served successfully with a Fumé Blanc or a Blanc de Pinot Noir.

2 California chiles (see Note)

3 tablespoons oil

4 green onions, finely chopped

4 large tomatoes, peeled, seeded, and chopped

¼ teaspoon salt

⅛ teaspoon finely ground pepper

1 tablespoon finely chopped cilantro

3 cups (¾ pound) shredded Cheddar cheese

1 ripe avocado

½ cup sour cream

1 tablespoon finely chopped cilantro

1 recipe Basic Pizza Dough (page 78)

1 For topping: To peel chiles, place on broiler pan and broil approximately 6 inches from heat until blackened on all sides. Use tongs to turn chiles.

2 Put chiles in a plastic bag and close tightly. Let rest for 10 minutes.

3 Remove from bag, drain chiles, and peel off skin. Make a slit in each chile and open it up. Core and cut off stem. Scrape off seeds and ribs from chiles. Drain and finely chop chiles.

4 Heat 1 tablespoon of the oil in a medium skillet over low heat. Add green onions and sauté until soft. Add tomatoes, salt, and pepper and cook, stirring occasionally, about 10 minutes, or until mixture is dry. Add cilantro and chiles. Taste for seasoning.

5 Oil 2 baking sheets. Knead dough again briefly, divide into 2 equal parts, and put each on a baking sheet. With oiled hands, pat each piece of dough out to a 9- to 10-inch circle with the rim slightly higher than rest of circle. Alternatively, use a rolling pin to roll out dough on a floured surface and transfer to baking sheets.

6 Divide tomato mixture among pizzas. Sprinkle each pizza with half the Cheddar cheese. Brush rim of pizzas with remaining oil.

7 Let rise about 15 minutes. Preheat oven to 400°F.

8 Bake for about 30 minutes, or until the dough is golden brown and firm but not hard.

9 Peel and dice avocado. Garnish pizza with diced avocado, sour cream, and chopped cilantro. Serve immediately.

VARIATION:

Use 4 corn tortillas instead of pizza dough. In Step 3, oil 2 baking sheets. Put 2 tortillas on each one. Bake for 5 minutes to crisp tortillas. Divide tomato mixture among tortillas. Sprinkle each with ¼ of the Cheddar cheese. Bake for about 10 minutes, or until cheese melts. When the "pizzas" are ready, garnish each as above. Serve immediately.

ADVANCE PREPARATION:

Topping may be prepared up to 4 hours ahead through Step 4 and kept in refrigerator. Bring to room temperature before cooking.

NOTE:

If fresh chiles are not available, substitute canned California (Anaheim) chiles, drained and chopped. When working with chiles always wear rubber gloves. Wash the cutting surface and knife immediately afterward.

CALZONE WITH PROSCIUTTO AND SONOMA GOAT CHEESE

Yields 8 calzones

Calzone is an Italian specialty that has seen a strong revival of interest among Californians. Goat cheese and fresh herbs are added, elevating the usual filling ingredients while at the same time maintaining a certain earthiness. The filling with prosciutto ham is creamy in contrast to the crusty pizza dough. This calzone is sensational either as a first course or as a main dish with Jerusalem Artichoke–Spinach Salad.

RECOMMENDED CALIFORNIA WINE:

Serve with a buttery Chardonnay or a robust Zinfandel.

FOR FILLING:

8 ounces Sonoma goat cheese or
    French goat cheese
2 ounces prosciutto, thinly sliced

1 pound fresh buffalo mozzarella or
    cow's milk mozzarella cheese, sliced

2 tablespoons finely chopped
  fresh oregano, or ¾ teaspoon
  dried oregano

2 tablespoons finely chopped parsley

1 egg

⅛ teaspoon finely ground pepper

1 recipe Basic Pizza Dough (page 78)

¼ cup olive oil

1 For filling: Scrape rind off goat cheese with a serrated knife, removing as thin a layer as possible. In a large bowl, crumble or mash goat cheese. Add remaining filling ingredients. Taste for seasoning.

2 Oil 2 baking sheets. Knead dough again briefly and divide into 8 equal parts. On a lightly floured surface, shape dough into ovals approximately 7½ by 6½ inches.

3 Brush olive oil on dough, leaving ½ inch free at edges. Brush the remaining ½-inch edge with water. Put about 3 heaping tablespoons filling on bottom half of oiled dough and fold top over like a turnover. Press edge with tines of fork to seal. Place on a baking sheet. Brush again with olive oil. Make a slash for a steam vent with serrated knife. Repeat with remaining dough and filling.

4 Let rise about 30 minutes. Preheat oven to 400°F.

5 Bake for 25 to 30 minutes, or until dough is puffed, golden brown, and firm but not too hard. Serve hot.

VARIATION:

For 1 pound buffalo mozzarella, substitute ½ pound cow's milk mozzarella and ½ pound Italian Fontina, shredded. You may add to filling 1 medium tomato, peeled, seeded, chopped, and drained of all excess juice in a strainer.

ADVANCE PREPARATION:

Filling may be prepared up to 4 hours ahead and kept in refrigerator. Remove from refrigerator 1 hour before using and bring to room temperature.

VEGETABLE FRITTATA

Serves 4 to 6

Although it originated in Italy, the ethnic influences in this frittata are both Italian and Mexican. This colorful California version calls for Spicy Red Salsa. Californians serve frittatas at lunch, brunch, and for supper, either hot or at room temperature. Serve with Orange, Kiwi, and Jicama Salad with Lime Dressing; finish with Cinnamon-Pecan Coffee Cake and freshly roasted coffee.

1 bunch spinach (about ½ pound)

2 tablespoons unsalted butter

1 tablespoon oil

2 shallots, finely chopped

½ pound mushrooms, thinly sliced

2 small zucchini, thinly sliced

¾ teaspoon salt

¼ teaspoon finely ground pepper

12 eggs

1½ cup (6 ounces) shredded sharp
   Cheddar or Gruyère cheese

FOR GARNISH:

¼ cup chopped fresh parsley

1 cup sour cream

½ cup Spicy Red Salsa (page 282)

1 Preheat oven to 425°F. Remove spinach stems and rinse leaves thoroughly.

2 Heat butter and oil in a 12-inch skillet with an ovenproof handle over medium-high heat (see Note). Add shallots and sauté until soft but not brown, about 3 minutes. Add mushrooms and sauté for 1 to 2 minutes. Add zucchini and continue cooking 2 minutes. Stir in spinach, cover, and cook until spinach is wilted. Season with ¼ teaspoon salt and a pinch of the pepper. Set aside.

3 In a large bowl, combine eggs, the remaining salt, and remaining pepper and whisk until well blended. Stir in 1¼ cups of the shredded cheese.

4 Pour egg mixture over vegetables in skillet and cook over medium-low heat, stirring occasionally, until bottom of mixture is lightly browned, about 5 minutes. Sprinkle with remaining ¼ cup cheese.

5 Transfer skillet to oven and bake until frittata is puffed and browned, about 10 to 15 minutes.

6 Remove from oven and invert onto a plate. Invert again onto a serving platter, with browned top facing up. Sprinkle with parsley and place a dollop of sour cream and a ring of salsa in the center. Cut frittata into wedges and serve immediately. Pass remaining sour cream and salsa separately.

ADVANCE PREPARATION:

May be prepared up to 2 hours ahead through Step 2 and kept covered at room temperature. Although it will be substantially different in texture and taste, the frittata may be made 1 day ahead, refrigerated, and served at room temperature.

NOTE:

Use a nonstick pan, if possible, for ease in inverting frittata.

FRITTATA WITH ZUCCHINI,
SPICY SAUSAGE, AND RED PEPPERS

Serves 4 to 6

Although Italian sausage is easier to find and is recommended in this recipe, you might try Mexican chorizo if it is available. Either way, the zucchini, red pepper, and sausage combination gives the frittata a memorable zing reminiscent of the early California-Mexican favorite, huevos rancheros. Serve with corn tortillas and butter.

2 tablespoons oil

1 spicy Italian-style sausage
   (about 3 ounces)

2 tablespoons unsalted butter

1 small zucchini, cut into thin slices

1 teaspoon salt

¼ teaspoon finely ground pepper

1 red bell pepper, cut into thin strips

½ teaspoon finely chopped fresh thyme,
   or ¼ teaspoon dried thyme

12 eggs

¾ cup freshly grated Parmesan cheese

1 In a medium skillet, heat 1 tablespoon of the oil over medium heat. Add sausage and sauté, stirring, until browned on all sides. Remove and drain on paper towels. Cut into ¼-inch slices.

2 Heat butter and remaining 1 tablespoon oil in a 12-inch skillet with an ovenproof handle over medium heat (see Note). Add zucchini, half the salt, and a pinch of the pepper and sauté for 1 minute on each side. Remove from skillet using a slotted spoon.

3 Add bell pepper to skillet and sprinkle with thyme, the remaining salt, and another pinch of pepper. Sauté over medium heat for 3 minutes, or until tender. Push to center of skillet.

4 Arrange sausage slices in a ring along border of skillet. Arrange zucchini slices in a ring inside sausage ring.

5 Preheat oven to 425°F. In a large bowl, combine eggs, half the Parmesan cheese, and the remaining pepper. Whisk until well blended.

6 Pour egg mixture over vegetables in skillet. Cook over medium-low heat, without stirring, until bottom is lightly browned, about 5 minutes. Sprinkle with remaining cheese.

7 Transfer skillet to oven and bake until frittata is puffed and browned, about 10 to 15 minutes.

8 Remove from oven and invert onto a plate. Invert again onto a serving platter, with browned top facing up. Cut frittata into wedges and serve immediately.

ADVANCE PREPARATION:

May be prepared up to 2 hours ahead through Step 4 and kept covered at room temperature. Although it will be substantially different in texture and taste, the frittata may be made 1 day ahead, refrigerated, and served at room temperature.

NOTE:

Use a nonstick pan, if possible, for ease in inverting frittata.

CORN AND SHRIMP FRITTATA

Serves 4 to 6

The combination of corn and shrimp is a frequent one in Baja California, where most of the Southwest's shrimp are caught. In this recipe the corn makes a crust on the bottom of the frittata. Jack cheese and chives are placed on top for a flavorful decorative touch. A spicy cheese bread and Sautéed Baby Tomatoes make excellent accompaniments.

3 ears of corn

2 tablespoons unsalted butter

1 tablespoon oil

½ pound raw shrimp, shelled,
   deveined, and cut in half lengthwise

½ teaspoon salt

¼ teaspoon finely ground pepper

12 eggs

2 tablespoons minced chives

1½ cups (6 ounces) shredded Monterey
   jack cheese

FOR SERVING:
   ½ cup Spicy Red Salsa (optional; page 282)

1 Preheat oven to 425°F. Scrape kernels off corncobs, using a sharp knife.

2 Heat butter and oil in a 12-inch skillet with an ovenproof handle over medium heat (see Note). Add shrimp, half the salt, and a pinch of the pepper and sauté, stirring, for 1 minute on each side. Add corn and continue to sauté for another minute.

3 Combine eggs, chives, remaining salt, and remaining pepper and whisk until well blended. Stir in ¾ cup of the shredded cheese.

4 Pour egg mixture over shrimp mixture in skillet. Cook over medium-low heat, without stirring, until bottom of mixture is lightly browned, about 5 minutes. Sprinkle with remaining cheese.

5 Transfer skillet to oven and bake until frittata is puffed and browned, about 10 to 15 minutes.

6 Remove from oven and invert onto a plate. Invert again onto a serving platter, with browned top facing up. Cut frittata into wedges and serve immediately. Pass salsa separately, if desired.

ADVANCE PREPARATION:

May be prepared up to 2 hours ahead through Step 2 and kept covered at room temperature. Although it will be substantially different in texture and taste, the frittata may be made 1 day ahead, refrigerated, and served at room temperature.

NOTE:

Use a nonstick pan, if possible, for ease in inverting frittata.

SALADS

CALIFORNIANS ENJOY SALAD VIRTUALLY ANY-
WHERE ON THE MENU AND AT ANY TIME OF DAY. A salad
may be a first course, an accompaniment, or a main course.
Pasta salads, vegetable salads, and green salads are among
the types included in this chapter. There is ample opportu-
nity for innovation in salad making, and the combinations
included here demonstrate the vast creativity of the cuisine
of California.

SAUTÉED RED CABBAGE SALAD WITH PANCETTA
AND BROILED GOAT CHEESE

WARM SCALLOP SALAD DRESSED WITH
TOMATO, MINT, AND LIME

VENTURA LIMESTONE LETTUCE WITH TOASTED
PINE NUTS AND RASPBERRY VINAIGRETTE

THREE-LETTUCE SALAD

CAESAR SALAD

JERUSALEM ARTICHOKE-SPINACH SALAD

TRICOLOR VEGETABLE SALAD WITH MUSTARD VINAIGRETTE

LEMON-MINT CABBAGE SALAD

ORANGE, KIWI, AND JICAMA SALAD WITH LIME DRESSING

GREEN BEAN-JICAMA SALAD

STIR-FRIED CHINESE VEGETABLE SALAD

BEET AND WALNUT SALAD WITH BLUE CHEESE

SLICED VEGETABLE SALAD WITH FENNEL
AND GORGONZOLA

SATURDAY SALAD

ORIENTAL-STYLE CHICKEN SALAD

CALIFORNIA DUCK SALAD WITH ORANGES AND WILD RICE

COLD CHINESE NOODLES IN PEANUT-SESAME SAUCE

COUNTRY GARDEN PASTA SALAD

SUMMER PASTA SALAD

SEAFOOD PASTA SALAD WITH LEMON-DILL DRESSING

CHICKEN PASTA SALAD WITH AVOCADO
AND SPICY RED SALSA

CHICKEN PASTA SALAD WITH SPICY GARLIC MAYONNAISE

SAUTÉED RED CABBAGE SALAD WITH
PANCETTA AND BROILED GOAT CHEESE

Serves 4

This is a delicious variation on warm spinach salad that uses year-round red cabbage to an advantage with crispy pancetta and goat cheese. The goat cheese is lightly breaded and then broiled just enough to melt and to lightly toast the bread crumbs for added crunch. I like to serve it as a main course for lunch with warm sourdough bread, or as a first course with Lemon-Herb Chicken and steamed zucchini and carrots.

RECOMMENDED CALIFORNIA WINES:

This can be served equally well with white or red wine. A big Napa or Sonoma Chardonnay melds the goat cheese and sherry vinegar flavors. The goat cheese will reduce the seemingly excessive tannin of a full-bodied Cabernet Sauvignon.

½ pound pancetta, sliced	1 small red cabbage, cored and
6 ounces Sonoma goat cheese or	thinly sliced or shredded
French goat cheese	2 large shallots, finely chopped
½ cup olive oil	3 tablespoons sherry vinegar
2 tablespoons French bread or	¼ teaspoon salt
whole-wheat bread crumbs	⅛ teaspoon coarsely cracked pepper

1 In a medium skillet, cook pancetta over medium-low heat until crisp and lightly browned. Remove and place on paper towels to drain. Crumble into small pieces and reserve.

2 Slice goat cheese into 4 equal portions. Place on broiler pan and brush each piece with 1 tablespoon of the olive oil. Sprinkle with bread crumbs so that they adhere to the cheese. Refrigerate for 1 hour.

3 Remove and discard all but 1 tablespoon of pancetta drippings and add 3 tablespoons olive oil to skillet. Add cabbage and sauté until it begins to wilt. Remove to a bowl.

4 Add the remaining ¼ cup olive oil to pan. Add shallots and sauté until soft. Add sherry vinegar and boil about 3 minutes. Season with salt and pepper and pour over cabbage. Add pancetta and mix well.

5 Preheat broiler if necessary. Broil coated goat cheese just until it is golden brown. Watch carefully, as it burns easily.

6 Place cabbage mixture on 4 individual plates and set goat cheese in center. Serve immediately.

ADVANCE PREPARATION:

May be prepared up to 4 hours ahead through Step 4. Serve at room temperature. Cheese may be breaded up to 6 hours ahead and refrigerated.

WARM SCALLOP SALAD DRESSED WITH TOMATO, MINT, AND LIME

Serves 4 as main course or 6 as appetizer

In California, warm salads are appearing with increasing regularity on lunch and dinner menus. Here, sweet, succulent scallops are quickly sautéed and then placed in the center of a bed of crisp green watercress. The cooling tomato-mint dressing is then spooned around the scallops for a stunning visual presentation. Whatever size scallop you use, remember that bay scallops cook much more quickly than do ocean scallops. Serve as a main course with lunch or at dinner before Turkey Sauté with Lemons, Mushrooms, and Capers.

RECOMMENDED CALIFORNIA WINE:
Serve with a dry Sauvignon Blanc or a Blanc de Noirs sparkling wine.

FOR DRESSING:

⅓ cup olive oil

2 shallots, finely chopped

2 tablespoons freshly squeezed lime juice

½ teaspoon salt

½ teaspoon coarsely cracked black pepper

2 tomatoes, peeled, seeded, and chopped

2 tablespoons finely chopped fresh mint

1 pound scallops, well drained and
    patted dry
2 tablespoons olive oil
¼ teaspoon salt

Pinch of coarsely cracked black pepper
3 bunches watercress,
    large stems removed (see Note)

1 For dressing: Heat olive oil in a medium skillet. Add shallots and sauté 2 minutes, or until soft. Add lime juice, salt, and pepper. Remove from heat and add tomatoes and mint. Set aside.

2 If using sea scallops, remove small white muscle at side of each. If scallops are 1 inch in diameter or larger, cut in half before using.

3 In another medium skillet, heat 2 tablespoons olive oil. Add scallops and sauté over medium-high heat for 3 to 5 minutes, turning often. They should be slightly translucent in the middle. Remove from heat.

4 Pour half of dressing mixture over warm scallops, add salt and pepper, and mix.

5 Divide watercress evenly among individual plates. Spoon scallops with some dressing in center of each plate. Spoon additional tomato-mint dressing around scallops.

ADVANCE PREPARATION:

This dish may be prepared up to 6 hours ahead through Step 4 and served cold on the bed of watercress.

NOTE:

Spinach may be substituted for watercress. Use 2 medium bunches. Clean, remove stems, and tear leaves into bite-sized pieces.

VENTURA LIMESTONE LETTUCE WITH TOASTED PINE NUTS AND RASPBERRY VINAIGRETTE

Serves 4 to 6

Limestone lettuce is now grown hydroponically year-round in Southern California. The taste is closest to butter lettuce, but there is less waste, and limestone lettuce has a pronounced, sweet, buttery flavor. In combination with ruby red radicchio, Belgian endive, and thin enoki mushrooms, the salad greens are out of the ordinary. Sweet, acidic raspberry vinaigrette accents the salad, and toasted pine nuts add a crunchy finish. If necessary, substitute butter lettuce for limestone and omit the radicchio if unavailable. Serve with Three-Onion Soup for a satisfying complete meal. I also like this salad as a first course before Pesto-Stuffed Chicken Breasts.

¼ cup pine nuts

FOR VINAIGRETTE:

2 tablespoons olive oil

2 tablespoons vegetable oil

2 tablespoons raspberry vinegar

1 small shallot, minced

1 teaspoon Dijon mustard

2 teaspoons whipping cream

Salt and finely ground pepper to taste

2 heads Ventura limestone lettuce, cut into bite-sized pieces

2 Belgian endives, thinly sliced

4 ounces enoki mushrooms, roots cut off

1 small head radicchio, torn into bite-sized pieces

FOR GARNISH:

8 cherry tomatoes, halved

1 Preheat oven to 350°F. Toast pine nuts in oven for 5 minutes, or until lightly browned.

2 For vinaigrette: Mix together all ingredients with a whisk or in a blender until well combined.

3 Place limestone lettuce, endive, mushrooms, and radicchio in a salad bowl. Garnish with cherry tomato halves and toasted pine nuts.

4 Pour approximately ¼ cup of raspberry vinaigrette over salad and toss. Taste for seasoning and serve.

ADVANCE PREPARATION:

Vinaigrette may be kept up to 1 week in refrigerator. Salad may be prepared up to 4 hours ahead through Step 3 and kept in refrigerator. Remove from refrigerator ½ hour before serving.

THREE-LETTUCE SALAD

Serves 6 to 8

Bright red radicchio, peppery arugula, and sweet limestone lettuce give this salad a contrasting mix of textures, colors, and tastes. The unusual dressing carries both the bite of mustard and the nuttiness of hazelnut oil. The recipe can be varied according to whatever lettuce you can find locally to create your own Three-Lettuce Salad, as long as you keep in mind that the tastes and textures should be complementary. This salad can begin the meal and is also quite refreshing following the entrée. Serve after Crispy Duck with Cranberry, Pear, and Pistachio Dressing to cleanse the palate, or serve before Springtime Vegetable Pasta.

1 cup hazelnuts
2 heads radicchio, torn into
   bite-sized pieces

FOR VINAIGRETTE:

3 tablespoons red wine
   or balsamic vinegar
1 teaspoon Dijon mustard
1 teaspoon whipping cream

2 bunches arugula, torn into
   bite-sized pieces
1 head limestone or butter lettuce,
   torn into bite-sized pieces

¼ cup hazelnut oil
¼ cup oil
½ teaspoon salt
¼ teaspoon finely ground pepper

1 Preheat oven to 350°F. Toast hazelnuts in oven for 10 minutes. Rub toasted nuts between a kitchen towel to remove skins. Coarsely chop nuts with a knife.

2 In a medium salad bowl, combine lettuces. Sprinkle hazelnuts over top.

3 For vinaigrette: Combine vinegar, mustard, and cream in a small mixing bowl. Slowly whisk in oils until blended. Add salt and pepper and taste for seasoning.

4 Pour dressing over salad and toss.

ADVANCE PREPARATION:

May be prepared up to 4 hours ahead through Step 3 and kept in refrigerator. Remove from refrigerator ½ hour before serving.

CAESAR SALAD

Serves 4 to 6

Originally conceived in a small hotel in Tijuana, Caesar salad is still enjoyed today with simple grilled entrées or in larger portions as a main course. This variation calls for anchovy paste, which is easy to work with, and elephant garlic, a mild, giant-cloved variety of garlic from Northern California. If elephant garlic is unavailable, substitute one medium clove for one elephant clove. Some people think it's sacrilege to garnish this wonderful salad with tomatoes, but I love it. It goes especially well with Grilled Chicken with Salsa and Mustard Butter.

FOR CROUTONS:

¼ cup olive oil

1 large clove elephant garlic, crushed

8 (½-inch-thick) slices sourdough bread, crusts removed, cut into ½-inch cubes (about 2 cups)

1 large clove elephant garlic, minced

Juice of 1 lemon

2 teaspoons anchovy paste

¼ teaspoon salt

¼ teaspoon finely ground black pepper

1 egg

½ cup olive oil

3 heads romaine lettuce, dark outer leaves
   removed, torn into bite-sized pieces

½ cup freshly grated Parmesan cheese

4 to 6 slices ripe tomato

1 In a medium skillet, heat olive oil over medium heat and add garlic. Sauté 1 minute and discard garlic.

2 Increase heat to high and add bread cubes, turning frequently so that they brown evenly on all sides and are crisp and golden. Add more oil if necessary to keep them from burning. Drain on paper towels. Reserve.

3 For dressing: Combine minced garlic, lemon juice, anchovy paste, salt, and pepper in a large salad bowl. Whisk until blended.

4 Immerse whole egg in a small pan of boiling water and cook for exactly 1 minute. Remove and crack egg into salad bowl. Whisk egg and other dressing ingredients until combined. Add oil in steady stream and whisk until smooth.

5 Add lettuce, Parmesan cheese, and croutons to bowl. Toss and taste for seasoning. Place on individual plates and garnish each with tomato slice. Serve immediately.

ADVANCE PREPARATION:

Salad should be made immediately before serving so all ingredients are at their crispy best.

JERUSALEM ARTICHOKE-SPINACH SALAD

Serves 6

The sunchoke, or Jerusalem artichoke, is a small tuber grown from the sunflower plant. It has a sweet, moist interior and is left unpeeled for this salad. Fresh green baby spinach leaves are joined with sunchokes for a contrast of soft texture and bright color. Balsamic Vinaigrette, with its heady rich taste, finishes the salad. Serve this before Lamb Stew with Rosemary or with Springtime Vegetable Pasta.

1 pound Jerusalem artichokes

2 bunches baby spinach (about 1 pound)

1 teaspoon chopped fresh basil

1 teaspoon chopped fresh parsley

1 teaspoon chopped chives

½ cup Balsamic Vinaigrette (page 282)

1 Scrub artichokes to remove excess dirt. (Do not peel.) Cut into thin slices. Place in a large salad bowl.

2 Remove spinach stems. Rinse and dry leaves thoroughly. Tear spinach into bite-sized pieces. Place in salad bowl with artichokes. Sprinkle herbs on top.

3 Add Balsamic Vinaigrette and toss. Taste for seasoning and serve.

ADVANCE PREPARATION:

May be prepared up to 1 hour ahead through Step 2 and refrigerated.

TRICOLOR VEGETABLE SALAD WITH MUSTARD VINAIGRETTE

Serves 6

When living in France, I became accustomed to the traditional crudité salad available in most charcuteries and bistro-style restaurants. This California adaptation uses the domestically grown thin string beans, which are similar to the French haricot verts. If they are unavailable, cut large string beans in half lengthwise. Try serving this at large gatherings, as this salad can easily be made in quantity. Use a food processor to shred the carrots and the beets. Complementary additions to this include Chicken Pasta Salad with Spicy Garlic Mayonnaise, marinated mushrooms, and Tomatoes with Fresh Mozzarella and Basil.

RECOMMENDED CALIFORNIA WINE:

This is especially good with a big oaky Chardonnay, though it can be served with any dry red wine.

3/4 cup Basic Vinaigrette (page 281)

2 teaspoons Dijon mustard

3 tablespoons chopped fresh parsley

1/2 pound French green beans
(haricots verts), ends cut off

6 carrots, peeled and shredded

4 small beets, peeled and shredded

FOR GARNISH:

Lettuce leaves

1 Combine Basic Vinaigrette with mustard and 2 tablespoons of the parsley. Mix well. Taste for seasoning.

2 Immerse green beans in a pan of boiling water and boil for 5 to 7 minutes, or until cooked but slightly crisp. Remove from heat, drain, and rinse with cold water to stop the cooking process. In a small bowl, combine beans with 1/4 cup of the vinaigrette. Let marinate 15 minutes.

3 In another small bowl, combine 1/4 cup of the vinaigrette with carrots and let marinate for 15 minutes.

4 Combine remaining vinaigrette with beets and let marinate for 15 minutes.

5 Place lettuce leaves on a large serving platter or individual plates. Arrange 3 mounds of vegetables on top of lettuce and garnish with remaining parsley.

ADVANCE PREPARATION:

May be prepared up to 4 hours ahead through Step 4 and kept covered in refrigerator.

LEMON-MINT CABBAGE SALAD

Serves 6 to 8

Citrus flavor is a frequent note in our salads. In this cabbage salad, a blend of fresh Middle Eastern herbs is combined with a tart lemon dressing. Exotic additions are vivid red pomegranate seeds and black currants. Pomegranates are available in California from September to December; if they are unavailable, double the amount of currants. Serve as a first course followed by Marinated Roast Rack of Lamb with Spicy Peanut Sauce.

FOR DRESSING:

2 cloves garlic, minced

½ teaspoon salt

Pinch of finely ground pepper

½ teaspoon sugar

⅓ cup freshly squeezed lemon juice

⅓ cup olive oil

3 cups finely shredded cabbage

1 tablespoon fresh dill,
 or 1 teaspoon dried dill

2 tablespoons chopped fresh mint

2 tablespoons chopped cilantro

FOR GARNISH:

2 tablespoons pomegranate seeds

2 tablespoons currants

1 For dressing: Place garlic, salt, pepper, sugar, and lemon juice in a bowl. Slowly add olive oil, whisking until blended. Taste for seasoning.

2 Place cabbage in a medium bowl and sprinkle with herbs. Garnish with pomegranate seeds and currants.

3 Pour dressing over salad and toss. Taste for seasoning and serve.

ADVANCE PREPARATION:

May be prepared up to 4 hours ahead though Step 2 and kept in refrigerator.

ORANGE, KIWI, AND JICAMA SALAD
WITH LIME DRESSING

Serves 6 to 8

This is a particularly pleasing accompaniment to Sunday brunch. Mexican jicama, navel oranges, and kiwi provide an exotic flavor combination, typical of California cooking. Today almost all of the world's kiwi fruits are grown in either California or New Zealand, and California supplies the majority for the American market. Serve this salad after Vegetable Frittata.

1 head salad bowl lettuce,
    separated into leaves
1 head romaine lettuce, torn into
    small pieces
2 stalks celery, thinly sliced
½ pound jicama, peeled and
    diced (see Note)

2 green onions, thinly sliced
3 kiwi, peeled and sliced ¼ inch thick
3 navel oranges, peel and pith removed,
    sliced ¼ inch thick
1 small red onion, thinly sliced into rings

FOR DRESSING:

Juice of 2 limes
Juice of 1 orange
½ teaspoon salt

Finely ground pepper to taste
¼ cup walnut oil

1 Line a serving bowl with salad bowl lettuce leaves.

2 In a medium bowl, combine romaine, celery, jicama, and green onions. Toss well, then mound in center of lettuce leaves in serving bowl. Top with circle of overlapping kiwi and orange slices. Arrange onion rings on top.

3 For dressing: In small bowl, combine lime juice, orange juice, salt, and pepper. Whisk in walnut oil.

4 Pour dressing over salad and refrigerate until ready to serve.

ADVANCE PREPARATION:

May be prepared up to 4 hours ahead through Step 3 and kept in refrigerator.

NOTE:

Water chestnuts or Jerusalem artichokes can be substituted for the jicama.

GREEN BEAN-JICAMA SALAD

Serves 4 to 6

A refreshing change from the traditional green bean and slivered almond combination, this crisp salad borrows from Mexico for its distinctive taste. Jicama, a slightly sweet, turniplike vegetable from Mexico, adds crunch and mild flavor to the sweet string beans and onion. It is perfect for a buffet table or as an accompaniment to a main course, such as Swordfish Brochette, for a light and satisfying meal.

¾ pound green beans,
   ends cut off, halved

¼ pound jicama, peeled, sliced,
   and cut into matchstick pieces
½ small red onion, thinly sliced

FOR DRESSING:

1 teaspoon freshly squeezed lemon juice
1 teaspoon grainy mustard
1 shallot, finely chopped

⅛ teaspoon finely ground pepper
¼ cup Basic Vinaigrette (page 281)

FOR GARNISH:

8 cherry tomatoes, halved
1 tablespoon chopped fresh parsley

1 Cook green beans in a 2-quart saucepan filled with boiling water for about 10 minutes, or until tender but slightly crisp. Drain. Pour cold water over vegetables to stop the cooking process. Drain thoroughly.

2 For dressing: Mix lemon juice, mustard, shallot, and pepper with Basic Vinaigrette in a medium bowl.

3 In another medium bowl, combine green beans, jicama, and onion. Add dressing and toss. Taste for seasoning. Place in a serving dish and surround with cherry tomato halves. Sprinkle with chopped parsley.

ADVANCE PREPARATION:

May be kept up to 1 day in refrigerator. Garnish with tomatoes and parsley just before serving.

STIR-FRIED CHINESE VEGETABLE SALAD

Serves 4 to 6

In stir-frying, vegetables are brought to their peak of flavor, color, and crispness and served immediately. This variation was created from already cooked and chilled vegetables, which are terrific in a salad. In this cold version, the sauce, which is flavored with garlic and soy, becomes the dressing. Serve as an accompaniment to Braised Spicy Eggplant and Oriental-Style Chicken Salad.

RECOMMENDED CALIFORNIA WINE:
Serve with a full-bodied Chardonnay or a Blanc de Pinot Noir.

½ cup plus 2 tablespoons peanut oil

¾ pound cauliflower, divided into
    small florets

¾ pound broccoli, divided into
    small florets

½ pound mushrooms, cut into quarters
    or into same size as florets

1 large red bell pepper, seeded and cut
    into strips

½ pound Chinese snow peas, cleaned

FOR DRESSING:

1 cup chicken stock (page 276)

¼ cup soy sauce

1 clove garlic, minced

2 tablespoons sherry

2 tablespoons sesame oil

1 In a wok, heat 2 tablespoons of the peanut oil over high heat. Add cauliflower and stir-fry for about 3 minutes, or until cooked but still crunchy. Place in a colander set over a bowl and drain.

2 Add 2 more tablespoons peanut oil to wok. When hot, add broccoli and stir-fry for about 3 minutes, or until cooked but still crunchy. Drain in colander.

3 Add 2 more tablespoons peanut oil to wok. When hot, add mushrooms and stir-fry for 2 minutes, or until just cooked. Drain in colander.

4 Add 2 more tablespoons peanut oil to wok. When hot, add red pepper strips and stir-fry for 2 minutes, or until cooked but still crunchy. Drain in colander.

5 Add remaining oil if wok is dry. Add snow peas and stir-fry for 1 minute, or until cooked but still crunchy. Drain in colander.

6 Remove vegetables from colander and place in a large bowl.

7 With a bulb baster, remove fat from drained vegetable juices in bowl.

8 For dressing: Place juice from vegetables and chicken stock in a medium saucepan. Add soy sauce, garlic, and sherry. Bring to a boil; boil until reduced to 1 cup. Add sesame oil and pour over vegetables. Refrigerate for at least 2 hours before serving.

This dish may also be eaten warm as a vegetable side dish. Serve immediately.

May be kept up to 1 day in refrigerator.

BEET AND WALNUT SALAD WITH BLUE CHEESE

Serves 4 to 6

Balsamic vinegar is as carefully aged as fine wine. I like to add it to walnut oil for an especially delectable salad dressing. Heavily French influenced, this salad mixes beets, walnuts, endive, and blue cheese. It is quite versatile: Without the beets it becomes an excellent after-dinner salad, since the cheese and nuts are emphasized; or serve it as a first course before Sautéed Chicken Breasts with Mustard and Tarragon and Sauté of Julienned Garden Vegetables.

4 baby beets

¼ cup walnut pieces

2 bunches watercress,
    large stems removed

2 Belgian endives, thinly sliced

¼ cup (about 2 ounces) crumbled
    blue cheese

⅓ cup Balsamic Vinaigrette
    made with walnut oil (page 282)

1. Cook beets in a medium saucepan in boiling water for 15 to 20 minutes, or until tender when pierced with a knife. Peel and cut into 1½-inch dice.

2. Preheat oven to 350°F. Toast walnuts in oven for 7 to 10 minutes, or until lightly browned. Remove and cool.

3. In a medium salad bowl, combine watercress and endive and toss. Arrange beets on outer edge of bowl. Sprinkle walnuts and blue cheese in center.

4. Toss with vinaigrette, taste for seasoning, and serve immediately.

ADVANCE PREPARATION:

May be prepared up to 4 hours ahead through Step 3 and kept in refrigerator. Remove from refrigerator 1 hour before serving.

SLICED VEGETABLE SALAD
WITH FENNEL AND GORGONZOLA

Serves 4 to 6

Fennel adds its crunchy texture to a variety of colorful raw vegetables in this European-style salad. Available in the fall and winter months, fennel is a celerylike bulb. Unlike celery, the long stalks are cut off, leaving the bulb, which is sliced into ¼-inch slices. The feathery leaves may be used in garnishes. Here, the light lemon salad dressing brings out the Gorgonzola's creamy, pungent taste. Serve with fresh sourdough bread as a light meal, or serve as a first course to Grilled Chicken with Basil and Garlic and Sautéed Sugar Snap Peas and Red Peppers. Try it before Pasta with Santa Barbara Calamari.

FOR DRESSING:

¼ cup freshly squeezed lemon juice

2 teaspoons Dijon mustard

½ cup olive oil

¼ teaspoon salt

Pinch of finely ground pepper

1 bulb fennel, thinly sliced

6 red radishes, thinly sliced

¼ pound mushrooms, thinly sliced

½ small red onion, thinly sliced

2 carrots, peeled and thinly sliced

¼ pound jicama, peeled and
    thinly sliced

¼ European cucumber, thinly sliced

2 stalks celery, peeled and thinly sliced

1 tablespoon finely chopped chives

1 tablespoon finely chopped fresh parsley

½ cup (about ¼ pound) crumbled
    Gorgonzola cheese

Green lettuce leaves

1 tablespoon finely chopped fresh parsley

1 For dressing: Mix lemon juice and mustard in a small bowl. Slowly whisk in oil until combined. Season with salt and pepper. Set aside.

2 In a medium bowl, combine vegetables and herbs. Sprinkle with Gorgonzola cheese.

3 Toss vegetables with dressing. Taste for seasoning. Arrange lettuce leaves on salad plates and top with vegetables. Garnish with parsley and serve.

ADVANCE PREPARATION:

May be prepared up to 2 days ahead through Step 1 and kept in refrigerator.

SATURDAY SALAD

Serves 4 as main course

My friend Barbara Windom makes this salad every Saturday at her house by the beach. It is so special because the chicken breasts are first marinated and then baked, and the juices from the baked chicken are used as the basis for the fragrant vinegar-garlic dressing. Serve either before Chilled Cucumber-Avocado Soup or all by itself.

RECOMMENDED CALIFORNIA WINE:

This can be served with an oaky white wine—Chardonnay or dry Sauvignon Blanc—or with a Zinfandel.

Salads

½ cup walnut pieces

½ pound pancetta, sliced

3 tablespoons Dijon mustard

1 tablespoon chopped fresh tarragon,
   or 1 teaspoon dried tarragon

1 clove garlic, minced

2 tablespoons freshly squeezed
   lemon juice

2 whole chicken breasts,
   skinned and boned

1 clove garlic, minced

¾ cup Basic Vinaigrette (page 281)

6 Belgian endives

¼ pound mushrooms, thinly sliced

1 large tomato, peeled and cut into
   bite-sized pieces

2 tablespoons finely chopped chives

1. Preheat oven to 350°F. Toast walnuts in oven for 7 to 10 minutes, or until lightly browned. Reserve.

2. Cook pancetta in a medium skillet over medium-low heat until crisp and slightly brown. Drain on paper towels. Crumble pancetta and reserve.

3. For marinade: Combine ingredients in a medium bowl. Place chicken breasts in marinade and marinate for at least 30 minutes in refrigerator.

4. Put chicken breasts in a baking dish and cover with aluminum foil. Bake for 20 minutes at 350°F. Remove from oven, let cool, and cut into 2-inch pieces. Reserve juices from chicken.

5. In a small bowl, combine chicken-cooking juices with minced garlic and Basic Vinaigrette. Taste for seasoning.

6. In a medium bowl, combine pancetta, endive, mushrooms, tomato, and chives. Add chicken breasts and walnuts.

7. Pour dressing over salad; toss and serve immediately.

ADVANCE PREPARATION:

May be prepared up to 2 hours ahead through Step 3 and kept in refrigerator.

ORIENTAL-STYLE CHICKEN SALAD

Serves 6 to 8

I will go anywhere for good chicken salad, especially this one, which is crunchy, spicy, and slightly sweet. This Oriental version is adapted from one found at a Malibu beach restaurant, the Whalewatch. Different from other Oriental chicken salads in that it gets its crunch from cucumber and sesame seeds rather than from deep-fried rice noodles, it is very refreshing. Serve with Cold Chinese Noodles in Peanut-Sesame Sauce and Stir-Fried Chinese Vegetable Salad for an informal buffet or picnic luncheon.

RECOMMENDED CALIFORNIA WINE:

This is one of those rare dishes that will work with almost any dry wine with moderate fruit: Chardonnay, Fumé Blanc, Riesling, or Chenin Blanc, in their drier versions; Cabernet Sauvignon, Pinot Noir, or Zinfandel. Each gives a slightly different and pleasing effect.

FOR DRESSING:

1 clove garlic, minced	¼ cup soy sauce
1 tablespoon peanut butter	¼ cup rice wine vinegar
Pinch of sugar	2 tablespoons Hot Pepper Oil (page 279)
Pinch of Chinese hot mustard	¼ cup sesame oil

3 cups chicken stock (page 276) or water combined with ½ teaspoon salt	1 medium European cucumber, julienned
2 pounds chicken breasts, boned	2 green onions, thinly sliced on diagonal
1 tablespoon sesame seeds, toasted	2 tablespoons finely chopped cilantro

1 For dressing: Combine all ingredients except the oils and whisk well to combine. Slowly whisk oils into dressing until combined. Set aside.

2 In a medium, deep skillet or a large saucepan, bring chicken stock or enough water to cover chicken to a simmer. If stock doesn't cover chicken, add water to cover. Add chicken breasts and simmer for 10 to 12 minutes, depending on size, or until just tender.

3 Cool chicken in liquid. Drain chicken and remove skin. Shred by tearing meat into long, thin pieces (or slice with a knife, if desired). Reserve in a medium serving bowl.

4 To toast sesame seeds, place in dry medium skillet over high heat. Shake until seeds turn light brown, about 2 minutes. Remove immediately from skillet. Reserve.

5 Add cucumber, green onions, and 1 tablespoon cilantro to bowl with chicken. Add dressing and mix well. Taste for seasoning. Garnish with sesame seeds and remaining cilantro.

May be prepared up to 8 hours ahead through Step 3 and kept in refrigerator. Toss with dressing just before serving.

CALIFORNIA DUCK SALAD WITH ORANGES AND WILD RICE

Serves 4 to 6

Most people are familiar with oranges and wild rice as accompaniments to hot roast duck. In this striking presentation, a classic French recipe is adapted to a California-style salad. This is actually a combination of two salads: a rice and mushroom salad as a base and a duck salad with toasted walnuts on top. A garnish of orange segments and walnuts surrounds this exquisite dish. Serve as a main-course luncheon entrée.

RECOMMENDED CALIFORNIA WINE:

A wine with vigorous fruit to match the citrus acidity is the key here: a chilled Gamay, a dry Chenin Blanc, or a very fruity Chardonnay.

1 five-pound duck, quartered

3 medium cloves garlic, minced

½ teaspoon salt

½ teaspoon finely ground pepper

1 tablespoon unsalted butter

2 medium shallots, finely chopped

½ cup wild rice, washed thoroughly and drained

1¼ cups chicken stock (page 276)

FOR VINAIGRETTE:

⅓ cup red wine vinegar

1 tablespoon Dijon mustard

½ cup olive oil

½ cup walnut oil

Salt and finely ground pepper to taste

⅓ cup coarsely chopped
   toasted walnuts
⅓ cup finely diced celery

½ pound mushrooms, thinly sliced
2 ½ medium oranges,
   peeled and sectioned

Red leaf lettuce
½ medium orange, peeled
   and sectioned

2 tablespoons toasted walnut halves
1 tablespoon chopped fresh parsley

1 Rub duck with garlic, salt, and pepper. Pierce skin ¼-inch deep all over, particularly in fatty areas around thigh and in wing area. (Do not pierce meat.)

2 Preheat oven to 425°F. Put duck skin side down on rack in a roasting pan and cover with parchment paper. Roast 30 minutes. Turn duck, remove paper, and roast 30 minutes more. Allow to cool. Remove skin and bones and cut meat into ½-inch pieces.

3 For rice salad: In a medium skillet, melt butter until foaming. Add shallots and sauté over low heat until soft and transparent. Rinse wild rice thoroughly with cold water in strainer. Drain. Add rice and mix thoroughly. Add chicken stock, cover, and simmer about 30 minutes, until liquid is absorbed and rice is tender but still a bit crunchy. Cool.

4 For vinaigrette: Combine vinegar and mustard. Whisk in both types of oil. Season to taste with salt and pepper. Reserve.

5 At least 2 hours before serving, toss duck pieces with ¾ cup of the vinaigrette, or until moistened, and add chopped walnuts and celery.

6 To finish rice salad, marinate sliced raw mushrooms in remaining vinaigrette in a large bowl for 15 minutes. Cut orange sections into small pieces. Add to mushrooms along with cooled rice.

7 Just before serving, line a large platter with red lettuce leaves. Make a flat layer of the rice salad, allowing lettuce to show around edges. Mound duck salad in center of rice salad. Garnish with whole orange sections, walnut halves, and parsley.

ADVANCE PREPARATION:

Can be kept up to 4 hours in refrigerator. Remove from refrigerator ½ hour before serving.

COLD CHINESE NOODLES IN PEANUT-SESAME SAUCE

Serves 8 to 10

Cold salads are very important in California cooking because of our year-round warm weather. Chinese-influenced dishes often appear as cold variations of typical hot Chinese dishes. Here, set off by crunchy peanuts and cucumbers, cold noodles in a smooth and spicy dressing make a lovely party dish. Serve this exotic side dish with Oriental-Style Chicken Salad and Braised Spicy Eggplant, or as an accompaniment to simple grilled chicken.

1 pound Chinese-style wheat and egg noodles

2 tablespoons dark sesame oil

FOR DRESSING:

6 tablespoons peanut butter

¼ cup water

3 tablespoons light soy sauce

6 tablespoons dark soy sauce

6 tablespoons tahini (sesame paste)

½ cup dark sesame oil

2 tablespoons sherry

4 teaspoons rice wine vinegar

¼ cup honey

4 medium cloves garlic, minced

2 teaspoons minced fresh ginger

1 to 2 tablespoons Hot Pepper Oil
   (page 279)

½ cup hot water

FOR GARNISH:

1 carrot, peeled and shaved into curls

½ firm medium cucumber, peeled,
   seeded, and julienned

½ cup roasted peanuts, coarsely chopped

2 green onions, sliced

1 Cook noodles in a large pot of boiling unsalted water over medium heat until barely tender and still firm.

2 Drain immediately and rinse with cold water until cold. Drain well and toss noodles with dark sesame oil so that they don't stick together. Reserve.

3 For dressing: Combine all ingredients except hot water in a blender or a food processor fitted with the steel blade and blend until smooth. Thin with hot water to the consistency of whipping cream. Reserve.

④ For garnish: Peel carrot in shavings about 4 inches long. Place in ice water for 30 minutes to curl.

⑤ Just before serving, toss noodles with sauce. Garnish with cucumber, peanuts, green onion, and carrot curls. Serve at room temperature.

ADVANCE PREPARATION:

May be prepared up to 1 day ahead through Step 3 and kept in refrigerator. Dressing will keep indefinitely in refrigerator.

COUNTRY GARDEN PASTA SALAD

Serves 6

Start with this dressing of garlic, mustard, and lemon. Add cooked and cooled pasta, then use your imagination and whatever's in season to create your own distinctive salad. You might also try a little cooked shrimp or chicken for another variation. Serve with Swordfish in Lemon-Ginger Marinade.

RECOMMENDED CALIFORNIA WINE:

This can be served with a Blanc de Pinot Noir or a particularly fruity Zinfandel.

2 tablespoons oil
1 teaspoon salt
1 pound fusilli or small shell pasta

4 cups vegetables (carrots, zucchini, broccoli, sugar snap peas, or any other vegetables of your choice), cut into matchsticks (see Note)

FOR DRESSING:

¼ cup grainy mustard
2 medium cloves garlic, minced
¼ cup freshly squeezed lemon juice
2 tablespoons sherry vinegar

¼ teaspoon salt
¼ teaspoon coarsely ground pepper
½ cup olive oil

¼ cup finely chopped fresh basil
½ cup freshly grated Parmesan cheese

1 Add 1 tablespoon oil and salt to a large pot of boiling water. Add pasta and cook over high heat 10 minutes, or until al dente. Drain and remove to a bowl of ice water mixed with 1 tablespoon oil until cool. Drain thoroughly.

2 Immerse vegetables in a large pan of boiling water and boil about 3 to 4 minutes, or until barely tender. Drain and pour cold water over vegetables to stop the cooking process. Drain thoroughly.

3 For dressing: Combine mustard, garlic, lemon juice, sherry vinegar, salt, and pepper. Slowly whisk in the olive oil until blended.

4 In a medium bowl, combine drained pasta and dressing. Add cooked vegetables, basil, and cheese. Toss well. Taste for seasoning. Refrigerate 1 hour before serving.

ADVANCE PREPARATION:

May be kept up to 4 hours in refrigerator. Do not add basil until immediately before serving. Remove from refrigerator ½ hour before serving.

NOTE:

This is a basic recipe for a salad in which you can use any vegetables of your choice. Make sure they have been cooked but still retain some crunch. Try to include some contrasting colors, and make sure vegetables are all cut into pieces of about the same size.

SUMMER PASTA SALAD

Serves 4 to 6

Fresh tomatoes and basil are at their peak in summer. Serve this light pasta salad with cold roast chicken and Green Bean-Jicama Salad for picnics or informal lunches.

RECOMMENDED CALIFORNIA WINE:

This can be served with any light picnic or lunch wine; try it with a Blanc de Pinot Noir or a Zinfandel Rosé.

2 tablespoons oil

1 teaspoon salt

1 pound fusilli or corkscrew-
shaped pasta

2 medium zucchini, julienned

4 large tomatoes, peeled, seeded,
and coarsely chopped

½ cup sliced black olives

1 tablespoon red wine vinegar

1 teaspoon minced garlic

2 tablespoons finely chopped
fresh parsley

3 tablespoons chopped fresh basil

1 teaspoon salt

½ teaspoon finely ground pepper

2 tablespoons olive oil

¼ cup freshly grated Parmesan cheese

1 Add 1 tablespoon of the oil and the salt to large pot of boiling water. Add pasta and cook over high heat for 10 minutes, or until al dente. Drain and remove to a bowl of ice water mixed with the remaining 1 tablespoon oil until cool. Drain thoroughly. Reserve.

2 Immerse zucchini in a 2-quart saucepan of boiling water and boil 2 minutes. Drain and pour cold water over zucchini to stop the cooking process. Drain thoroughly.

3 For dressing: In a large mixing bowl combine vinegar, garlic, parsley, basil, salt, and pepper. Slowly whisk in oil to blend. Add Parmesan cheese and whisk to combine.

4 Add drained pasta to bowl with dressing. Add zucchini, tomatoes, and olives. Toss well. Taste for seasoning. Chill or serve at room temperature.

ADVANCE PREPARATION:

May be kept up to 4 hours in refrigerator. Do not add basil until immediately before serving. Remove from refrigerator ½ hour before serving.

SEAFOOD PASTA SALAD WITH LEMON-DILL DRESSING

Serves 6

For a party or a picnic, prepare this combination of fresh pink shrimp, Dungeness crab, black olives, and crisp, colorful vegetables. The tangy dill-flavored dressing complements the flavors of the seafood. Start with Chilled Fresh Tomato-Basil Soup for a light lunch or dinner.

RECOMMENDED CALIFORNIA WINE:

This can be served with a Chardonnay, Fumé Blanc, or Blanc de Pinot Noir.

2 tablespoons olive oil

1 teaspoon salt

1 pound small pasta shells

¼ pound Chinese snow peas, julienned

1 cup water

1 cup dry white wine

1 bay leaf

1 pound raw medium shrimp, shelled and deveined

1 small red bell pepper, seeded and julienned

1 small red onion, thinly sliced

1 cup whole black olives, pitted

1 medium carrot, peeled and julienned

½ pound cooked Dungeness crabmeat, torn into small pieces

FOR DRESSING:

3 tablespoons finely chopped fresh dill

2 medium cloves garlic, minced

½ cup freshly squeezed lemon juice

½ cup olive oil

1 teaspoon salt

¼ teaspoon finely ground pepper

1 Add 1 tablespoon of the olive oil and the salt to a large pot of boiling water. Add pasta shells and cook over high heat 10 minutes, or until al dente. Drain and remove to a bowl of ice water mixed with 1 tablespoon olive oil until cool. Drain thoroughly.

2 Immerse snow peas in a small saucepan of boiling water and boil 1 minute. Drain and pour cold water over to stop the cooking process. Drain thoroughly. Place in a large bowl.

3 Combine water, wine, and bay leaf in a medium saucepan and bring to boil. Add shrimp and cook over low heat for 3 to 5 minutes, or until shrimp are pink on outside and just cooked in center. Remove shrimp with a slotted spoon to bowl. Reserve cooking liquid in pan.

4 Immerse bell pepper in shrimp-cooking liquid and boil 1 minute. Drain and pour cold water over pepper to stop cooking process. Drain thoroughly. Put pepper in a large mixing bowl. Add onion, olives, carrot, and crabmeat and stir to combine.

5 For dressing: Combine dill, garlic, and lemon juice in a small bowl. Whisk in olive oil slowly until blended. Season with salt and pepper.

6 Add drained pasta to a large mixing bowl. Add dressing and toss to coat ingredients. Taste for seasoning. Chill or serve at room temperature.

ADVANCE PREPARATION:

May be kept up to 4 hours in refrigerator. Remove from refrigerator ½ hour before serving.

CHICKEN PASTA SALAD WITH AVOCADO AND SPICY RED SALSA

Serves 6

An intriguing mixture of Italian and Mexican influences, this refreshing salad uses a spicy salsa-flavored sauce to dress the al dente linguine and creamy, mild avocado. The poached chicken adds a hearty meatiness. Serve with Green Bean-Jicama Salad or alone.

RECOMMENDED CALIFORNIA WINE:

Serve with a Blanc de Pinot Noir.

1 tablespoon olive oil

1 teaspoon salt

1 pound linguine

3 cups chicken stock (page 276)
  or water mixed with ½ teaspoon salt

Salt to taste

2 whole medium chicken breasts, boned

2 medium avocados

2½ cups Spicy Red Salsa (page 282)

1. Add olive oil and salt to a large pot of boiling water. Add linguine and cook over high heat for 10 minutes, or until al dente. Drain and remove to a bowl of ice water until cool. Drain thoroughly.

2. In a deep, medium skillet or a medium saucepan, bring chicken stock or enough water to cover chicken to a simmer. If stock doesn't cover chicken, add water to cover. Add chicken breasts and simmer for 10 to 12 minutes, depending on their size, or until just tender.

3. Remove from heat. Cool chicken in liquid. Drain chicken and remove skin. Cut into small pieces.

4. Peel and dice 1 avocado. In a serving bowl combine salsa, chicken, and diced avocado. Carefully add cooled pasta and toss well. Season to taste with salt.

5. Slice remaining avocado into ½-inch slices. Garnish salad with avocado slices around outside edge of bowl.

ADVANCE PREPARATION:

May be prepared up to 2 hours ahead through Step 4 and kept in refrigerator. Garnish with avocado immediately before serving.

❧

CHICKEN PASTA SALAD WITH SPICY GARLIC MAYONNAISE

Serves 6

Roasted red pepper, capers, and a vinaigrette-accented mayonnaise dressing add zest to poached chicken in this cold pasta salad. Serve with Pacific Coast Eggplant or marinated mushrooms for a luncheon or informal dinner menu.

RECOMMENDED CALIFORNIA WINE:

This can be served equally well with a Chardonnay, Fumé Blanc, or Blanc de Pinot Noir.

½ cup Spicy Garlic Mayonnaise (page 289)

2 tablespoons Basic Vinaigrette (page 281)

3 cups chicken stock or water mixed
  with ½ teaspoon salt (optional)

1 to 1½ teaspoons salt

2 whole chicken breasts, boned

1 tablespoon olive oil

1 pound linguine

1 red bell pepper

4 green onions, thinly sliced

¼ cup chopped parsley

2 tablespoons capers, drained

1 tablespoon chopped parsley

1 For dressing: In a small bowl, combine mayonnaise with vinaigrette and whisk well. Set aside.

2 In a deep medium skillet or a medium saucepan, bring chicken stock or enough water to cover chicken to a simmer. If stock doesn't cover chicken, add water to cover. Add chicken breasts and simmer for 10 to 12 minutes, depending on size, or until just tender.

3 Cool chicken in liquid. Drain chicken and remove skin. Cut into small pieces.

4 Add oil and 1 teaspoon salt to a large pot of boiling water. Add linguine and cook over high heat 10 minutes, or until al dente. Drain and remove to a bowl of ice water mixed with 1 tablespoon olive oil until cool. Drain thoroughly.

5 To peel bell pepper, place on broiler pan and broil approximately 6 inches from heat until blackened on all sides. Use tongs to turn pepper.

6 Put pepper in a plastic bag and close tightly. Let rest 10 minutes.

7 Remove from bag, drain pepper, and peel off skin. Make a slit in pepper and open it up. Core and cut off stem. Scrape off seeds and ribs from pepper. Cut pepper in ¼-inch dice.

8 In a large bowl, combine chicken, pepper, green onions, parsley, and capers with mayonnaise-vinaigrette mixture. Carefully add cooled pasta and toss well. Taste for seasoning. Garnish with parsley and serve.

ADVANCE PREPARATION:

May be kept up to 1 day in refrigerator.

MAIN COURSES

$\mathcal{T}$HIS CHAPTER REFLECTS THE LIGHT, INFORMAL STYLE OF CALIFORNIA COOKING. Seafood has become the California entrée of choice. With sushi bars fast becoming commonplace, the Japanese concepts of simple preparation and brief cooking time have inspired California fish cookery. Chicken, turkey, duck, and squab served in myriad ways are a close second in popularity as entrées. Because of the contemporary shift away from eating meat, this chapter contains only a limited selection of veal, lamb, pork, and beef dishes. Some of these recipes use veal stock as a base, avoiding the heavier beef stock. Lamb is available from California ranches or imported from New Zealand. Pork is frequently used in Mexican- and Italian-influenced dishes. I have also included several innovative beef recipes.

Grilling is the signature of California Cuisine, and many grilled dishes are included in this chapter. The barbecue has played an important part in the casual California lifestyle, an outgrowth of fair weather and informal entertaining. In California cooking, briquets derived from burning oak, mesquite, hickory, or other hardwoods are used instead of ordinary charcoal. Their smoky-sweet taste enhances the flavor of seafood, poultry, and meat.

SEAFOOD

Swordfish in Lemon-Ginger Marinade
Swordfish Brochette

Sea Bass with Garlic Mayonnaise
Steamed Sea Bass and Fresh Spinach with
Cabernet Sauvignon Sauce

Grilled Trout with Lemon-Curry Butter
Whitefish with Tomato Béarnaise Sauce

Cold Poached Salmon with
Tomato-Basil Vinaigrette
Fillet of Salmon Glazed with
Pesto Hollandaise Sauce

Halibut with Apples, Ginger, and Cider Vinegar
Fresh Tuna with Sautéed Peppers
and Garlic in Parchment

Skewered Shrimp with Cilantro and Green Salsa
Shrimp and Leek Stir-Fry with Toasted Pine Nuts

Scallops with Fresh Tomatoes,
Herbs, and White Wine
Cold Mussels in Tomato-Saffron Sauce

Grilled Lobster with Garlic Butter
Seafood Quartet

California Fish Stew

POULTRY

GRILLED CHICKEN WITH BASIL AND GARLIC

Grilled Lemon-Mustard Chicken

GRILLED CHICKEN WITH SALSA AND MUSTARD BUTTER

Lemon-Herb Chicken

PESTO-STUFFED CHICKEN BREASTS

Spicy Sautéed Chicken Breasts

**SAUTÉED CHICKEN BREASTS WITH
MUSTARD AND TARRAGON**

Chicken with Pancetta and Zinfandel

MEXICAN CHICKEN WITH RAISINS AND ALMONDS

Chicken with Tomatoes and Sausages

**ROAST CHICKEN STUFFED UNDER THE SKIN
WITH GOAT CHEESE-LEEK FILLING**

Crispy Duck with Cranberry, Pear,
and Pistachio Dressing

**BARBECUED ROAST DUCK WITH
RED WINE AND BLACK CURRANTS**

Grilled Squab with Basil Butter

TURKEY SAUTÉ WITH LEMON, MUSHROOMS, AND CAPERS

Sautéed Chicken Livers with Green Peppercorns

MEATS

GRILLED VEAL CHOPS WITH ROSEMARY

VEAL MEDALLIONS WITH LIME-GINGER SAUCE

**VEAL STEW WITH BABY ONIONS,
WILD MUSHROOMS, AND SPINACH**

VEAL AND CHICKEN SAUSAGES
WITH CHILES AND CILANTRO

**SAUTÉED LAMB CHOPS WITH MADEIRA,
CARROTS, AND GREEN BEANS**

SAUTÉED LAMB MEDALLIONS ON A BED OF EGGPLANT
WITH RED PEPPERS

LEG OF LAMB, CALIFORNIA STYLE

MARINATED ROAST RACK OF LAMB
WITH SPICY PEANUT SAUCE

LAMB STEW WITH ROSEMARY

LOIN OF PORK WITH RHUBARB-GINGER SAUCE

STUFFED PORK WITH APPLES AND PRUNES

PORK TACOS, CALIFORNIA STYLE

SAUSAGES WITH LENTILS AND ANCHO CHILE BUTTER

NEW YORK STEAKS WITH ROQUEFORT SAUCE

GRILLED STEAKS WITH ANCHO CHILE BUTTER

TENDERLOIN OF BEEF WITH
ROASTED SHALLOTS AND TARRAGON

SWORDFISH IN LEMON-GINGER MARINADE

Serves 6

Barbecuing over mesquite, with its special, smoky-sweet flavor, has become a trademark of California cooking. Swordfish steaks prepared in this manner assume an added tang when marinated in lemon and ginger for a special sweet-tart contrast. Serve with Green Vegetable Rice and steamed zucchini and carrots.

RECOMMENDED CALIFORNIA WINE:

A full-bodied Napa Chardonnay with plenty of fruit and oak combines deliciously with the grilled and citrus flavors.

FOR MARINADE:

½ cup freshly squeezed lemon juice	1 tablespoon olive oil
2 medium cloves garlic, minced	2 tablespoons oil
1½ teaspoons minced fresh ginger	¼ teaspoon salt
1 teaspoon minced lemon zest	⅛ teaspoon finely ground pepper

6 swordfish steaks, ⅓ to ½ pound each
   and no more than 1 inch thick (see Notes)

1 For marinade: Combine ingredients in a medium bowl. Whisk until blended.

2 In a large shallow nonaluminum dish, arrange fish steaks and pour marinade over. Marinate fish for 2 to 4 hours in refrigerator.

3 Prepare barbecue for medium-heat grilling. Remove fish from marinade. Grill fish about 3 inches from heat for 5 minutes on each side.

4 Heat remaining marinade in a small saucepan over medium heat.

5 Pour some of the remaining marinade over and serve immediately.

VARIATION:

Freshly squeezed lime juice and minced zest may be substituted for lemon.

ADVANCE PREPARATION:

May be made ahead through Step 2 up to 4 hours ahead and refrigerated.

(1) *Other firm-fleshed fish that may be used include shark, tuna, and halibut.*
(2) *When barbecuing with mesquite charcoal or any other charcoal that burns at very high temperatures, cut the fish into pieces that are no more than 1 inch thick so the surface does not burn before the center is cooked.*

SWORDFISH BROCHETTE

Serves 4

Rice wine vinegar mixes with cumin to highlight the flavor of the swordfish in this easy dish. Sweet red bell pepper, cherry tomatoes, and other vegetables add a delightful freshness when threaded between chunks of the fish. Serve with Green Vegetable Rice.

RECOMMENDED CALIFORNIA WINE:

Choose a full-bodied, rich, buttery Chardonnay from Napa or Sonoma to complement the soy and cumin flavors.

FOR MARINADE:

½ cup rice wine vinegar
½ cup dry white wine
¼ cup soy sauce
½ teaspoon cumin

1½ pounds swordfish, skin removed, cut into 1½-inch chunks
1 large zucchini, cut into thick slices
1 large red bell pepper, seeded and cut into chunks

4 green onions, cut into 2-inch pieces and halved
8 mushrooms
8 cherry tomatoes

1 Combine marinade ingredients in a small bowl. Mix well.

2 In a large, shallow nonaluminum dish, arrange fish pieces and pour marinade over. Marinate fish for 2 to 4 hours.

3 Prepare barbecue for medium-heat grilling or preheat broiler, if necessary.

4 Dip vegetables in marinade before placing on skewer. To skewer, thread items in this order: zucchini, fish, red pepper, fish, green onion, mushroom, fish, tomato, fish; repeat.

5 Grill brochette about 3 inches from heat for about 5 minutes on each side. Fish should be slightly underdone in the center. Serve immediately.

ADVANCE PREPARATION:

May be prepared up to 4 hours ahead through Step 4 and kept in refrigerator. Remove from refrigerator before continuing.

SEA BASS WITH GARLIC MAYONNAISE

Serves 6

The sauce, made of lime juice and garlic mayonnaise, transforms Pacific Coast sea bass into a simple but elegant main course. Atlantic sea bass may be substituted. Serve with Leek Timbale and Mustard-Baked Tomatoes.

RECOMMENDED CALIFORNIA WINE:

Serve with a medium- to full-bodied Chardonnay from Napa, San Luis Obispo, or Santa Barbara Counties.

1 tablespoon freshly squeezed lime juice
¾ cup Fresh Garlic Mayonnaise (page 288)
6 sea bass fillets or steaks, ⅓ to ½ pound each

FOR GARNISH:

1 tablespoon chopped fresh parsley

1. Preheat oven to 450°F. Combine lime juice with Fresh Garlic Mayonnaise.

2. Spread half the mayonnaise on top of fish and place fish on broiler pan.

3. Bake for 5 to 7 minutes in hot oven, then transfer to broiler.

4. Preheat broiler, if necessary. Broil fish about 3 inches from heat source until side spread with mayonnaise browns, then turn over. Spread with remaining mayonnaise. Return to broiler and broil until bubbly and well browned. Be careful not to let fish burn. Sprinkle with parsley and serve immediately.

VARIATION:
Add 1 teaspoon chopped shallot to mayonnaise.

ADVANCE PREPARATION:
May be prepared up to 1 day ahead through Step 1 and kept in refrigerator.

STEAMED SEA BASS AND FRESH SPINACH WITH CABERNET SAUVIGNON SAUCE

Serves 4

Steaming is an effective means of bringing both spinach and sea bass to their fullest flavor. In this blend of local ingredients, steamed sea bass sits atop fresh chopped spinach. The rose-colored Cabernet Sauvignon Sauce is poured across the white fish for a beautiful contrast of colors and flavors. You may substitute Atlantic sea bass if Pacific fish is unavailable. Serve with steamed white rice.

RECOMMENDED CALIFORNIA WINE:

Serve with one of the lighter, silkier versions of Napa Valley Cabernet Sauvignon.

4 bunches spinach (about 2 pounds)

1 quart fish stock (page 277) or water

4 sea bass fillets, ½ pound each and
   no more than 1¼ inches thick

¼ cup Cabernet Sauvignon

2 tablespoons Cabernet Sauvignon (red)
   wine vinegar

3 medium shallots, minced

½ teaspoon salt

¼ teaspoon finely ground white pepper

1 cup (2 sticks) unsalted butter,
   chilled and cut into small cubes

1 Remove spinach stems and rinse leaves thoroughly. Chop leaves coarsely.

2 Put spinach in a medium saucepan, cover, and cook 2 minutes over medium heat or until just wilted but still green. Drain and keep warm.

3 Pour stock or water into a deep medium skillet or a steamer. Place steamer rack in pan and heat liquid until simmering.

4 Place fish fillets on steamer rack and cover. Steam for 6 minutes, or until just done (cooking time depends on thickness of fish). Test with a skewer; you should be able to penetrate fish easily. Cover fish and keep warm.

5 In a small heavy saucepan, boil wine, vinegar, and shallots until about 2 tablespoons liquid remain. Add salt and white pepper.

6 Over low heat, add cubes of butter to shallot mixture, whisking constantly; add butter 1 or 2 cubes at a time and wait until they are absorbed before adding more. The sauce should thicken, but butter should not melt. If pan begins to get very hot, remove it from heat and add some butter cubes off heat to cool sauce slightly. Remove from heat as soon as last butter cube is added.

7 Strain sauce if a smoother consistency is desired. Taste for seasoning. Keep warm.

8 To serve, place ¼ of spinach in center of each plate. Top with a fish fillet and spoon Cabernet sauce over. Serve remaining sauce separately.

GRILLED TROUT WITH LEMON-CURRY BUTTER

Serves 6

Trout is best enjoyed fresh and simply prepared. In this rendition, the trout is filleted and then grilled quickly with a lemon curry butter. It is moist and very colorful, for a presentation that is characteristic of California cooking at its best. Serve with Spicy Brown Rice with Eggplant and Tomatoes.

RECOMMENDED CALIFORNIA WINE:
Serve with a well-balanced, slightly buttery Napa Valley Chardonnay.

½ cup (1 stick) unsalted butter, softened

1 medium onion, finely chopped

2 teaspoons curry powder

1 teaspoon freshly squeezed lemon juice

½ teaspoon salt

½ teaspoon cayenne pepper

6 trout, about 6 ounces each, filleted

½ teaspoon salt

¼ teaspoon finely ground pepper

1 For lemon-curry butter: Heat 1 tablespoon of the butter in a skillet, add onion, and cook over low heat until very soft but not browned. Add curry powder and continue to cook, stirring, for about 2 minutes. Remove from heat and let cool.

2 In a bowl, beat remaining butter until smooth. Gradually beat in lemon juice. Stir in onion mixture, salt, and cayenne pepper.

3 Season trout with salt and pepper. Spoon approximately 1 tablespoon curry butter into cavity of each trout. Spread more butter over outer surfaces of fish.

4 Prepare barbecue for medium-heat grilling. Place fish in grilling basket if available; if not, be sure to arrange fish on grill carefully. Grill about 3 inches from heat source or 3 to 4 minutes on each side or until just tender when pierced with a skewer. Serve immediately.

ADVANCE PREPARATION:

Curry butter may be prepared up to 3 days ahead and kept in refrigerator.

WHITEFISH WITH TOMATO BÉARNAISE SAUCE

Serves 6

Whitefish is caught mainly in the Great Lakes but is found in other areas as well. In this recipe, whitefish is quickly poached and glazed with a tarragon-tomato sauce that brings out the best of the naturally mild fish flavor. Serve with Parsleyed Cucumbers.

Serve with an oaky, dry Sauvignon Blanc.

1 quart of fish stock (page 277) or water
6 whitefish fillets, ⅓ to ½ pound each
¾ cup Tomato Béarnaise Sauce (page 285)
2 tablespoons finely chopped fresh parsley

1 In a skillet, bring stock to simmer; gently lay fish in skillet side by side. Stock or water should just cover fish. Poach about 5 minutes on each side. Remove to broiler pan. Preheat broiler, if necessary.

2 Prepare Tomato Béarnaise Sauce.

3 Spoon sauce over top of fillets to lightly cover. Broil 3 inches from heat for 1 to 2 minutes until glazed and light brown. Be careful not to let burn. Garnish with parsley and serve immediately.

COLD POACHED SALMON
WITH TOMATO-BASIL VINAIGRETTE

Serves 4

Rather than the customary dill or cucumber sauce, I like to accent cold poached salmon with fresh tomato-basil vinaigrette. Wrap the salmon in cheesecloth when cooking to keep it moist and tender throughout. Another method is to use a fish poacher. Serve with Green Bean-Jicama Salad and marinated mushrooms for a refreshing summer luncheon or evening meal.

Serve a fresh, crisp, very fruity young Chardonnay. The tomato will take much of the edge off the wine and make it taste more rounded and mature than it actually is.

1 cup Basic Vinaigrette (page 281)

1 medium tomato, peeled, seeded,
   and finely chopped

1 tablespoon finely chopped fresh basil

1 quart fish stock (page 277) or water

2 pounds fresh salmon, in 1 piece cut
   from center portion, bones removed

FOR GARNISH:

Red leaf lettuce

Fresh basil leaves

Cucumber, cut into thin slices

① Combine all ingredients for vinaigrette and taste for seasoning.

② In a large (at least 4-quart) saucepan, bring fish stock to a slow simmer.

③ Wrap salmon in cheesecloth, twirl the ends, and tie with string. Place salmon in simmering fish stock or water. Stock or water should just cover fish. Partially cover and simmer about 20 minutes, depending on thickness of fish. (It will take 6 to 10 minutes per pound, depending on thickness.) The salmon should remain moist.

④ Remove pan from heat. Allow salmon to cool in fish stock. Remove salmon from stock and unwrap cheesecloth. Peel skin away if desired. Chill at least 2 hours.

⑤ Cut salmon in 4 equal slices and place on serving plates garnished with red leaf lettuce. Spoon a dollop of tomato-basil vinaigrette along the side. Garnish with fresh basil leaves and thinly sliced cucumbers.

VARIATION:

Serve with Spinach-Watercress Sauce (page 291) or Cucumber-Mustard Dill (page 292).

ADVANCE PREPARATION:

May be prepared up to 1 day ahead through Step 4 and kept in refrigerator.

FILLET OF SALMON GLAZED WITH
PESTO HOLLANDAISE SAUCE

Serves 6

This recipe brings together two entirely different sauces. Pesto without cheese is added to hollandaise for a zesty and fragrant blend. This green-flecked sauce is spooned quickly over the cooked pink salmon fillets and glazed briefly. Serve the additional sauce on the side with Steamed New Potatoes with Chive Butter and steamed zucchini and carrots.

RECOMMENDED CALIFORNIA WINE:

This dish is ideal for those magnificent oaky, buttery Chardonnays that seem too big for most dishes.

FOR PESTO HOLLANDAISE SAUCE:

¾ cup Hollandaise Sauce (page 284)
¼ cup Pesto Sauce (page 290), without cheese

6 salmon fillets, ⅓ to ½ pound each
1 tablespoon freshly squeezed lemon juice

1 For sauce: Prepare Hollandaise Sauce in a medium bowl. Add pesto and whisk to combine. Pour into a warmed 1-quart thermos. (It will keep warm for up to 1 hour.)

2 Preheat broiler, if necessary. Place salmon fillets on broiler pan and brush lemon juice on each fillet. Broil for 3 to 5 minutes on each side, depending on thickness of fish.

3 Spoon Pesto Hollandaise Sauce on flesh side of fish. Broil about 3 inches from heat source for about 1 minute, or until lightly glazed and browned. Be careful not to burn. Serve immediately.

HALIBUT WITH APPLES, GINGER, AND CIDER VINEGAR

Serves 4

California has several abundant apple orchard areas. In the apple-harvesting months of October through February, fresh cider, cider vinegar, and apples of all varieties can be purchased from roadside stands. This recipe uses these ingredients to their utmost advantage. Aromatic fresh ginger blends discreetly with the tart apple and the cider vinegar to heighten the flavor of Pacific halibut. The combination of light sautéing and quick steaming leaves the fish firm and flavorful. Steamed green beans or zucchini is all that is needed to complete the main course.

RECOMMENDED CALIFORNIA WINE:
Serve with an excellent, very fruity young Chardonnay or dry Chenin Blanc.

5 tablespoons unsalted butter

1 medium pippin or other tart apple, peeled, cored, and cut into ⅛-inch wedges

4 halibut fillets, ½ pound each

2 tablespoons all-purpose flour

2 medium shallots, finely chopped

¼ cup cider vinegar

½ cup fish stock (page 277)

1 cup whipping cream

2 teaspoons julienned fresh ginger

Salt and finely ground white pepper to taste

FOR GARNISH:
Parsley sprigs

1 In a medium skillet, melt 2 tablespoons of the butter over medium heat. Add apple wedges and sauté until slightly brown but not soft. Set aside.

2 Sprinkle halibut fillets with flour; shake off excess.

3 In a medium skillet, melt the remaining 3 tablespoons butter. Add fillets and sauté over medium heat for about 3 to 4 minutes, until lightly browned on both sides. Cover and steam for 2 minutes. Remove fish to platter and cover.

4 Discard all but 1 tablespoon of the butter from skillet. Add shallots and sauté over low heat for about 3 minutes. Add vinegar and fish stock and boil to reduce liquid by half. Add cream and continue to reduce, until sauce is slightly thickened. Add ginger and simmer for 1 minute.

5 Strain sauce into a bowl. Taste for seasoning.

6 Reheat apples until hot.

7 Place fillets on a serving plate and surround with sautéed apple slices. Spoon sauce over fish. Garnish with parsley sprigs.

ADVANCE PREPARATION:

Can prepare sauce (Steps 4 and 5) 2 hours ahead. Cover and keep at room temperature.

FRESH TUNA WITH SAUTÉED PEPPERS AND GARLIC IN PARCHMENT

Serves 2

Cooking fish in parchment is a healthful technique that Californians are using more often. The fish retains its natural moisture through this process. Patricia Unterman, food writer and owner of the Hayes Street Grill in San Francisco, introduced me to this recipe. Chiles, peppers, and garlic are placed atop a tuna fillet, which is then wrapped in parchment. The spicy aroma of peppers and herbs is released when the packets are opened at the table. This is an easy, informal dinner entrée that may be doubled or tripled if desired. Serve with Rice with Clams and Cilantro Butter.

RECOMMENDED CALIFORNIA WINE:

Serve with Blanc de Pinot Noir, a slightly oaky Chardonnay, or a slightly oaky version of dry Sauvignon Blanc.

1 tablespoon olive oil

1 red bell pepper, seeded and julienned

2 small cloves garlic, minced

1 teaspoon finely chopped fresh oregano, or ½ teaspoon dried oregano

2 slices tuna, 8 ounces each and cut from center (no bone)

1 small green chile, seeded and finely chopped (see Note)

2 thin slices red onion

Salt and finely ground pepper to taste

1 tablespoon unsalted butter

1. Preheat oven to 425°F. Cut 2 pieces parchment paper or aluminum foil into large heart or rectangular shapes. Set aside.

2. In a 9-inch skillet, heat olive oil over medium heat. Add red pepper and sauté for about 2 minutes. Add garlic and oregano and continue cooking for 30 seconds. Remove from heat.

3. Place tuna slice in center of parchment paper. Top with sautéed red pepper, then add chile and red onion and sprinkle with salt and pepper. Dot top of vegetable mixture with small pieces of butter.

4. Fold parchment in half over fish. Overlap edges, holding down creased edges with one index finger, using the other thumb and index finger to pinch and fold. Tuck under excess parchment and place package on baking sheet.

5. Bake for 6 minutes. (Fish should be medium-rare.) Serve immediately.

ADVANCE PREPARATION:

May be prepared up to 6 hours ahead through Step 4 and kept in refrigerator. Remove from refrigerator ½ hour before placing in oven.

NOTE:

When working with chiles always wear rubber gloves. Wash cutting surface and knife immediately afterward.

SKEWERED SHRIMP WITH CILANTRO AND GREEN SALSA

Serves 6

Cilantro-flavored marinade infuses the sweet shrimp with a subtle flavor that grilling brings out fully. Mexican green tomatillos are small, green, ripe tomatoes that contribute color and flavor to the salsa. Serve with Autumn Rice with Red Peppers and Pine Nuts.

RECOMMENDED CALIFORNIA WINE:

Serve with a dry Sauvignon Blanc.

1½ pounds raw jumbo or large shrimp (24 jumbo or 30 large)

2 tablespoons chopped cilantro

2 medium cloves garlic, minced

2 tablespoons freshly squeezed lime juice

1 tablespoon vegetable oil

¼ teaspoon salt

FOR GARNISH:

6 red lettuce leaves

12 cherry tomatoes

1 jicama, peeled and cut in thin slices

FOR SERVING:

1 cup Green Chile Salsa (page 283)

1 Shell and devein shrimp. Put them in a shallow nonaluminum dish and add cilantro, garlic, lime juice, and oil. Mix well and leave to marinate for 30 minutes.

2 Meanwhile, prepare barbecue for medium-heat grilling or preheat broiler, if necessary. Remove shrimp from marinade and season with salt. Thread lengthwise on skewers, pushing skewer through shrimp near each end of shrimp but leaving center of shrimp free.

3 Grill or broil about 3 inches from heat source for 2 minutes per side, or until just firm.

4 Serve shrimp on lettuce leaves and garnish with cherry tomatoes and jicama slices. Serve salsa separately.

ADVANCE PREPARATION:

Marinade may be prepared 1 day in advance and refrigerated. Shrimp may be marinated up to 4 hours ahead and kept in refrigerator.

SHRIMP AND LEEK STIR-FRY
WITH TOASTED PINE NUTS

Serves 4

Tender leeks quickly stir-fried with California shrimp are complemented by a sweet and spicy blend of Chinese flavorings. Try it with steamed white rice or Spicy Chinese Noodles with Vegetables.

RECOMMENDED CALIFORNIA WINE:

Serve with a well-balanced Chardonnay from Napa or San Luis Obispo County.

3 tablespoons pine nuts

3 tablespoons peanut oil

4 leeks, white part only,
   cleaned and cut into thin strips

2 teaspoons finely chopped fresh ginger

3 cloves garlic, minced

2 pounds shrimp, peeled and deveined

¼ cup sherry

¼ cup soy sauce

2 tablespoons dark sesame oil

2 teaspoons Hot Pepper Oil (page 279)

① Preheat oven to 350°F. Toast pine nuts in oven for 5 minutes, or until lightly browned. Reserve.

② Heat peanut oil in a wok over high heat.

③ Stir in leeks and stir-fry 3 minutes, or until tender but still crisp.

④ Add ginger and garlic and continue stir-frying until softened. Add shrimp and stir until pink, about 3 minutes.

⑤ Add sherry and soy sauce and bring to boil. Add pine nuts, sesame oil, and hot pepper oil and cook for 1 minute. Taste for seasoning. Serve immediately.

VARIATION:

Use scallops in place of shrimp.

SCALLOPS WITH FRESH TOMATOES, HERBS, AND WHITE WINE

Serves 4 as main course or 6 as first course

California cooking eschews the use of heavy cream sauces, so rather than being served in such a sauce, scallops are often sautéed, baked, or barbecued quickly to retain their natural flavor. In this uncomplicated preparation, fresh tomatoes and herbs bring out the sweet taste of the scallops. It can be served either as a first course or as a main course with Saffron Rice and steamed green beans.

RECOMMENDED CALIFORNIA WINE:

Serve with a dry Sauvignon Blanc.

2 pounds fresh bay or sea scallops
    (see Note)

¼ cup olive oil

2 medium shallots, finely chopped

3 large tomatoes, peeled, seeded,
    and diced

⅔ cup dry white wine

1 teaspoon finely chopped fresh basil,
    or ½ teaspoon dried basil

1 teaspoon finely chopped fresh thyme,
    or ½ teaspoon dried thyme

1 teaspoon finely chopped fresh rosemary,
    or ½ teaspoon dried rosemary

1 tablespoon finely chopped fresh parsley

2 medium cloves garlic, minced

¼ teaspoon salt

Pinch of finely ground pepper

1 tablespoon all-purpose flour

FOR GARNISH:

2 tablespoons chopped fresh parsley

1. If using sea scallops, remove small white muscle at side of each. Cut sea scallops in half horizontally.

2. Heat 2 of the tablespoons oil in a medium skillet over medium heat. Add shallots and sauté for 3 minutes, or until soft. Add tomatoes, wine, herbs, and garlic. Simmer for 5 minutes, or until slightly reduced. Add salt and pepper and taste for seasoning.

3. Pat scallops dry. Sprinkle with flour; shake off excess.

4. Heat remaining oil in a large skillet. Place scallops in skillet and sauté

over medium-high heat, turning frequently, about 2 minutes per side, or until lightly browned and tender. This should be done in batches if scallops don't fit in one layer. Bay scallops require less cooking time than do sea scallops.

5 Spoon scallops onto serving plates and pour sauce over each serving. Sprinkle with chopped parsley.

May be prepared up to 8 hours ahead through Step 2 and kept in refrigerator. Reheat before continuing.

NOTE:

Scallop shells make attractive containers for serving the scallops.

COLD MUSSELS IN TOMATO-SAFFRON SAUCE

Serves 4 to 6 as first course

Pacific Coast mussels are seasonal and can be found fresh only between November and April. Experimental attempts at cultivation are now being performed off the Santa Barbara coast. Here, the mussels are steamed open, cooled, and dressed with a light tomato-saffron sauce. Serve slightly chilled as a first course or as part of a cocktail buffet.

RECOMMENDED CALIFORNIA WINE:

Serve with a crisp Fumé Blanc.

2 pounds mussels (see Note)	¾ cup fresh tomato sauce
½ cup water	⅛ teaspoon saffron threads
½ cup dry white wine	1 tablespoon whipping cream

FOR GARNISH:

2 tablespoons chopped fresh parsley

1 Clean mussels by soaking in cold water 15 minutes. Pull beard away from shell and brush mussels vigorously under cold running water to remove excess sand. Place in bowl with cold water for 15 minutes. Repeat process, making sure all sand is washed off.

2 Bring water and wine to boil in stockpot. Add mussels. Cover tightly and boil over high heat. Hold handles of pot and shake vigorously so that mussels will cook evenly. The mussels should open after 5 minutes. Remove from heat immediately and let cool.

3 Strain ¼ cup mussel cooking liquid through cheesecloth to remove excess sand; reserve.

4 Separate mussel shells, discarding the top shell and leaving mussels in bottom shell. Arrange on a large platter in concentric circles.

5 Combine reserved mussel juice, tomato sauce, saffron, and cream in a skillet and boil to reduce to about ¾ cup. Taste for seasoning. Pour over mussels and refrigerate at least 2 hours.

6 Garnish with parsley and serve slightly chilled.

ADVANCE PREPARATION:

May be kept up to 6 hours in refrigerator.

NOTE:

To determine freshness, press the shell between your thumb and forefinger. If they can be pried open easily, discard them.

❧

GRILLED LOBSTER WITH GARLIC BUTTER

Serves 2

Garlic and parsley are added to melted butter, which accentuates the lobster taste. The lobster is slightly undercooked during boiling so that the meat does not dry out on the barbecue. To give an outdoor character, buttered lobster tail is finished on a grill. Serve with Rosemary Potatoes Steamed in Foil and start with Caesar Salad.

RECOMMENDED CALIFORNIA WINE:

Serve with a fine Napa Valley Chardonnay with lots of body, fruit, and oak.

2 tablespoons unsalted butter

2 medium cloves garlic, finely minced

1 teaspoon chopped fresh parsley

1 lemon, cut into slices

12 peppercorns

2 bay leaves

1 sprig fresh thyme, or 1 teaspoon
dried thyme

1 teaspoon salt

1 (2½ pound) live lobster

1 For garlic butter: Melt butter in a small saucepan over low heat and add garlic and parsley. Remove from heat and cool.

2 Fill a 16-quart pot two-thirds full of water. Squeeze some juice from lemon slices into pot. Add lemon slices, peppercorns, bay leaves, thyme, and salt. Bring to rapid boil.

3 Add live lobster to pot, cover, and cook for about 10 minutes.

4 Remove lobster and cool slightly. With poultry shears, cut shell in half lengthwise and divide lobster in two. Remove stomach sac.

5 Brush meat side and shell side with garlic butter, reserving about 2 teaspoons for final basting.

6 Prepare barbecue for high-heat grilling. Grill lobster about 3 inches from heat, meat side down, for 2 minutes. Turn and grill shell side down for 2 minutes while basting with reserved garlic butter. Serve immediately.

May be prepared 4 hours ahead through Step 4 and kept in refrigerator.

SEAFOOD QUARTET

Serves 4 to 6 as main course or 8 to 10 as first course

A piquant marinade brings out the individual flavor of each type of fish, while separate dipping sauces further enhance their taste. This straightforward, easily prepared dish with its informal presentation lends itself well to the California lifestyle. The seafood is placed on a large round platter with dipping sauces in the center. Provide your guests with separate plates and let them choose what they want. I like to serve Lemon-Chive Sabayon Sauce, Spicy Garlic Mayonnaise, and Cucumber-Mustard Dill Sauce for a variety that indulges the whole spectrum of tastes, from hot to tart to creamy and mild. Serve as a first course on red leaf lettuce or as a main dish on a bed of Green Vegetable Rice.

RECOMMENDED CALIFORNIA WINE:

Serve with an oaky Chardonnay or dry Sauvignon Blanc.

FOR MARINADE:

½ cup Chardonnay (white) wine vinegar

1 tablespoon freshly squeezed lemon juice

1 cup oil

1 tablespoon finely chopped chives

½ teaspoon salt

¼ teaspoon finely ground pepper

1 pound scallops

12 raw unshelled jumbo shrimp, cleaned

1 pound salmon fillet, cut into
  1½-inch chunks

1 pound swordfish, cut into
  1½-inch chunks

1 cup Lemon-Chive Sabayon Sauce
  (page 293)

1 cup Spicy Garlic Mayonnaise
  (page 289)

1 cup Cucumber-Mustard Dill Sauce
  (page 292)

Salt to taste

1 For marinade: Combine marinade ingredients in a small bowl. Whisk until blended.

2 If using sea scallops, remove small white muscle at side of each. Wash shrimp and arrange along with salmon and swordfish in a large shallow nonaluminum dish; pour marinade over. Marinate for 30 minutes to 1 hour.

③ Prepare dipping sauces for serving.

④ Prepare barbecue for medium-heat grilling.

⑤ Remove shrimp from marinade. Thread lengthwise on skewers, pushing skewer through shrimp near each end of shrimp but leaving center of shrimp free. Thread other types of seafood lengthwise on separate skewers.

⑥ Place shrimp, salmon, and swordfish on barbecue. Grill about 3 inches from heat for about 3 to 4 minutes on each side, depending on size of fish.

⑦ Place scallops on barbecue and grill for about 2 minutes on each side.

⑧ To serve, arrange seafood on a large platter, keeping each type separate. Put bowls of dipping sauces in center. The seafood may also be arranged on individual serving plates and the sauces passed separately.

ADVANCE PREPARATION:

May be prepared up to 4 hours ahead through Step 3 and kept in refrigerator.

CALIFORNIA FISH STEW

Serves 6 to 8

Typical of San Francisco fish stews, this hearty version is a combination of tomatoes, spices, and flavorful California Zinfandel. The choice of fish for the stew always depends on what is fresh and seasonal. What could be a better companion to this meal than a warm crusty loaf of sourdough bread?

RECOMMENDED CALIFORNIA WINE:

Serve with a lightly chilled Zinfandel.

½ cup olive oil

2 stalks celery, finely chopped

1 medium onion, finely chopped

1 medium carrot, peeled and
   finely chopped

2 medium leeks, white part only,
   cleaned and sliced

2 pounds tomatoes, peeled and coarsely
   chopped, or 1 (28-ounce) can Italian
   plum tomatoes, drained and
   coarsely chopped

6 tablespoons tomato paste

3 tablespoons freshly squeezed
  lemon juice

4 medium cloves garlic, minced

3 cups fish stock (page 277)

2 cups California Zinfandel

¼ cup dry California Marsala

Pinch of sugar

1 teaspoon fennel seeds

½ teaspoon saffron threads (optional)

Bouquet garni (see Note)

1 pound halibut, sea bass, or flounder,
  cut into bite-sized chunks

1 pound sole or red snapper,
  cut into bite-sized chunks

8 clams

16 mussels

1 pound scallops

1 pound raw shrimp,
  shelled and deveined

1 cooked Dungeness crab, cracked

1 cooked Pacific coast lobster,
  cut into pieces (optional)

¼ cup finely chopped fresh parsley

1 lemon, thinly sliced

1 Heat olive oil in a 6-quart nonaluminum Dutch oven or stockpot. Add celery, onion, carrot, and leeks and sauté, stirring occasionally, for about 5 minutes.

2 Add tomatoes, tomato paste, lemon juice, garlic, fish stock, wines, sugar, fennel, saffron, and bouquet garni. Cook 40 minutes on medium heat, partially covered. Taste for seasoning.

3 Add the halibut, sea bass, or flounder; cover and cook on medium heat about 3 minutes. Add sole or snapper, the clams, and mussels.

4 Cook for about 3 more minutes. Add scallops, shrimp, crab, and lobster. Continue cooking until clams and mussels open and other seafood is just cooked through. Remove bouquet garni.

5 Serve sprinkled with chopped parsley. Garnish with lemon slices.

ADVANCE PREPARATION:

May be prepared up to 3 days ahead through Step 2 and kept in refrigerator.

NOTE:

To make bouquet garni, wrap 1 bay leaf, ½ teaspoon each of fresh oregano, basil, thyme, and rosemary, and a 1-inch piece of orange zest in cheesecloth and tie with string.

GRILLED CHICKEN WITH BASIL AND GARLIC

Serves 6

Basil invariably dies when the weather turns cold, but California warmth makes for a longer season. Gilroy, just south of San Jose, is the center for garlic production. The combination of these two essential fresh ingredients brings out the best in grilled chicken. Through the cooking process the garlic becomes like a cream when squeezed from the cloves. It is then combined with the additional marinade ingredients into a unique sauce. Make sure your sauce is warm, and use a sparing quantity poured gently over the center of each boneless chicken breast. Serve with Sautéed Sugar Snap Peas and Red Peppers.

RECOMMENDED CALIFORNIA WINE:

Serve with a big, oaky Chardonnay or a Napa Cabernet Sauvignon or Zinfandel.

1 medium clove garlic, finely minced

½ cup fresh basil leaves

4 whole large chicken breasts,
    boned and halved

FOR MARINADE:

½ cup dry white wine

¼ cup olive oil

½ teaspoon salt

Finely ground pepper to taste

1 medium clove garlic, finely minced

1 cup veal stock (page 274)
    or chicken stock (page 276)

1 large head garlic, cloves separated
    but not peeled

2 tablespoons finely chopped fresh basil

2 tablespoons whipping cream

Salt and finely ground pepper to taste

FOR GARNISH:

Fresh basil leaves

1 Slide ¼ of the minced garlic and the basil leaves under skin of each chicken breast until breast is entirely covered with leaves. Reserve some basil leaves for marinade.

2 Combine marinade ingredients in a small bowl. Whisk until blended. Add remaining basil leaves.

3 In a large shallow nonaluminum dish, arrange chicken breasts and pour marinade over them. Marinate at least 2 to 4 hours in refrigerator.

4 In a medium saucepan, bring veal stock to boil. Add cloves of garlic, cover, and simmer for 30 minutes.

5 Remove garlic from pan and place in a food processor fitted with the steel blade and puree. Force garlic through a fine strainer and return to saucepan.

6 Prepare barbecue for medium-heat grilling. Grill chicken 3 inches from heat for 6 to 8 minutes on each side. Transfer to individual plates.

7 In a medium saucepan, combine remaining marinade, pureed garlic, basil, and cream. Whisk until combined. Boil until slightly thickened. Taste for seasoning. Pour sauce over chicken and garnish plates with fresh basil.

ADVANCE PREPARATION:

May be prepared up to 4 hours ahead through Step 5 and kept in refrigerator. Remove from refrigerator ½ hour before continuing.

GRILLED LEMON-MUSTARD CHICKEN

Serves 6

This is one of my most frequently used recipes. It is a satisfying dish and it demands little preparation time. The mustard, lemon, and herbs in the marinade are low in calories yet add a rich, full flavor to the chicken. You can broil the chicken if a barbecue is not available. Spicy Brown Rice with Eggplant and Tomatoes, Stir-Fried Broccoli, or Pacific Coast Eggplant make good accompaniments.

RECOMMENDED CALIFORNIA WINE:

This flexible dish works equally well with Chardonnay, Cabernet, and Zinfandel, and can be served with a crisp, refreshing Fumé Blanc in the summer.

½ cup freshly squeezed lemon juice

1 tablespoon minced lemon zest

¼ cup Dijon mustard

¼ cup finely chopped fresh herbs
  (any combination of rosemary, thyme,
  basil, oregano, and parsley)

¾ teaspoon salt

¼ teaspoon coarsely cracked pepper

4 whole large chicken breasts, skinned,
  boned, and halved

Parsley sprigs

Lemon slices

Fresh herb leaves used in marinade

1 For marinade: Combine marinade ingredients in a small bowl. Mix well.

2 In a large, shallow, nonaluminum dish, arrange chicken pieces and pour marinade over them. Marinate for 2 to 4 hours in refrigerator.

3 Prepare barbecue for medium-heat grilling. Remove chicken from marinade and grill 3 inches from heat for 6 to 8 minutes on each side.

4 Place on individual plates or on a platter surrounded by parsley sprigs, lemon slices, and fresh herb leaves.

May be prepared up to 4 hours ahead through Step 2 and refrigerated.

GRILLED CHICKEN WITH SALSA AND MUSTARD BUTTER

Serves 6

The mixture of Dijon-style mustard and Spicy Red Salsa elevates plain broiled chicken to a zesty California-style original. The chicken is garnished with a slice of compound spicy butter. Serve with Gratin of Vegetables, Baked Japanese Eggplant with Herbs, or Baked Black Beans with Sour Cream.

RECOMMENDED CALIFORNIA WINE:
Serve with a Fumé Blanc or a Blanc de Pinot Noir.

FOR MARINADE:

⅔ cup Spicy Red Salsa (page 282)

⅓ cup Dijon mustard

1 tablespoon freshly squeezed lemon juice

4 whole large chicken breasts, boned and halved

3 tablespoons unsalted butter, softened

1 For marinade: Mix ingredients together in a medium bowl. Reserve 1 tablespoon of mixture for mustard butter.

2 In a large, shallow, nonaluminum baking dish, arrange chicken breasts and pour marinade over them. Marinate for 1 to 4 hours in refrigerator.

3 To make mustard butter, combine butter and reserved marinade mixture and whip until smooth. Place on a waxed paper sheet and roll up in form of a log. Refrigerate until ready to use.

4 Preheat broiler, if necessary. Place chicken breasts skin side down on broiler pan and broil 3 inches from heat for 6 to 8 minutes on each side. When turning skin side up, spoon additional marinade over top and broil until very brown and bubbly.

5 Place chicken on individual serving dishes.

6 Slice mustard butter in equal pieces and arrange slices on chicken pieces. Serve immediately.

(1) *May be cooked on barbecue grill if desired.*

(2) *Grainy mustard may be substituted for Dijon style.*

ADVANCE PREPARATION:

May be prepared up to 4 hours ahead through Step 3 and kept in refrigerator.

LEMON-HERB CHICKEN

Serves 6

Highly appealing for its tangy and fragrant flavor, Lemon-Herb Chicken is a most versatile entrée. The chicken breasts are first marinated in lemon and fresh herbs, then quickly sautéed. A sauce is prepared with the remaining marinade, which becomes a light lemon cream. Serve the chicken breasts hot for a dinner menu with Autumn Rice with Red Peppers and Pine Nuts or Stuffed Zucchini with Banana Squash Puree, or serve it chilled for lunch with sliced tomatoes with fresh basil.

RECOMMENDED CALIFORNIA WINE:

This is delicious with a fine Chardonnay or one of the gentler coastal county Pinot Noirs.

FOR MARINADE:

2 tablespoons minced lemon zest

½ cup freshly squeezed lemon juice

2 tablespoons oil

¼ cup finely chopped fresh herbs
   (any combination of rosemary, thyme,
   parsley, basil, and oregano)

½ cup dry white wine

1 teaspoon honey

½ teaspoon salt

¼ teaspoon coarsely cracked pepper

4 whole large chicken breasts, skinned,
   boned, and halved

2 tablespoons unsalted butter

2 tablespoons oil

6 tablespoons whipping cream

Salt to taste

Coarsely cracked black pepper

2 tablespoons finely chopped fresh parsley

FOR GARNISH:

1 bunch fresh watercress

1 lemon, sliced

2 tablespoons finely chopped fresh parsley

1 For marinade: Combine marinade ingredients in a small bowl. Whisk until blended.

2 In a large, shallow, nonaluminum dish, arrange chicken pieces and pour marinade over them. Let marinate for 4 hours in refrigerator.

3 Remove chicken pieces and pat dry. Reserve marinade.

4 Melt butter and oil in a large skillet or sauté pan over medium-high heat. Add chicken breasts and sauté for 5 to 7 minutes on each side until tender and brown. Remove to a dish. Remove excess oil and butter.

5 Add reserved marinade to pan and boil until reduced to about ½ cup. Add cream and boil for about 3 more minutes. Season with salt and pepper to taste. Add chopped parsley.

6 Return chicken breasts to sauce and allow to heat through.

7 Place chicken breasts on a platter and surround with fresh watercress, lemon slices, and chopped parsley.

VARIATION:

This dish is also delicious served cold.

ADVANCE PREPARATION:

May be prepared up to 4 hours ahead through Step 5; keep sauce and chicken covered at room temperature.

PESTO-STUFFED CHICKEN BREASTS

Serves 4 to 6

This recipe works well for parties and entertaining, as it may be easily doubled. The spinach-ricotta stuffing seasoned with pesto is an outstanding combination with chicken breasts. A light mushroom sauce is served on the side. Round out the menu with Sautéed Baby Tomatoes and steamed green beans.

RECOMMENDED CALIFORNIA WINE:

Serve with a Chardonnay, Cabernet Sauvignon, or Zinfandel.

FOR FILLING:

¼ cup pine nuts

2 bunches spinach (about 1 pound)

2 tablespoons unsalted butter

3 medium shallots, finely chopped

½ cup ricotta cheese

¼ cup Pesto Sauce (page 290)

1 egg yolk

⅛ teaspoon finely ground pepper

3 slices prosciutto, ⅛ inch thick,
   cut in half

3 whole large chicken breasts, skinned,
   boned, halved, and flattened

FOR BASTING:

3 tablespoons unsalted butter, melted

3 tablespoons freshly squeezed lemon juice

FOR SAUCE:

3 tablespoons unsalted butter

½ pound mushrooms, sliced

1 cup chicken stock (page 276)

¾ cup dry white wine

½ cup whipping cream

2 tablespoons chopped fresh basil

1 For filling: Preheat oven to 350°F. Toast pine nuts in oven for 5 minutes, or until lightly browned. Reserve.

2 Remove spinach stems and rinse leaves thoroughly. Put spinach in a 10-inch skillet and partially cover. Steam spinach over medium-high heat for about 2 minutes. Remove from heat and place in a strainer. Pour cold water over spinach to stop the cooking process. Drain carefully and place spinach in a dry kitchen towel. Wring spinach until all excess liquid is removed. Chop medium-fine.

3 Heat butter in small skillet. Add shallots and sauté over low heat until soft but not brown.

4 Increase oven temperature to 375°F. Generously butter a medium baking dish.

5 Mix pine nuts, spinach, and shallots with remaining filling ingredients. Taste for seasoning. Put a slice of prosciutto on each chicken breast half. Spread filling evenly over prosciutto. Fold chicken breast and prosciutto over in half. Place in baking dish.

6 For basting: Mix together melted butter and lemon juice in a small bowl. Spoon over chicken. Bake chicken, basting occasionally with juices in pan, for 30 minutes or until just tender. Remove chicken to a platter and cover to keep warm. Set baking dish aside, reserving drippings.

7 For sauce: In a medium skillet heat butter over medium heat. Add mushrooms and sauté 3 minutes. Remove mushrooms and reserve. Add chicken stock to skillet and boil until reduced to ¼ cup. Add white wine and boil until reduced to ½ cup. Add whipping cream and boil until reduced to ¾ cup. Return mushrooms to skillet and stir.

8 Remove fat from baking dish. Heat juices in baking dish on top of stove and add sauce. Raise heat to medium-high and bring to a boil, stirring. Add basil and taste for seasoning.

9 To serve, arrange chicken breasts on a platter and pass sauce separately.

ADVANCE PREPARATION:

May be prepared up to 4 hours ahead through Step 5 and kept in refrigerator. Remove from refrigerator ½ hour before baking.

SPICY SAUTÉED CHICKEN BREASTS

Serves 4 to 6

This is an adaptation on a specialty that was served to me by Mark Miller, owner of the Fourth Street Grill in Berkeley. When I ate it, I was grateful for the slice of lime, which was just the right balance for the very spicy chicken. The dish is easy to prepare but should be reserved for those who like it hot. Serve with Oven-Roasted Potatoes or Sautéed Sugar Snap Peas and Red Peppers.

RECOMMENDED CALIFORNIA WINE:

Serve with a crisp Fumé Blanc or a Blanc de Pinot Noir.

FOR MARINADE:

1 fresh hot green chile (jalapeño or
    Serrano), finely chopped (see Note)
1 medium clove garlic, minced
1 teaspoon ground cumin

¼ teaspoon chili powder
⅛ teaspoon cayenne pepper
½ teaspoon salt
1 teaspoon freshly squeezed lime juice

3 whole chicken breasts, skinned,
    boned, and halved
⅓ cup clarified butter

FOR GARNISH:

Paprika
1 tablespoon chopped cilantro
1 lime, cut into thin slices

① For marinade: Mix chile with garlic, cumin, chili powder, cayenne pepper, salt, and lime juice. Thoroughly rub mixture into chicken breasts. (Wash your hands immediately because of contact with the chile.) Leave chicken breasts to marinate at room temperature ½ hour or in the refrigerator for 2 to 3 hours.

② Heat clarified butter in skillet until foaming. Add chicken breasts and sauté over medium-high heat until lightly browned on both sides. Cover and continue cooking over low heat for about 7 minutes, or until just tender.

③ Sprinkle with paprika. Place on a platter or individual plates.

④ Garnish with cilantro and slices of lime and serve.

ADVANCE PREPARATION:

May be prepared up to 3 hours ahead through Step 1 and refrigerated. Remove from refrigerator ½ hour before continuing.

NOTE:

When working with chiles always wear rubber gloves. Wash cutting surface and knife immediately afterward.

SAUTÉED CHICKEN BREASTS WITH MUSTARD AND TARRAGON

Serves 4 to 6

This is a favorite of my students because it is easy to prepare and makes an excellent party dish. It is best to make this recipe during the spring and summer months, when fresh tarragon is at its peak. Serve with Lemon Rice with Capers and Parsley and Sauté of Julienned Garden Vegetables.

RECOMMENDED CALIFORNIA WINE:

Serve with an elegant Chardonnay from Napa or San Luis Obispo County.

3 tablespoons unsalted butter

2 tablespoons oil

3 whole large chicken breasts, skinned, boned, and halved

2 medium shallots, finely chopped

½ cup white wine

1 cup chicken stock (page 276)

2 medium cloves garlic, minced

¾ cup whipping cream

3 tablespoons grainy mustard

1 tablespoon finely chopped fresh tarragon, or 1 teaspoon dried tarragon

1 teaspoon finely chopped fresh thyme, or ½ teaspoon dried thyme

½ teaspoon salt

Pinch of coarsely ground white pepper

FOR GARNISH:

1 tablespoon chopped fresh parsley

1 In a large skillet, heat 2 tablespoons of the butter and 1 tablespoon of the oil over medium-high heat. Add chicken breasts and sauté over medium-high heat until golden brown on both sides; this ensures that the juices will be seared in. Remove to a dish and cover to keep warm.

2 Add the remaining butter and oil to skillet and heat until foamy. Add shallots and sauté for about 2 minutes, or until softened. Add wine, stock, and garlic and bring to boil. Boil until liquid is reduced to about ½ cup.

3 Whisk in cream and mustard and bring to boil. Cook until slightly thickened. Add tarragon, thyme, salt, and pepper and whisk well. Taste for seasoning.

4 Return chicken breasts and extra juice from chicken to skillet and cook about 5 minutes longer, until warmed but not overcooked.

5 Garnish with fresh parsley.

ADVANCE PREPARATION:
May be prepared up to 2 hours ahead through Step 3 and kept at room temperature; keep chicken well covered.

CHICKEN WITH PANCETTA AND ZINFANDEL

Serves 4

The secret of this updated version of the classic coq au vin is marinating the chicken in spicy Zinfandel for at least 8 hours to intensify the taste of the finished dish. California chickens are young; thus, cooking time is shorter than average. By cooking the chicken until it is just done and reserving it, the flesh remains moist and juicy. The substitution of Italian-cured bacon for the pork sets it apart from other versions. Although this dish takes some time to prepare, it may be made completely in advance and then reheated. Serve with Steamed New Potatoes with Chive Butter and steamed zucchini and carrots. Finish the meal with Apricot-Currant Bread Custard.

RECOMMENDED CALIFORNIA WINE:
This dish is best with a fine fresh Zinfandel.

1 medium onion, thinly sliced

2 medium carrots, peeled and
   thinly sliced

Bouquet garni (see Note)

1 bottle full-bodied Zinfandel

½ teaspoon coarsely ground pepper

1 (3½- to 4-pound) chicken,
   cut into pieces

⅓ pound pancetta, sliced and cut into
   ¼-by-1-inch pieces

2 tablespoons unsalted butter

2 tablespoons oil

3 tablespoons California brandy

1 medium onion, diced

2 tablespoons all-purpose flour

3 medium cloves garlic, minced

1 tablespoon tomato paste

Bouquet garni (see Note)

1 teaspoon salt

¼ teaspoon finely ground pepper

1 tablespoon oil

1 tablespoon unsalted butter

1 pound mushrooms, quartered if large

18 to 20 white pearl onions

1 tablespoon oil

1 tablespoon unsalted butter

½ cup chicken (page 276)
   or veal stock (page 274)

Bouquet garni (see Note)

Salt and pepper to taste

2 tablespoons chopped fresh parsley

1 For marinade: Combine ingredients in a small bowl. Mix well.

2 In a large shallow nonaluminum dish, arrange chicken pieces and pour marinade over them. Marinate chicken 8 to 12 hours in refrigerator.

3 Preheat oven to 450°F. Remove chicken from marinade, reserving marinade, and pat dry with paper towels.

4 For sauce: In a medium ovenproof nonaluminum casserole, cook pancetta over medium-low heat until much of the fat has been rendered and the

pancetta is slightly crisp. Drain on paper towels and reserve. Remove all but 2 tablespoons drippings from casserole.

5 Add 1 tablespoon of the butter and 1 tablespoon of the oil to casserole. Heat until bubbling over medium-high heat. Add chicken pieces, cook until browned, and ignite it with long match, averting your face and making sure that the overhead fan is not on.

6 In a separate small skillet, heat remaining 1 tablespoon oil. Add onion and sauté until soft and light brown. Reserve.

7 Sprinkle chicken with flour until evenly coated. Place casserole in oven and bake, uncovered, for about 7 minutes, or until flour is lightly browned. Remove casserole from oven and place on burner. This will establish a base for the sauce and give it a deep color.

8 Strain marinade into casserole and boil for about 2 minutes to reduce alcohol. Add sautéed onions, minced garlic, tomato paste, and a fresh bouquet garni. Cover and simmer for about 20 to 25 minutes, or until chicken is tender but not overdone. Remove chicken from casserole and set aside. Add salt and pepper to casserole and bring sauce to boil. Boil for about 10 minutes, or until sauce is slightly thickened. Taste for seasoning. Remove and discard bouquet garni.

9 For mushrooms: Heat oil and butter. When foaming, add mushrooms. Sauté for 3 to 5 minutes, or until mushrooms are slightly soft. Reserve.

10 For onions: To peel onions, first immerse in boiling water for 10 seconds, then rinse in cold water. Trim off top and bottom portions and remove outside skin and first layer with fingers. Pierce a cross shape at root end so that onions will cook evenly and not burst.

11 Heat oil and butter in a medium skillet over medium heat. Add onions and brown for about 10 minutes. Use a large spoon to rotate them, or roll them by shaking skillet.

12 Add stock, a fresh bouquet garni, salt, and pepper. Cover and simmer slowly for about 30 minutes. Onions should be tender and retain their shape, and liquid should have evaporated. Watch carefully toward the end of the cooking time to avoid burning. Remove and discard bouquet garni.

13 When ready to serve, combine mushrooms, onions, chicken, and reserved pancetta with sauce and mix well. Heat until bubbling, taste for seasoning, and garnish with fresh parsley. Serve immediately.

May be kept up to 2 days in refrigerator. Bring to room temperature and reheat slowly.

To make a bouquet garni, wrap a parsley sprig, bay leaf, and a sprig of fresh thyme in cheesecloth and tie with string.

MEXICAN CHICKEN WITH RAISINS AND ALMONDS

Serves 6

Chicken has such a marvelous versatility that it is adaptable to almost any vegetable or herb. The Mexican influence in this dish is strong, but the addition of raisins and almonds at the end stamps it California as well. You will need nothing more than warm tortillas and Green Chile Salsa to complete this entrée. Start with Guacamole or Spicy Lemon Shrimp.

RECOMMENDED CALIFORNIA WINE:

Although beer or margaritas are a first choice, this can be served with one of the bigger dry Sauvignon Blancs or with a Blanc de Noirs. Their flavors are unfazed by any degree of spiciness, despite the seeming lightness of the wine.

⅓ cup dry sherry

3 tablespoons golden raisins

2 tablespoons slivered almonds

½ pound pork chorizo

¼ cup oil

6 chicken quarters (about 4 ½ pounds)

1 medium onion, thinly sliced

2 Serrano chiles, seeded and finely
    chopped (see Note)

¾ cup chicken stock (page 276)

1 pound tomatoes, peeled, seeded,
    and pureed

2 medium cloves garlic, minced

¼ cup freshly squeezed lime juice

½ pound carrots, peeled and cut into
    2-inch-long matchsticks

¾ pound zucchini, cut into
    2-inch-long matchsticks

1. In a small saucepan, heat sherry until simmering. Place raisins in a small bowl and pour sherry over them. Cover and leave for 2 to 4 hours.

2. Preheat oven to 350°F. Toast almonds in oven for 7 to 10 minutes, or until lightly browned.

3. In a large skillet, fry chorizo until well cooked and slightly crisp. Remove and drain on paper towels. Reserve. Discard drippings from sauté pan.

4. In a sauté pan heat oil over medium-high heat. Add chicken pieces in 2 batches and brown well on all sides. Remove from pan and reserve.

5. Add onion and chiles to pan and sauté for about 5 minutes, or until soft. Remove from pan and reserve. Drain excess oil from pan but do not wash pan.

6. Return pan to heat and add chicken stock. Boil 3 minutes, stirring and scraping bits from the bottom of the pan. Boil until reduced to ½ cup.

7. Add pureed tomatoes and garlic and cook 5 more minutes over medium-high heat.

8. Add chorizo, lime juice, and chicken. Cover and simmer for 15 minutes.

9. Add the sherry the raisins soaked in, the onions, chiles, carrots, and zucchini. Simmer another 15 minutes or until chicken is tender. Taste for seasoning. Add about 1½ tablespoons of the almonds and all of the raisins.

10. To serve, transfer to a platter and garnish with remaining almonds.

ADVANCE PREPARATION:

May be kept up to 1 day in refrigerator. Reheat gently over low heat. Do not add almonds until reheating.

NOTE:

When working with chiles, always wear rubber gloves. Wash cutting surface and knife immediately afterward.

CHICKEN WITH TOMATOES AND SAUSAGES

Serves 6 to 8

Always a family and guest favorite, this zesty entrée combines sweet and hot sausages with Marinara Sauce, peppers, and chicken. It may be served as a meal by itself or with fresh pasta. Follow with fresh Banana or Strawberry Sorbet.

RECOMMENDED CALIFORNIA WINE:
This is very good with dry Sauvignon Blanc in the summer and spicy Zinfandel in the winter.

4 sweet sausages (about 1 pound)	3 pounds chicken, cut into pieces
4 hot sausages (about 1 pound)	1 cup dry red wine
2 medium onions, sliced	3 cups Marinara Sauce (page 278)
1 large green bell pepper, seeded and cut into 1-inch strips	3 tablespoons chopped fresh parsley
	2 teaspoons finely chopped fresh oregano, or 1 teaspoon dried oregano
1 large red bell pepper, seeded and cut into 1-inch strips	2 teaspoons finely chopped fresh basil, or 1 teaspoon dried basil
½ pound mushrooms, sliced	
2 medium cloves garlic, minced	1½ teaspoons salt
2 tablespoons olive oil	½ teaspoon finely ground pepper

FOR GARNISH:

2 tablespoons chopped fresh parsley

Freshly grated Parmesan cheese (optional)

1 In a large skillet, brown sausages over medium heat. Place on paper towels or a brown paper bag to absorb excess fat. Let cool and slice on the diagonal into 1½-inch pieces.

2 Remove and discard all but 2 tablespoons drippings from skillet. Add onions to skillet and sauté for 3 minutes. Add peppers and mushrooms. Continue cooking another 5 minutes over high heat, stirring often. Add garlic and cook for 1 minute. Remove to platter.

3 Add olive oil to skillet and heat. Add chicken pieces and sauté until golden brown, about 5 minutes on each side. Remove to platter.

④ Remove excess oil. Pour red wine into pan. Bring to boil, stirring and scraping up the browned bits. Add Marinara Sauce, herbs, salt, and pepper. Bring to a simmer. Return chicken and vegetables to sauce and simmer until tender, about 15 to 20 minutes, depending on size of pieces. Add sausages to warm them.

⑤ Taste for seasoning. Skim off excess fat if necessary. Transfer to a serving platter and sprinkle with fresh parsley. If desired, pass Parmesan cheese separately.

ADVANCE PREPARATION:

May be kept up to 2 days in refrigerator.

ROAST CHICKEN STUFFED UNDER THE SKIN WITH GOAT CHEESE-LEEK FILLING

Serves 4

This recipe is an adaptation of cookbook author Richard Olney's Stuffed Baked Chicken. The filling is fragrant with goat cheese, herbs, watercress, and leeks. It is stuffed under the skin, which keeps the chicken moist and juicy. The final presentation is beautiful to behold, with its plump brown crispy skin. For ease in serving, slice chicken in large pieces, or quarter the chicken. Begin the meal with Garlic-Vegetable Soup; serve the chicken with steamed seasonal vegetables.

RECOMMENDED CALIFORNIA WINE:

This can be served with a fine Chardonnay, Cabernet, Sauvignon, or Zinfandel.

1 (4½ pounds) roasting chicken

FOR MARINADE:

1 tablespoon dry white wine

3 tablespoons olive oil

1 teaspoon chopped fresh thyme,
    or ½ teaspoon dried thyme

¼ teaspoon salt

Pinch of finely ground pepper

2 cups fresh watercress leaves

2 tablespoons unsalted butter

2 medium leeks, white part only,
cleaned and finely chopped

4 small green onions, white part and
1 inch of green part, thinly sliced

6 ounces Sonoma goat cheese
or French goat cheese

6 ounces fresh buffalo mozzarella or cow's
milk mozzarella, coarsely chopped

2 tablespoons finely chopped
Italian parsley

2 tablespoons finely chopped fresh thyme

⅛ teaspoon finely ground pepper

½ cup chicken stock (page 276)

Fresh watercress

1 Cut wing tips off chicken.

2 Combine marinade ingredients in a bowl.

3 Moisten fingers with marinade. Separate skin from meat at neck end
of chicken, leaving the tail end intact. (Use rubber gloves if you have long
fingernails.) Being careful not to rip the skin, carefully slip moistened fingers under skin of legs, thighs, and breast portion of chicken.

4 Place chicken in a large bowl. Pour marinade over and marinate for 1 to
2 hours in refrigerator.

5 For filling: Immerse watercress in a pan of boiling water and boil 10
seconds. Remove from pan and run cold water over leaves. With a kitchen
towel, wring all excess moisture out of watercress. Place in a bowl.

6 In a medium skillet, melt butter over moderate heat. Add chopped leeks
and green onions and sauté until tender.

7 Remove rind from goat cheese. Combine all ingredients for filling and mix
well. (This may be done in the food processor for finer texture.) If making by
hand, mash the goat cheese and mozzarella and add remaining ingredients.

8 Preheat oven to 400°F. Stuff chicken by taking small handfuls of stuffing
and pushing it evenly under the skin. The legs should have as much stuffing
as the breasts. Pat the chicken all around, so that the stuffing is distributed
evenly. Tie wings and legs to body to make a tight package.

9 Set chicken on a rack in a roasting pan and roast for 15 minutes. Reduce
oven temperature to 375°F. Continue roasting for 1 hour, basting with pan
juices every 15 to 20 minutes. The bird should be nicely browned.

10 Place chicken on a carving board. Remove trussing string and quarter chicken with poultry shears. Garnish with fresh watercress.

ADVANCE PREPARATION:

Stuffing may be prepared up to 1 day ahead and kept in refrigerator. Remove from refrigerator 1 hour before stuffing chicken to soften filling.

CRISPY DUCK WITH CRANBERRY, PEAR, AND PISTACHIO DRESSING

Serves 6 to 8

Crispy duck is a wonderful fall or holiday-season main course. The ducks are roasted at a high temperature briefly, then at a lower temperature, so that the dressing can bake with them. The dressing may also be served with Cornish game hens or turkey. In contemporary California cooking, duck is often served medium-rare. In this recipe, the ducks are roasted for a longer period of time in a more traditional method of preparation. The cranberry-pear marinade becomes a glaze when the ducks are roasted, which keeps them moist during the long roasting. The ducks are quartered and placed on a platter surrounded by tiny poached pears and fresh cranberries. Serve with simple steamed green beans and the dressing on the side.

RECOMMENDED CALIFORNIA WINE:

Serve this with full-bodied elegant wines with vigorous fruit—a big Chardonnay, Pinot Noir, or Zinfandel. Duck is a great tannin-cutter for big red wines. This is one of those rare dishes that can be served with late-harvest Zinfandel.

FOR MARINADE:

½ medium Bosc pear, coarsely chopped

1 cup cranberries

½ cup tawny port

1 cup freshly squeezed orange juice

¼ cup orange honey

½ teaspoon allspice

Pinch of salt and finely ground pepper

2 (4½-pound) ducks, necks and
    giblets removed

1 pound whole-wheat bread, cubed
(about 6 cups)

1 cup shelled pistachios

2 tablespoons unsalted butter

1 tablespoon oil

1½ medium onions, coarsely chopped

1 Bosc pear, peeled, cored,
and cut into medium dice

1 cup chicken stock (page 276)

2 eggs, slightly beaten

¼ cup finely chopped fresh parsley

1 tablespoon finely chopped orange zest

1 cup cranberries, coarsely chopped

3 cups duck stock (page 275)

10 tiny red pears, about 2 inches high

Parsley sprigs

¼ cup cranberries

1 For marinade: Combine all ingredients in a blender or a food processor fitted with the steel blade and puree.

2 Put ducks in a large bowl and pour marinade over them. Marinate for 2 to 4 hours in refrigerator.

3 Remove ducks from marinade and pat dry. Reserve marinade. Prick duck skin ¼-inch deep all over, particularly in fatty area around thigh and in wing area. Do not pierce meat.

4 Preheat oven to 425°F. To truss ducks, pull neck skin over breast and tie legs together. Pull string around body, then tie wings together. Place on a rack in a roasting pan large enough to hold both ducks.

5 Roast ducks for 20 minutes. Reduce oven temperature to 350°F and continue roasting for 1 hour and 15 minutes.

6 Meanwhile, prepare dressing. Toast bread in oven for 15 minutes. In a separate pan, toast pistachios in oven for 10 minutes.

7 In a medium skillet, heat butter and oil over low heat. Add onions and sauté until soft, about 5 minutes. Remove to a large bowl.

8 Add bread cubes, pistachios, pear, chicken stock, eggs, parsley, orange zest, and cranberries. Toss to combine.

9 Generously butter a 2½-quart soufflé dish. Spoon dressing mixture into dish.

10 Put dressing in oven after duck has been roasting about 45 minutes. Bake for 45 minutes, or until golden brown.

11 For garnish: In a medium saucepan, combine pears and the remaining marinade. Poach pears for 20 minutes over medium heat, covered. Turn pears after 10 minutes to cook evenly. Remove pears and keep warm. Reserve marinade.

12 Remove roast ducks from oven. Drain and discard duck drippings. Add duck stock and remaining marinade from pears to pan. Bring to boil, stirring. Boil until sauce is reduced to 3 cups.

13 When dressing is done, remove from oven. Raise oven temperature to 450°F.

14 Quarter ducks and place on an ovenproof platter. Surround with pears. Spoon ½ cup sauce over pieces and return to oven for 15 minutes, or until nicely browned.

15 Arrange ducks on a platter and garnish with pears. Decorate with small bunches of parsley sprigs; lay fresh cranberries on top of parsley. Serve dressing and sauce on side.

VARIATION:

Pippin or other tart apples may be used instead of pears. Walnuts or pecans may be substituted for pistachios.

ADVANCE PREPARATION:

Duck may be prepared up to 2 hours ahead through Step 5; keep at room temperature, covered lightly with aluminum foil. Dressing may be prepared up to 6 hours ahead through Step 10 and kept in refrigerator. Bring to room temperature before baking.

BARBECUED ROAST DUCK WITH RED WINE
AND BLACK CURRANTS

Serves 3 to 4

Here, the duck is first roasted to remove excess fat. Then it is grilled on a medium-hot mesquite barbecue. Make sure the fire is not too hot or flames will erupt from the duck drippings. The duck should be cooked until medium-rare. A reduction of the wine and currant marinade is added to reserved duck stock for a light and complementary sauce. Don't be discouraged from trying this slightly unusual method for cooking duck if you don't have fresh black currants; just omit them. Serve with Sauté of Carrots and Turnips or Sweet Potato–Shallot Sauté.

RECOMMENDED CALIFORNIA WINE:

Big Cabernet Sauvignons or Zinfandels shine with this dish, especially if you match the grape varietal used in the marinade with the finer version you are drinking with the dish.

FOR MARINADE:

3½ cups dry red wine

½ cup black currant syrup

2 bay leaves

1 medium onion, thinly sliced

1 medium carrot, peeled and thinly sliced

6 black peppercorns

1 teaspoon whole cloves

1 (4½-pound) duck, neck and
    giblets removed

¼ teaspoon salt

⅛ teaspoon finely ground pepper

FOR SAUCE:

1 cup duck stock (page 275)

¼ teaspoon salt

Pinch of finely ground white pepper

¼ cup fresh black currants (optional)

2 tablespoons unsalted butter

FOR GARNISH:

Fresh black currants (optional)

1. Combine marinade ingredients and place in a large mixing bowl.

2. Cut wing tips off duck, using a heavy knife or cleaver, and save for stock. Halve duck by splitting backbone and breastbone, using a heavy knife or cleaver.

3. Place duck halves in marinade. Marinate for 6 to 12 hours in refrigerator, turning frequently.

4. Prepare barbecue for medium-heat grilling (fire should not be too hot). Preheat oven to 475°F.

5. Remove duck from marinade, reserving marinade, and pat duck dry. Prick skin about ¼-inch deep all over, particularly in fatty areas around thigh and in wing area. Do not pierce meat.

6. Season duck with salt and pepper. Place duck on a roasting rack in a roasting pan and roast in oven for 20 minutes to remove some of the fat.

7. Strain 2 cups marinade and place in a 2-quart saucepan. Boil over high heat until reduced to ½ cup, about 15 minutes. Skim if necessary.

8. Transfer duck to barbecue grill, breast side down. Grill 3 inches from heat for about 25 to 30 minutes. Turn duck halves over and grill for about 5 more minutes.

9. Meanwhile, to make sauce, add duck stock to reduced marinade. Boil until reduced to 1 cup; season with salt and pepper. Add currants. Whisk in butter to finish sauce. Taste for seasoning.

10. Remove duck from grill and place on a platter. Quarter duck and slice breasts. Garnish with fresh black currants. Serve sauce separately.

ADVANCE PREPARATION:

May be prepared 12 hours ahead through Step 3 and refrigerated.

GRILLED SQUAB WITH BASIL BUTTER

Serves 6 to 8

Have your poultry dealer split and remove the breastbone from the squab, for ease of preparation and a more refined presentation. After marinating, the squabs are placed flat on a grill. Since the meat is dark and richly flavored, small servings are sufficient. The meat should be cooked to the point where it is just pink in the breast portion. The fragrant basil butter will blend with the natural flavor and juices of the squab. A wild rice salad with carrots and oranges is an unusually good accompaniment.

RECOMMENDED CALIFORNIA WINE:

This is another flexible dish that works equally well with fine Chardonnay, Fumé Blanc, Cabernet Sauvignon, or Zinfandel, depending on your mood and the weather.

½ cup fresh basil leaves

4 whole baby squabs, split in half
    lengthwise, breastbone removed

FOR MARINADE:

½ cup dry white wine

¼ cup olive oil

1 teaspoon salt

¼ teaspoon finely ground pepper

FOR BASIL BUTTER:

½ cup (1 stick) unsalted butter

2 tablespoons chopped fresh basil

¼ teaspoon salt

Pinch of finely ground black pepper

1 Slide enough basil leaves under skin of each squab breast to cover breast. Be careful not to tear skin.

2 For marinade: Combine ingredients in a small bowl. Whisk until blended. Add remaining whole basil leaves.

3 In a large shallow nonaluminum dish, arrange squab pieces and pour marinade over them. Marinate 2 to 4 hours in refrigerator.

4 For basil butter: Combine butter, basil, salt, and pepper in a medium bowl. Place on sheet of waxed paper, roll up in form of a log, and put in refrigerator until ready to use.

5 Prepare barbecue for medium-heat grilling. Remove squabs from marinade and grill 3 inches from heat for 5 to 7 minutes on each side for medium-rare. For medium to medium-well-done squabs, cook for 10 to 12 minutes on each side. Remove from grill.

6 Carve a leg off each squab half and reserve. Slice breasts into thin slices and arrange on plate, overlapping slightly. Place a leg next to breast slices and arrange basil leaves for garnish.

7 Cut basil butter into thin slices and place over the sliced breast. Serve immediately.

VARIATIONS:

(1) *Chicken breasts may be used instead of squab.*
(2) *The squab breast and leg may be served whole rather than sliced. Place the pieces on a plate surrounded by basil leaves for a different presentation.*

ADVANCE PREPARATION:

May be prepared up to 4 hours ahead through Step 4 and kept in refrigerator.

TURKEY SAUTÉ WITH LEMON, MUSHROOMS, AND CAPERS

Serves 8

Sliced California turkey breast has become widely available, but you can ask your butcher to slice it for you if it has not already been done. This variation on a classic veal scallopine is simple to prepare and is less expensive than veal. It is essential to cook the turkey very quickly over medium-high heat to keep it moist and tender. The light lemon-caper finish enhances the flavor. Serve with Baked Yams with Sour Cream and Chives or Sauté of Carrots and Turnips.

Turkey in this or any other form is best accompanied by a big, rich California Chardonnay.

¼ cup all-purpose flour (approximately)

2 tablespoons olive oil

6 tablespoons (¾ stick) unsalted butter

2 pounds turkey breast, thinly sliced
   and pounded thin

Salt and finely ground pepper to taste

½ pound mushrooms, thinly sliced

½ cup dry white wine

¾ cup chicken stock (page 276)

3 tablespoons freshly squeezed
   lemon juice

4 tablespoons chopped fresh parsley

2 tablespoons capers, drained and rinsed

FOR GARNISH:

1 bunch fresh parsley

2 lemons, fluted with a citrus stripper
   and cut into thin slices

1 Spread flour on a flat plate. Heat oil and 2 tablespoons of the butter in a medium skillet over medium-high heat. (It should be quite hot so that the turkey will cook quickly, or it will become leathery.)

2 Dip both sides of turkey slices in flour and shake off excess. Add enough slices to pan to fit comfortably, and sauté until they are browned on one side. Turn over and brown other side for up to 2 minutes. Transfer to a warm platter and season with salt and pepper. Continue with remaining turkey.

3 Add 2 tablespoons of the butter to a skillet and heat. Add mushrooms and sauté, stirring to cook them evenly, about 3 minutes.

4 Add wine, stock, and lemon juice to skillet and boil for 3 minutes, or until slightly thickened. Whisk in the remaining 2 tablespoons butter and add 2 tablespoons of the chopped parsley. Taste for seasoning.

5 Add turkey to quickly reheat, then arrange meat on a serving platter. Spoon sauce over meat and sprinkle capers and remaining chopped parsley on top. Arrange sprigs of parsley around platter and place lemon slices on top. Serve immediately.

SAUTÉED CHICKEN LIVERS WITH GREEN PEPPERCORNS

Serves 2

This is a delicious variation on the usual chicken liver, onions, and bacon. Here the flavors are combined to create an outstanding main course. The green peppercorns add zest, while the cream softens the sauce to give it elegance as well as spice. Serve with steamed white rice and Sauté of Julienned Garden Vegetables.

RECOMMENDED CALIFORNIA WINE:

This is delicious with big, oaky Chardonnays and big Pinot Noirs.

¼ pound pancetta or bacon,
    thinly sliced
2 tablespoons unsalted butter
2 tablespoons oil
1 pound fresh chicken livers
2 medium shallots, finely chopped
¾ pound mushrooms, thinly sliced
⅓ cup white wine vinegar
    or green peppercorn vinegar

¾ cup chicken stock (page 276)
    or veal stock (page 274)
⅓ cup whipping cream
½ teaspoon green peppercorns,
    rinsed well
¼ teaspoon salt
Pinch of finely ground pepper to taste

1 In a medium skillet, fry pancetta or bacon over medium heat until crisp. Drain on paper towels and crumble. Drain off drippings.

2 To skillet, add 1 tablespoon of the butter and 1 tablespoon of the oil and heat over medium-high heat. Add livers and brown over very high heat, turning frequently, for about 2 to 3 minutes. Remove from pan and reserve.

3 Add remaining butter and oil to pan. Add shallots and sauté over medium heat until softened. Add mushrooms and continue cooking for 2 minutes. Remove vegetables. Drain off excess fat but do not wash pan.

4 Place pan back on medium heat and add vinegar and stock. Bring to boil, stirring and scraping browned bits. Boil for about 1 minute, until reduced to ½ cup. Add cream and green peppercorns and simmer until slightly thickened. Add salt and pepper.

5 Add livers, bacon, and vegetables to reheat and taste for seasoning. Serve immediately.

GRILLED VEAL CHOPS WITH ROSEMARY

Serves 4

Veal, virgin olive oil, and fresh rosemary come alive in this quickly prepared entrée. The mesquite charcoal seals the brilliant flavor in with its searing heat. Start with Pasta with Fresh Mushroom Sauce and accompany with Sautéed Sugar Snap Peas and Red Peppers.

RECOMMENDED CALIFORNIA WINE:

Serve with a graceful Cabernet Sauvignon from Napa or Alexander Valley, or with a big, lively Chardonnay.

4 veal loin chops, 6 to 8 ounces each

2 tablespoons virgin olive oil

2 (2-inch) sprigs fresh rosemary

Juice of 1 medium lemon

Salt and finely ground pepper to taste

1 Brush veal chops liberally on each side with olive oil.

2 Strip leaves off rosemary sprigs and press leaves into both sides of each veal chop. Sprinkle lemon juice on each side and refrigerate 1 hour.

3 Prepare barbecue for medium-heat grilling or preheat broiler, if necessary. Grill veal about 3 inches from heat for 5 to 7 minutes on each side. The veal should be very pink inside. Take veal off grill and sprinkle with salt and pepper. Serve immediately.

VEAL MEDALLIONS WITH LIME-GINGER SAUCE

Serves 4

As an outgrowth of their willingness to experiment with new ideas, Californians appreciate the combination of citrus with spice. In this recipe, which was adapted from Bernard's restaurant in Los Angeles, tangy lime and ginger combine to bring out the veal medallions' natural sweetness. Serve this with Leek Timbale or Sauté of Julienned Garden Vegetables.

Serve with a Cabernet Sauvignon from Napa or Alexander Valley, or with a lush, full-flavored Chardonnay.

6 tablespoons (¾ stick) unsalted butter	3 tablespoons freshly squeezed lime juice
4 veal loin chops, bone removed	1 cup veal stock (page 274)
(½ pound each and no more than	¼ teaspoon salt
1 inch thick)	Pinch of coarsely cracked pepper
1 tablespoon julienned fresh ginger	

FOR GARNISH:

1 lime, sectioned

1. Melt 4 tablespoons of the butter over medium heat in a medium skillet. Soften remaining 2 tablespoons butter.

2. Place veal in skillet and brown for approximately 4 to 5 minutes on each side. The meat will turn dark brown around the edges.

3. Remove veal from pan. Discard butter remaining in pan. Add ginger, lime juice, and veal stock. Stir over high heat. Boil until reduced to ½ cup, about 3 minutes. Strain and return to pan.

4. Lower heat and add softened butter in pieces, whisking until blended. Season with salt and pepper. Taste for seasoning. Return veal to sauce to heat it.

5. Spoon 1 tablespoon of sauce onto each of 4 individual plates. Place veal on top and spoon over additional sauce. Garnish with lime sections. Serve immediately.

VEAL STEW WITH BABY ONIONS, WILD MUSHROOMS, AND SPINACH

Serves 6

Notably different from the classic white veal stew, this main dish uses fresh California green spinach strips and rich yellow orange chanterelle mushrooms. It is appealing as a hearty meal in itself, or serve it with Saffron Rice or steamed white rice with parsley.

RECOMMENDED CALIFORNIA WINE:

Serve with a full-bodied Chardonnay or a light Pinot Noir.

2½ pounds veal shoulder
   or veal stew meat
½ pound veal bones or veal breast
1 quart veal stock (page 274) or water
1 medium onion, quartered
1 medium clove garlic, quartered
Bouquet garni (see Notes)
½ teaspoon salt
¼ teaspoon finely ground pepper

½ pound baby onions
3 tablespoons unsalted butter
¼ pound chanterelles or other fresh
   wild mushrooms, rinsed carefully
   (see Notes)
1 tablespoon all-purpose flour
1 bunch spinach (½ pound), leaves only,
   cut into thin strips
¼ cup whipping cream

1 Cut veal shoulder into 2-inch pieces. Put in a large saucepan with bones, stock, onion, garlic, and bouquet garni. Add ¼ teaspoon of the salt and ⅛ teaspoon of the pepper. Bring to boil. Cover and cook over low heat for about 1 hour and 15 minutes or until veal is nearly tender. Remove and discard bouquet garni, onion, and garlic.

2 Add baby onions to pan and simmer for about 15 minutes, or until veal and onions are tender.

3 Heat 2 tablespoons of the butter in a skillet. Add wild mushrooms, the remaining ¼ teaspoon salt, and the remaining ⅛ teaspoon pepper and sauté over medium-high heat for about 5 minutes, or until tender and any liquid has evaporated.

4 When the veal and onions are tender, remove them with a slotted spoon. Discard veal bones but reserve pieces of veal breast with the shoulder meat.

5 Boil the veal-cooking liquid until reduced to about 2 cups.

6 Mash the remaining butter in a bowl. Stir in flour to obtain a smooth paste. Gradually whisk mixture into the simmering liquid. Return to a boil, whisking constantly.

7 Add spinach to sauce and simmer for about 2 minutes, or until just wilted. Return veal and onions to sauce and add wild mushrooms. Simmer for 2 minutes longer. Add cream and bring just to a boil. Taste for seasoning. Serve immediately in individual bowls.

ADVANCE PREPARATION:

May be kept up to 1 day in refrigerator. Bring to room temperature before reheating. Gently reheat and serve immediately.

NOTES:

(1) *To make a bouquet garni, wrap a parsley sprig, bay leaf, and a sprig of fresh thyme in cheesecloth and tie with string.*
(2) *Substitute small button mushrooms if wild mushrooms are unavailable.*

VEAL AND CHICKEN SAUSAGES
WITH CHILES AND CILANTRO

Serves 6

With the addition of chiles and cilantro to white veal sausage, this dish becomes spicy yet delicate, with a light Mexican touch. Serve with scrambled eggs or use in Frittata with Zucchini, Spicy Sausage, and Red Peppers. It also makes a delicious supper served with Oven-Roasted Potatoes and a simple green salad.

RECOMMENDED CALIFORNIA WINE:

Beer and margaritas are the first choice, but these sausages are delicious with a Blanc de Pinot Noir or Fumé Blanc.

Small-diameter sausage casings

½ cup milk

⅓ cup white bread crumbs

1 onion, chopped

2 Serrano chiles, split and seeded
(see Notes)

½ pound veal meat

½ pound chicken meat,
without skin or bones

¼ pound pork fat

2 tablespoons chopped cilantro

2 large egg whites

Grated zest of 1 lemon

1 teaspoon salt

¼ teaspoon finely ground pepper

FOR FRYING:

¼ cup (½ stick) unsalted butter (optional)

1　Soak casings in cold water for about 2 hours.

2　Bring milk to a boil. Pour it over bread crumbs and let cool.

3　Grind onion, chiles, veal, chicken, pork fat, and cilantro in a meat grinder using the fine plate, or in a food processor fitted with the steel blade. Mixture should be a fine paste.

4　Add egg whites, bread crumb–milk mixture, lemon zest, salt, and pepper to meat mixture and mix thoroughly in a food processor or by hand in a bowl.

5　Drain casings. Tie one end closed. Insert a sausage stuffer or funnel into other end and spoon in meat mixture. Carefully push mixture down into casing. Do not fill casings too tightly or they will burst. Tie them with string into 6-inch sausages.

6　To cook sausages, bring a large pan of salted water to simmer. Add sausages, cover, and cook over low heat for 20 minutes. (See Notes.) Let cool in liquid.

7　To serve, drain sausages. Melt butter in a skillet over medium heat. Add sausages and sauté until golden brown and heated through. Or, heat in broiler, turning to brown them evenly. They may also be grilled on the barbecue.

VARIATION:

Omit chiles and cilantro and add ¼ teaspoon freshly grated nutmeg and ½ teaspoon allspice. Serve with sliced apples that have been sautéed in butter until just tender.

ADVANCE PREPARATION:

May be prepared up to 2 days ahead through Step 6 and kept in refrigerator.

(1) *When working with chiles always wear rubber gloves. Wash cutting surface and knife immediately afterward.*

(2) *Sausage mixture may be spooned out in tablespoons and sautéed in butter if you prefer not to stuff in casings.*

SAUTÉED LAMB CHOPS WITH MADEIRA, CARROTS, AND GREEN BEANS

Serves 6

Sautéing lamb results in an unusual flavor. A simple arrangement of deliciously cooked vegetables finishes off the tender lamb. The green al dente beans and orange carrots that surround the lamb chops provide a colorful balance of taste and appearance. Serve with Baked Potato Rose or Saffron Rice.

RECOMMENDED CALIFORNIA WINE:

Serve with a Cabernet Sauvignon or Pinot Noir.

FOR GLAZED CARROTS:

1½ pounds carrots
½ teaspoon salt
1 teaspoon sugar
1 tablespoon unsalted butter

¾ pound thin French green beans
   (haricots verts) or regular green
   beans, julienned
1 teaspoon salt
2 tablespoons oil

2 tablespoons unsalted butter
12 small-rib or lion lamb chops,
   up to ¾ inch thick
¼ teaspoon finely ground pepper
⅓ cup Madeira

1 For glazed carrots: Peel and slice carrots and put them in a large saucepan. Add salt, sugar, butter, and water to barely cover. Cover pan and cook over low heat for about 20 minutes, or until nearly tender. If water evaporates before carrots are tender, add a few more tablespoons water.

2 When carrots are nearly tender, boil uncovered to evaporate excess water so that butter and sugar form a light glaze.

3 Immerse green beans in a large pan of boiling water, add ½ teaspoon of the salt, and boil for about 5 minutes, or until just tender. Drain thoroughly.

4 Meanwhile, heat oil and 1 tablespoon of the butter in a large skillet. Season lamb chops with the remaining ½ teaspoon salt and the pepper. Add chops to skillet in batches and sauté over medium-high heat for about 3 minutes on each side, or until lightly browned and tender but still pink inside.

5 Transfer lamb chops to an ovenproof platter and keep warm in low oven. Pour off drippings from pan.

6 Reheat pan used for sautéing lamb. Add Madeira and bring to a boil, stirring. Boil until reduced to about ¼ cup. Taste for seasoning.

7 Heat the remaining butter in a deep skillet, add green beans, and toss over low heat until just hot. Taste for seasoning.

8 Reheat carrots if necessary.

9 To serve, spoon carrots on one side of lamb chops and green beans on the other, on a platter or on individual plates. Serve sauce separately. Serve immediately.

ADVANCE PREPARATION:

May be prepared 4 hours ahead through Step 3 and kept at room temperature.

SAUTÉED LAMB MEDALLIONS
ON A BED OF EGGPLANT WITH RED PEPPERS

Serves 4

If possible, have your butcher remove the bones from the lamb chops and make sure to bring them home. The bones are browned and cooked with veal stock to give the lamb a sensational finish. Colorful and visually exciting to look at, with a sautéed red pepper topping, this entrée is nice for a small dinner party. Serve with steamed white rice.

RECOMMENDED CALIFORNIA WINE:

Serve with a zesty Zinfandel or Cabernet Sauvignon.

12 small-rib lamb chops

1 cup veal stock

2 small thin eggplants
(approximately 1 pound)

½ cup olive oil

½ teaspoon salt

¼ teaspoon finely ground pepper

2 medium cloves garlic, minced

3 tablespoons chopped fresh parsley

2 red bell peppers, seeded and cut
into thin strips

1 To make the medallions: Cut bones from the lamb chops, leaving the nugget of meat. Reserve bones. Refrigerate meat until ready to cook.

2 Preheat oven to 350°F. Brown lamb bones in a medium roasting pan in oven for about 1 hour.

3 Pour off drippings from roasting pan. Place pan over medium-high heat, add veal stock, and boil until reduced to ½ cup. Remove bones and set aside.

4 Cut each eggplant into 6 slices crosswise.

5 Reduce oven temperature to 300°F. Heat about ¼ cup of the oil in a skillet. Add enough eggplant slices to make one layer and sprinkle with a little salt and pepper. Fry over medium-high heat for about 5 minutes or until lightly browned on both sides and tender when pierced with fork. Drain on paper towels. Continue with remaining eggplant.

6 Add garlic and parsley to skillet and sauté lightly for 1 minute. Scatter mixture over eggplant. Keep warm in oven until ready to serve.

7 Add 2 tablespoons of the oil to skillet. Add peppers, ¼ teaspoon salt, and a pinch of pepper and sauté over medium heat, stirring often, for about 5 minutes, or until just tender.

8 Heat remaining oil in a large skillet. Lightly season lamb medallions with remaining salt and pepper. Add lamb to skillet in batches and sauté over medium-high heat for about 3 minutes on each side or until lightly browned and tender but still pink inside. Place lamb on a platter and keep warm.

9 Pour off drippings from skillet. Add reduced stock and bring to boil. Boil to reduce until slightly thickened. Taste for seasoning.

10 To serve, spoon a small amount of sauce on each plate. Place eggplant on sauce and top with red pepper and lamb medallions. Spoon additional sauce over lamb. Serve immediately.

ADVANCE PREPARATION:

May be prepared up to 1 day ahead through Step 3 and refrigerated. Remove from refrigerator 1 hour before finishing the dish.

LEG OF LAMB, CALIFORNIA STYLE

Serves 6 to 8

Using local wines and spirits, the marinade in this lamb dish provides a subtlety of flavor that will make this dish a favorite. Enhanced by citrus, the sauce is both a bit unusual and also slightly familiar. A butterflied leg of lamb works well for barbecuing or broiling. The thicker portion of the lamb can be pounded so that the meat will be of an even thickness and will cook evenly throughout. Serve with Baked Potato Rose and Mustard-Baked Tomatoes.

RECOMMENDED CALIFORNIA WINE:

Serve a full-bodied young red wine with plenty of fruit and vigorous flavors: Cabernet Sauvignon, Pinot Noir, or Zinfandel. Don't worry too much if the wine is a bit young and tannic; lamb is a great tannin eraser.

¼ cup soy sauce

½ cup California Burgundy

¼ cup brandy

Juice of 1 medium orange

Juice of 1 medium lemon

2 tablespoons honey

1 teaspoon dry mustard

1 large tomato, coarsely chopped

3 medium cloves garlic, finely minced

¼ teaspoon finely ground black pepper

1 (7-pound) leg of lamb, butterflied if
   possible (net weight 4½ to 5 pounds)
1 cup veal stock (page 274)

1 If leg of lamb isn't already butterflied, do it yourself. Remove excess fat. With a sharp boning knife, cut off tail bone. Cut along shank bone and scrape meat from bone. Remove shank bone.

2 Cut around ball joint, which is in the thickest part of leg. Make a cut into meat down leg bone toward knee joint. Scrape and pull away flesh from leg bone. Remove leg bone.

3 Carefully cut away tendons around knee joint. You may need to twist and break knee joint to remove bone.

4 Open lamb up all the way so that it is flat. Pound thicker portion of meat to same thickness as rest of meat.

5 Combine all marinade ingredients in a food processor fitted with the steel blade or a blender and process 15 seconds.

6 Twelve hours before serving, place lamb in large nonaluminum roasting pan and pour marinade over it. Marinate lamb 12 hours in refrigerator, turning every few hours.

7 Prepare barbecue for high-heat grilling; fire should be very hot. Remove lamb from marinade, reserving ½ cup marinade. Place lamb on grill 3 inches from heat. Grill each side for about 20 minutes, for a total cooking time of 40 minutes for medium-rare to medium. For medium well-done, cook 25 to 30 minutes on each side for a total cooking time of approximately 1 hour. The meat should be pink on the inside for best flavor and texture. Remove to wooden platter and slice against the grain in diagonal slices.

8 Combine reserved marinade with veal stock in a medium saucepan. Boil until reduced to about ¾ cup. Taste for seasoning. Serve separately.

Marinade may be prepared up to 2 days ahead and kept in refrigerator. Meat may be marinated up to 24 hours ahead and kept in refrigerator.

MARINATED ROAST RACK OF LAMB
WITH SPICY PEANUT SAUCE

Serves 4

Hot pepper oil and cilantro give this peanut sauce a spicy tang. Inspired by a recipe from the original Trader Vic's restaurant in Oakland, this rack of lamb has a piquant flavor reminiscent of Thailand. Serve with Lemon Rice with Capers and Parsley, Saffron Rice, or Potato-Leek Pancake.

RECOMMENDED CALIFORNIA WINE:

Serve with a big, oaky Chardonnay or full-bodied Pinot Noir.

FOR MARINADE:

1 medium clove garlic, minced

1 medium shallot, chopped

1 teaspoon dry mustard

¼ cup dry red wine

2 teaspoons curry powder

1 teaspoon chopped fresh thyme,
  or ½ teaspoon dried thyme

Zest of 1 medium lemon, finely chopped

Juice of 1 medium lemon

1 tablespoon honey

¼ teaspoon coarsely cracked pepper

1 bay leaf

2 medium racks of lamb, 2½ pounds
  each, chine bone removed

FOR PEANUT SAUCE:

½ cup crunchy peanut butter

2 tablespoons dark soy sauce

2 medium cloves garlic, minced

¼ cup chicken stock (page 276)

2 tablespoons honey

1 tablespoon hot pepper oil (page 279)

1 tablespoon finely chopped cilantro

2 tablespoons freshly squeezed
  lemon juice

1 For marinade: Combine all ingredients in a medium bowl. Put racks of lamb in a shallow nonaluminum dish and pour marinade over them.

2 Refrigerate 4 hours; turn meat several times to evenly distribute marinade.

3 For peanut sauce: Combine all ingredients in a small bowl. Whisk together until blended. The oils should be incorporated.

4 Preheat oven to 400°F. Remove racks from marinade and place in a roasting pan. Cover exposed bones with aluminum foil to avoid burning them. Roast meat for about 30 minutes, or until pink. Roasting time depends on thickness of meat. Turn meat once and baste frequently.

5 Preheat broiler, if necessary. Place lamb under broiler for 3 minutes to brown top of rack. Serve ½ rack per person. Whisk peanut sauce and pass it separately.

ADVANCE PREPARATION:

May be prepared up to 4 hours ahead through Step 3 and kept in refrigerator.

LAMB STEW WITH ROSEMARY

Serves 6

Fresh rosemary, available year-round, is the key ingredient in this recipe. Winter turnips and carrots add texture and color. The end result is a robust and satisfying main course. Serve with Steamed New Potatoes with Chive Butter and Olive Oil–Pine Nut Bread.

RECOMMENDED CALIFORNIA WINE:

Serve with a big young Zinfandel with plenty of fruit or with a Petite Sirah.

3 tablespoons oil

2 medium onions, finely chopped

3 pounds leg of lamb, cut into
    1½-inch cubes

1 tablespoon unsalted butter

1 tablespoon all-purpose flour

1 teaspoon salt

¼ teaspoon finely ground pepper

1 cup Petite Sirah or other mild
    dry red wine

4 ripe large tomatoes, peeled, seeded,
    and chopped; or 1 (28-ounce) can
    Italian plum tomatoes, throroughly
    drained and chopped

1 tablespoon tomato paste

2 cups veal stock (page 274)

1 medium clove garlic, minced

Bouquet garni (see Note)

2 medium turnips, peeled
   and cut into ¾-inch dice

1 cup shelled fresh peas
   (about 1 pound unshelled)

4 medium carrots, peeled and cut
   into ¾-inch dice

1 tablespoon chopped fresh rosemary

1 tablespoon finely chopped fresh parsley

1 Preheat oven to 450°F. Heat 1 tablespoon of the oil in a large skillet over medium heat. Add onions and sauté until softened. Remove from skillet and set aside.

2 Pat meat dry. Add the remaining oil and the butter to skillet. Add meat in small batches and brown on all sides. Transfer meat to a large ovenproof casserole but do not wash skillet.

3 Sprinkle browned meat with flour, salt, and pepper. Bake, uncovered, for 5 to 7 minutes, or until browned. Remove from oven.

4 Add wine to skillet and bring to boil, stirring. Add tomatoes, tomato paste, sautéed onions, veal stock, garlic, and bouquet garni. Simmer until reduced by half and add to meat in casserole.

5 Reduce oven temperature to 350°F. Cover casserole and bake for 1½ hours. Remove and discard bouquet garni.

6 Add vegetables and cook on top of stove over low heat about 15 minutes, until meat and vegetables are tender. Taste for seasoning.

7 If sauce is very thin, remove meat and vegetables with a slotted spoon and boil sauce to thicken it. Return meat and vegetables to casserole.

8 Garnish with fresh rosemary and parsley and serve immediately.

ADVANCE PREPARATION:

May be prepared up to 2 days ahead through Step 5 and kept in refrigerator. Reheat gently and add vegetables.

NOTE:

To make a bouquet garni, wrap a parsley sprig, bay leaf, a sprig of fresh thyme, and 2 large sprigs of rosemary in cheesecloth and tie with string.

LOIN OF PORK WITH RHUBARB-GINGER SAUCE

Serves 6

February through June is the peak season for rhubarb. When ripe, its stalk will be firm, crisp, and either a bright pink or cherry red. Tart rhubarb is mixed with sugar, water, port, and fresh ginger to yield an aromatic, sweet, yet slightly pungent sauce. The pork is cooked in this sauce until tender. Just before serving, sliced rhubarb and more grated ginger are added for extra texture and taste. Serve this unusual entrée with Sautéed Potatoes with Onion, Apple, and Mint or with Roasted Potato Fans.

RECOMMENDED CALIFORNIA WINE:
Serve with a fine Pinot Noir or a big fine Chardonnay.

1 tablespoon unsalted butter	1 pound rhubarb
1 tablespoon oil	1/3 cup sugar
3 pounds pork loin roast, boned	1/4 cup water
1/2 cup tawny port	4 teaspoons grated fresh ginger
2 cups chicken stock (page 276)	1 tablespoon whipping cream
or veal stock (page 274)	Salt and finely ground pepper to taste

FOR GARNISH:
1 bunch watercress

1. Preheat oven to 350°F. In a medium ovenproof enamel casserole, heat butter and oil. Add pork and, turning meat with 2 large spoons or with tongs, brown evenly on all sides.

2. Remove pork, set aside, and pour out excess drippings. Add port and stock to casserole and bring to boil, stirring and scraping bits from bottom of pan. Boil for 3 minutes.

3. Cut 1 stalk of the rhubarb into thin slices and reserve. Cut remaining rhubarb into 1-inch pieces. In a medium saucepan combine rhubarb pieces, sugar, and water. Cover and cook over medium heat for about 10 minutes, or until softened. Add 1 tablespoon of the ginger. Pour mixture into casserole.

4. Return pork to casserole and bring sauce to a simmer.

5 Cover casserole and bake for 1½ hours or until meat is tender and cooked to 160°F (test in thickest part with a meat thermometer).

6 Remove pork, cover, and keep warm. Add cream to cooking liquid and boil sauce over high heat until reduced to 2 cups. Add sliced rhubarb, reduce heat to medium, and continue cooking for 5 minutes. Add remaining ginger and taste for seasoning.

7 To serve, slice pork into ½-inch slices, arrange on a platter, and pour sauce over slices. Garnish with watercress leaves. Serve immediately.

ADVANCE PREPARATION:
May be prepared up to 1 day ahead through Step 6 and kept in refrigerator. Reheat gently and taste for seasoning.

STUFFED PORK WITH APPLES AND PRUNES

Serves 8

Loin of pork is an excellent cut for braising because it retains moisture during slow cooking. As the dish simmers, the complementary flavors of the sweet California dried prunes and tart apples intermingle with the rich taste of the pork. Make sure to have your butcher make a pocket and tie the roast for easy stuffing. Serve with Oven-Roasted Potatoes or Potato-Leek Pancake.

RECOMMENDED CALIFORNIA WINE:
Serve with a big, rich Chardonnay or a full-bodied, elegant Pinot Noir.

1 medium pippin apple or other firm, tart apple, peeled, cored, and coarsely chopped

6 ounces whole dried pitted prunes

½ cup dry white wine

¾ cup apple brandy

2 (2-pound) pieces eye of loin of pork, boned and tied

6 tablespoons (¾ stick) unsalted butter

2 tablespoons oil

¼ cup whipping cream

½ teaspoon salt

¼ teaspoon finely ground pepper

1 tablespoon finely chopped fresh parsley

1 Mix together apple and prunes in a bowl.

2 Boil wine and ½ cup of the apple brandy for 2 minutes, then pour over apple and prune mixture. Let macerate for 1 to 2 hours.

3 Stuff fruit into center hole of pork loin by pushing it through with the handle of a wooden spoon. Reserve remaining fruit and marinade.

4 In a casserole large enough to easily fit both pieces of pork, heat butter and oil over medium-high heat. Add pork and, turning meat with 2 large spoons or with tongs, brown evenly on all sides. (If casserole is not large enough, brown loins one at a time or in 2 separate casseroles.)

5 Add ¼ cup of the apple brandy and ignite it with a long match, averting your face and making sure overhead fan is not on. Cover and simmer over low heat for 45 minutes. Meat temperature should be 160°F and can be checked with a meat thermometer inserted into meat (not in stuffing).

6 Remove pork to a dish and add 1 cup fruit and marinade mixture to casserole. Boil for 2 minutes, stirring. Add cream and simmer for 5 minutes. Add salt and pepper and taste for seasoning.

7 To serve, slice pork into ½-inch slices and overlap slices slightly on a platter to reveal fruit-stuffed center. Spoon sauce over pork. Garnish with parsley and serve immediately.

ADVANCE PREPARATION:

May be prepared up to 4 hours ahead through Step 6 and kept in refrigerator. Reheat gently on low to heat through.

PORK TACOS, CALIFORNIA STYLE

Serves 6

The West Beach Café in Venice, California, makes every type of taco imaginable, including turkey, duck, filet of beef—even sweetbreads. Pork tacos are my favorite. The distinctive arrangement of the ingredients on the plate is characteristically Californian. Grilled pork is cut into bite-sized pieces and, along with guacamole, green onions, cilantro, and salsas, is arranged colorfully and artistically. The tortillas are soft, so they can be rolled with the filling ingredients inside. The meat is best when barbecued but can also be roasted.

RECOMMENDED CALIFORNIA WINE:

Although beer and margaritas work well, a crisp Fumé Blanc is also refreshing.

FOR MARINADE:

½ cup freshly squeezed orange juice

2 tablespoons freshly squeezed lime juice

1 teaspoon chopped fresh oregano,
    or ½ teaspoon dried oregano

¼ teaspoon cumin

½ teaspoon marjoram

2 tablespoons oil

½ teaspoon salt

¼ teaspoon finely ground pepper

2 pounds eye of loin of pork

6 green onions

12 small fresh corn tortillas

1 bunch cilantro, large stems removed

1 recipe Guacamole (page 19)

1 cup sour cream

1 cup Spicy Red Salsa (page 282)

1 cup Green Chile Salsa (page 283)

① Combine marinade ingredients in a medium bowl. Whisk until blended.

② Place pork in a shallow nonaluminum dish and pour marinade over it. Marinate for 6 to 12 hours.

③ Cut through green part of onion, making 2 slits all the way down to where the white part begins. This will give the onions a fan shape.

④ Preheat oven to 350°F. Prepare barbecue for medium-heat grilling. Grill pork about 3 inches from heat for 20 to 25 minutes on each side, or until interior temperature is 160°F (test with meat thermometer). Baste green onions with marinade and grill for about 3 minutes on each side. Remove meat and onions from barbecue, cut meat into small chunks, and reserve.

5 Wrap tortillas in aluminum foil and warm in oven for about 10 minutes. Keep warm while preparing plates.

6 On outer edges of individual serving plates, arrange a few sprigs of cilantro, a large dollop of guacamole, and a large dollop of sour cream. Place 2 warmed tortillas on side of each plate and arrange meat and grilled scallions in center. Pass both types of salsa in separate bowls. Serve immediately.

ADVANCE PREPARATION:

May be prepared up to 4 hours ahead through Step 4 and kept in refrigerator. To reheat meat, place in medium skillet over a medium-high heat. Stir meat to brown and heat through. Reheat scallions in hot skillet.

❧

SAUSAGES WITH LENTILS AND ANCHO CHILE BUTTER

Serves 4 to 6

This recipe is an adaptation from one at the Balboa Cafe in San Francisco, headed by Jeremiah Tower. It is ideal for the cooler months, when a hearty meal is desired. The lentils are cooked until tender with herbs, tomatoes, and cream. Sausages, with a fragrant slice of spicy Ancho Chile Butter, accompany the lentils. Start with a Caesar Salad and include warm chunks of sourdough bread.

RECOMMENDED CALIFORNIA WINE:

Serve with a robust Zinfandel.

1 pound lentils, rinsed and drained	1 tablespoon unsalted butter
1 medium onion, quartered	1 tablespoon oil
Bouquet garni (see Notes)	1 large onion, finely chopped
1 bay leaf	3 medium tomatoes, peeled,
5 cups chicken stock (page 276)	seeded, and finely chopped

2 large cloves garlic, crushed

1 teaspoon finely chopped fresh oregano,
   or ½ teaspoon dried oregano

1 teaspoon finely chopped fresh thyme,
   or ½ teaspoon dried thyme

½ cup plus 2 tablespoons whipping
   cream

¼ teaspoon salt

Freshly ground pepper to taste

2 pounds sausages, sweet or hot
   or a combination

½ cup Ancho Chile Butter (page 287)

1 Combine lentils, onion, bouquet garni, bay leaf, and chicken stock in a medium saucepan. Bring to boil, lower heat, and simmer, covered, for 40 minutes. Lentils should be tender but not falling apart.

2 In a medium skillet, heat butter and oil. Add chopped onion and sauté over medium heat until soft and transparent. Add tomatoes and garlic. Simmer, uncovered, for 10 minutes.

3 Remove bay leaf, onion, and bouquet garni from lentils and discard. Add tomato-onion mixture, oregano, thyme, and ½ cup of the cream. Cover and simmer 20 minutes, stirring occasionally, over low heat.

4 Add salt and pepper. Taste for seasoning. Add the remaining 2 tablespoons cream and mix well. Taste for seasoning. Mixture should be slightly soupy.

5 Preheat oven to 425°F. Line a baking sheet with double thickness of brown paper bags.

6 Prick sausages all over and arrange on paper bags. Bake for 15 minutes. Turn and continue baking until puffed and brown, about another 30 minutes, turning again if necessary so that they brown evenly (see Notes).

7 To serve, spoon lentils into large, shallow individual serving bowls. Arrange sausages in each bowl and top with a slice of Ancho Chile Butter. Serve immediately.

ADVANCE PREPARATION:

May be prepared 4 hours ahead through Step 4 and kept covered at room temperature. Reheat slowly.

NOTES:

(1) *To make a bouquet garni, wrap a parsley sprig, bay leaf, and a sprig of fresh thyme in cheesecloth and tie with string.*

(2) *The sausage may also be broiled or sautéed, if desired.*

NEW YORK STEAKS WITH ROQUEFORT SAUCE

Serves 2

This New York steak recipe combines California sweet tawny port with earthy, strong Roquefort cheese. Crushed green peppercorns add an extra zing. Enjoy this with Oven-Roasted Potatoes and steamed asparagus.

RECOMMENDED CALIFORNIA WINE:

The intense flavor of the sauce accommodates those big, spicy California Cabernet Sauvignons and Pinot Noirs that seem to have too much of every-thing—fruit, oak, tannin, and body. The excesses are tamed and balanced by strong food flavors.

2 tablespoons green peppercorns, rinsed	½ cup tawny port
2 tablespoons oil	⅓ cup whipping cream
2 New York steaks, ½ pound each	⅓ cup (about 3 ounces) Roquefort
1 medium garlic clove, minced	cheese, crumbled

FOR GARNISH:

2 teaspoons finely chopped fresh parsley

1 Crush green peppercorns with a mortar and pestle. Set aside.

2 In medium skillet large enough to fit steaks easily, heat oil over medium-high heat. Sear steaks about 4 minutes on first side and 3 minutes on second side. Transfer to a platter and cover to keep warm.

3 Pour excess drippings out of pan. Add garlic, green peppercorns, and port and boil over high heat until reduced to ¼ cup.

4 Add cream and stir to combine. Boil mixture until reduced by half. Whisk in Roquefort cheese to thicken sauce. Heat, whisking, until cheese melts.

5 Pour sauce on each serving plate and place steak on top of sauce, or slice steak for an attractive presentation. Garnish with parsley. Serve immediately.

GRILLED STEAKS WITH ANCHO CHILE BUTTER

Serves 6

When I was child, a standard favorite at our house was barbecued New York steaks basted with garlic and soy sauce: simple, but so delicious. A large green vegetable salad and baked potatoes were the only accompaniments. Today, this tradition takes on a slightly Mexican-French influence with the addition of hot chile compound butter. This is still barbecued steak, but with an update from the overpowering teriyaki-style sauce. Serve with Baked Yams with Sour Cream and Chives or Sautéed Potatoes with Onion, Apple, and Mint.

RECOMMENDED CALIFORNIA WINE:

Serve with a full-bodied Petite Sirah or Pinot Noir.

6 steaks (spencer, sirloin, or porterhouse),
     ½ pound each
½ teaspoon salt
Pinch of finely ground pepper
½ cup Ancho Chile Butter (page 287)

1 Prepare barbecue for medium-heat grilling. Preheat broiler if necessary. Grill or broil steaks about 3 inches from heat for about 4 minutes on each side, or until browned but still rare. Season lightly with salt and pepper.

2 Slice chile butter and place a slice on each steak. Serve immediately.

TENDERLOIN OF BEEF WITH
ROASTED SHALLOTS AND TARRAGON

Serves 4 to 6

Shallots, often described as a cross between onion and garlic, are a flavorful addition to this beef dish. Usually cooked on top of the stove, here shallots are glazed with a little veal stock and roasted in the oven with cream, Madeira, and tarragon. This special roasting allows them to brown and develop full depth of flavor. Sweet and pungent tarragon lends a complementary flavor to the shallots and the beef. Serve with Baked Potato Rose and steamed asparagus.

RECOMMENDED CALIFORNIA WINE:
Serve with a fine Cabernet Sauvignon or Pinot Noir.

1 whole tenderloin of beef, trimmed
    (about 3 to 4 pounds)
2 tablespoons unsalted butter, melted
2 tablespoons soy sauce
1 medium shallot, finely chopped

ROASTED SHALLOTS:

18 large shallots	1½ teaspoons chopped fresh tarragon,
1 tablespoon butter	or ½ teaspoon dried tarragon
½ cup whipping cream	¼ teaspoon salt
2 tablespoons Madeira	Pinch of finely ground white pepper

1 Preheat oven to 425°F. Prepare roast by tucking tail end under meat, so that meat is of even thickness. Tie meat tightly lengthwise and crosswise with string.

2 Combine butter, soy sauce, and chopped shallot and rub thoroughly over meat.

3 For roasted shallots: Peel shallots and cut fuzzy part of root end off. Make sure some root is left so that shallot will hold together.

④ Bring water to boil in a medium saucepan and immerse shallots. Boil 2 minutes. Drain thoroughly.

⑤ Place meat on a roasting rack so that it will cook evenly.

⑥ Roast the beef for 45 to 50 minutes, or until a meat thermometer registers 130°F for rare, 140°F for medium well-done.

⑦ Meanwhile, place shallots in a small shallow baking dish and dot with butter. Roast shallots for 10 minutes and remove from oven.

⑧ Mix cream with Madeira, tarragon, salt, and pepper. Pour mixture over shallots.

⑨ Return shallots to oven and roast an additional 30 to 35 minutes. Watch carefully at end so that cream does not separate.

⑩ Remove beef from oven and let rest for 10 minutes before cutting.

⑪ Slice roast and divide among plates. Spoon 3 shallots with a little of the juice from the pan onto each serving. Serve immediately.

VEGETABLES

$\mathcal{C}$ALIFORNIA HAS THE LARGEST AGRICULTURAL
OUTPUT OF ANY STATE, SO IT IS NO WONDER THAT FRESH
VEGETABLES ARE KEY INGREDIENTS IN CALIFORNIA CUISINE.
Interesting variations on simple vegetable dishes that require
more than ordinary steaming or blanching procedures are
included. In contemporary California cooking, a small serving of one or several vegetables is attractively placed on the
main course plate. Vegetables blend with the main course
rather than overpower it.

Braised Baby Artichokes

Warmed Asparagus with Hazelnut Oil Vinaigrette

Baked Black Beans with Sour Cream

Stir-Fried Broccoli

Parsleyed Cucumbers

Braised Spicy Eggplant

Baked Japanese Eggplant with Herbs

Pacific Coast Eggplant

Leek Timbale

Sautéed Swiss Chard

Stuffed Zucchini with Banana Squash Puree

Sautéed Baby Tomatoes

Mustard-Baked Tomatoes

Sauté of Julienned Garden Vegetables

Sauté of Carrots and Turnips

Sautéed Sugar Snap Peas and Red Peppers

Gratin of Vegetables

BRAISED BABY ARTICHOKES

Serves 4

The town of Castroville, located in the central Salinas Valley of California, produces and ships more artichokes than any other place in the United States. It is sometimes called "The Artichoke Capital of the World." This recipe uses baby globe artichokes. Their tough outer green leaves are removed, and the chokes are quartered before braising. Tender and moist, they are a good choice to accompany Grilled Veal Chops with Rosemary. You may also serve them chilled as an appetizer or first course.

1½ pounds baby globe artichokes (about 16)

2 tablespoons olive oil

2 medium shallots, finely chopped

1 pound plum tomatoes, peeled, seeded, and coarsely chopped

2 medium cloves garlic, minced

1 cup dry white wine

1 teaspoon finely chopped fresh rosemary, or ½ teaspoon dried

1 teaspoon finely chopped fresh basil, or ½ teaspoon dried basil

1 teaspoon finely chopped fresh oregano, or ½ teaspoon dried oregano

1 teaspoon finely chopped fresh thyme, or ½ teaspoon dried thyme

½ teaspoon salt

¼ teaspoon finely ground pepper

FOR GARNISH:
2 tablespoons finely chopped fresh parsley

1 Clean artichokes by removing all green outer leaves and trimming ¼ inch off top and bottoms. Cut artichokes in quarters so they are a uniform size.

2 In a large skillet, heat olive oil over medium heat. Add shallots and sauté for 2 minutes, or until softened.

3 Add artichoke quarters and continue sautéing until lightly cooked on all sides.

4 Add tomatoes, garlic, wine, and herbs. Bring to boil. Partially cover and simmer for 45 minutes to 1 hour over low heat, stirring occasionally, until artichokes are tender when pierced with a fork. Add salt and pepper and taste for seasoning. Garnish with fresh parsley and serve immediately.

May be kept for up to 1 day in refrigerator. Serve chilled as a first course or as part of a variety of vegetable salads. Taste for seasoning, as chilling may reduce their piquancy.

WARMED ASPARAGUS WITH HAZELNUT OIL VINAIGRETTE

Serves 4

California asparagus develops a distinctive nutty flavor with the addition of hazelnut oil vinaigrette. Fresh toasted hazelnuts provide a pleasing crunchy contrast to the soft asparagus. Try this as a first course preceding Sautéed Chicken Breasts with Mustard and Tarragon, or as a side dish for a simple grilled chicken or fish entrée.

½ cup hazelnuts

FOR HAZELNUT OIL VINAIGRETTE:

3 tablespoons hazelnut oil

3 tablespoons oil

2 tablespoons white wine vinegar

¼ teaspoon salt

⅛ teaspoon finely ground pepper

1 pound asparagus

Salt to taste

1 Preheat oven to 350°F. Toast hazelnuts on a baking sheet in oven for 10 minutes. Remove and rub off skins with a kitchen towel and coarsely chop. Reserve.

2 For hazelnut oil vinaigrette: Whisk all the ingredients together. Let stand at room temperature.

3 Peel asparagus and cut off 1 inch from bottom of each stalk. Bring a large sauté pan of salted water to boil and add asparagus. Boil for about 5 minutes, or until just tender. Remove stalks carefully with slotted spoon and set them on paper towels to drain.

4 Set asparagus on a platter and spoon vinaigrette over. Sprinkle with toasted hazelnuts; serve warm.

Vinaigrette may be kept up to 2 days in refrigerator. Bring to room temperature before serving. This may also be served slightly chilled.

BAKED BLACK BEANS WITH SOUR CREAM

Serves 4

A traditional Southern black bean dish is given a spicy and deliciously different twist, with jalapeño chile and cilantro contributing a tangy flavor. It is a good fall and winter lunch or supper dish and goes well with Grilled Chicken with Salsa and Mustard Butter. Begin with a Caesar Salad.

1 cup black beans	1 small jalapeño chile or other hot chile,
2 tablespoons oil	finely chopped (see Note)
3 medium onions, thinly sliced	3 tablespoons finely chopped cilantro
2 medium cloves garlic, minced	1 teaspoon salt

FOR GARNISH:

½ cup sour cream
1 tablespoon finely chopped cilantro

1 Soak beans overnight in cold water, or do a quick soak by bringing them to a boil in water to cover, boiling 2 minutes, covering, and letting stand 1 hour.

2 Drain soaked beans and put them in a large saucepan. Add enough water to cover generously. Bring to boil and simmer, uncovered, until tender, about 1½ to 2 hours.

3 Heat oil in a skillet. Add onions and cook over low heat until soft but not brown. Add garlic, chile, and 2 tablespoons of the chopped cilantro and continue to cook 1 minute longer. Remove from heat.

4 Preheat oven to 350°F. Drain beans, reserving ½ cup cooking liquid. Put beans in an oiled, small baking dish. Add reserved liquid and the onion mixture. Add salt to taste.

5 Bake for 30 to 40 minutes or until liquid is absorbed. Top each serving with 2 tablespoons sour cream and a sprinkling of chopped cilantro.

ADVANCE PREPARATION:

May be prepared up to 8 hours ahead through Step 4 and kept in refrigerator. Bring to room temperature before baking.

NOTE:

When working with chiles always wear rubber gloves. Wash cutting surface and knife immediately afterward.

STIR-FRIED BROCCOLI

Serves 6

Broccoli's natural deep green color is accented here by flakes of red pepper, a seasoning that also makes this vegetable dish slightly hot. This procedure differs from the usual stir-fry because the vegetable is only quickly stir-fried and then simmered in chicken stock to finish the cooking process. Serve with Brown Rice with Ginger and Shrimp or Lemon-Herb Chicken.

2 pounds broccoli

3 tablespoons olive oil

2 medium cloves garlic, minced

Pinch of crushed red pepper flakes

½ cup chicken stock (page 276)

½ teaspoon salt

1 Remove large stems from broccoli. Peel remaining smaller stems with vegetable peeler and cut into 1-inch pieces. Cut broccoli florets into 1-inch pieces.

2 Heat olive oil in a wok or large skillet. Add broccoli and stir-fry until well coated and partially cooked. Add garlic and red pepper flakes and continue to stir-fry for another minute.

3 Add chicken stock and partially cover. Simmer on medium heat for about 5 minutes, or until done to taste. Add salt. Taste for seasoning and serve immediately.

ADVANCE PREPARATION:

May be made up to 4 hours ahead through Step 2 and kept in refrigerator. Remove from refrigerator ½ hour before continuing.

PARSLEYED CUCUMBERS

Serves 6 to 8

Cucumbers are cool, fresh tasting, and slightly crunchy. Sautéing softens the texture, and the addition of parsley highlights the flavor. Parsleyed cucumbers go well with Fillet of Salmon Glazed with Pesto Hollandaise Sauce, White-fish with Tomato Béarnaise Sauce, or Sea Bass with Garlic Mayonnaise.

4 cucumbers

3 tablespoons unsalted butter

½ teaspoon salt

¼ teaspoon finely ground pepper

1 tablespoon chopped parsley

1 Peel cucumbers and cut in half lengthwise. With a spoon scoop out all seeds.

2 Cut each cucumber into 2-inch-long chunks. Place each chunk flat side down and quarter it lengthwise.

3 Immerse cucumbers in a large pan of boiling salted water and boil about 4 minutes. They should be crisp-tender. Immediately pour cold water over cucumbers to stop the cooking process. When cold, drain and set aside.

4 Melt butter in a medium skillet and add cucumbers. Sauté over medium heat for 4 to 5 minutes, rolling pieces frequently. Add salt, pepper, and parsley. Taste for seasoning and serve immediately.

ADVANCE PREPARATION:

May be prepared up to 4 hours ahead through Step 2 and kept covered at room temperature.

BRAISED SPICY EGGPLANT

Serves 4 to 6

To complement an Oriental-style entrée with a different taste, try this spicy eggplant. For more spice, use a greater quantity of chile paste. I recommend serving this chilled, with Cold Chinese Noodles in Peanut-Sesame Sauce and Stir-Fried Chinese Vegetable Salad. It may also be served at room temperature.

3 tablespoons peanut oil	2 tablespoons dry sherry
1 eggplant (about 1 pound) or 4	2 tablespoons soy sauce
Japanese eggplants, unpeeled	½ teaspoon sugar
and cut into 1-inch chunks	2 teaspoons cider vinegar
3 medium cloves garlic, minced	½ cup chicken stock (page 276)
2 tablespoons finely chopped fresh ginger	Salt to taste
4 green onions, finely chopped	2 teaspoons dark sesame oil (optional)
1 tablespoon chile paste with garlic	

1 Heat peanut oil in a wok. Add eggplant and stir-fry over high heat until coated and slightly browned.

2 Add garlic, ginger, and green onions and mix well.

3 Add remaining ingredients except salt and sesame oil. Cook over high heat for 3 minutes. Reduce heat, cover, and cook for 10 to 15 minutes, or until eggplant is tender. Add salt to taste.

4 Put on a platter and drizzle with sesame oil, if desired. Serve immediately, cool to room temperature for serving, or chill and serve cold.

ADVANCE PREPARATION:

If dish is to be served cold or at room temperature, it may be prepared up to 1 day ahead and kept in refrigerator. Remove from refrigerator at least ½ hour before serving.

BAKED JAPANESE EGGPLANT WITH HERBS

Serves 6 to 8

Available during the spring and summer months, small Japanese eggplants are a pleasure to use. Here the eggplants are spread with a fragrant herb paste and baked until soft inside and slightly crunchy outside. Serve with Marinated Roast Rack of Lamb with Spicy Peanut Sauce or Turkey Sauté with Lemon, Mushrooms, and Capers.

4 Japanese eggplants, halved lengthwise

FOR TOPPING:

½ cup chopped fresh parsley

2 medium shallots, finely chopped

2 large cloves garlic, minced

2 tablespoons chopped fresh basil

⅓ cup olive oil

2 tablespoons freshly grated
    Parmesan cheese

¼ teaspoon finely ground pepper

1 Preheat oven to 350°F. Place eggplant halves in a medium roasting pan. Prick the flesh to allow herbs to penetrate.

2 For topping: Combine all ingredients in a bowl. Mix to a smooth paste.

3 Spread paste evenly on top of eggplant halves.

4 Bake for 40 to 45 minutes, or until tender and top is lightly browned.

ADVANCE PREPARATION:

May be prepared up to 4 hours ahead through Step 3 and kept in refrigerator. Bring to room temperature before continuing.

PACIFIC COAST EGGPLANT

Serves 6 to 8

This summery, seaside vegetable dish uses bell peppers, tomatoes, and fresh herbs. It is delicious cold, warm, or at room temperature, and is excellent for buffets. Try it with Grilled Lemon-Mustard Chicken or Grilled Steaks with Ancho Chile Butter.

5 Japanese eggplants (about 1½ pounds), cut in half lengthwise

6 tablespoons olive oil

2 green bell peppers, seeded and sliced into ¼-inch slices

2 medium onions, sliced into ¼-inch slices

½ pound mushrooms, sliced

2 ripe large tomatoes, peeled, seeded, and chopped

3 large cloves garlic, minced

1 cup Marinara Sauce (page 278)

3 tablespoons chopped fresh basil, or 1 tablespoon dried basil

2 tablespoons chopped fresh parsley

2 teaspoons finely chopped fresh oregano, or ½ teaspoon dried oregano

Pinch of crushed red pepper flakes

10 pitted black olives, quartered lengthwise

Salt and pepper to taste

1 Preheat oven to 350°F. In a large skillet, heat 4 tablespoons of the olive oil over medium heat. Add eggplants and brown, skin side up, in batches if necessary. Then arrange skin side down in a single layer in a buttered baking dish.

2 Heat remaining oil in skillet. Add peppers and sauté 2 to 3 minutes, or until slightly soft. Add onions and sauté until softened but not browned. Add mushrooms and continue to sauté 2 more minutes.

3 When all vegetables are tender, add tomatoes and garlic and simmer 10 more minutes. Add Marinara Sauce, herbs, red pepper, and olives. Cook 10 minutes. Season to taste with salt and pepper.

4 Pour mixture over eggplants and bake for about 20 minutes, or until bubbly. Serve immediately, or serve at room temperature or slightly chilled.

May be prepared up to 1 day ahead through Step 3 and kept in refrigerator. Bring to room temperature and continue with Step 4. If dish is to be served cold or at room temperature, it may be completely prepared up to 1 day ahead and kept in refrigerator. Remove from refrigerator at least ½ hour before serving.

LEEK TIMBALE

Serves 6

A timbale is a vegetable custard cooked in a tall cylindrical mold. It can also be cooked in small ramekins and unmolded. This version takes the wintertime leek and combines it with cheese and custard for a light green–flecked vegetable dish. Serve with Sautéed Chicken Breasts with Mustard and Tarragon or Sautéed Lamb Medallions on a Bed of Eggplant with Red Peppers.

1 cup chicken stock (page 276)

3 medium leeks, cleaned and finely chopped (about 4 cups)

4 eggs

1½ cups half-and-half

½ cup grated Gruyère cheese

Pinch of freshly grated nutmeg

½ teaspoon salt

¼ teaspoon finely ground pepper

1 In a medium saucepan, bring chicken stock to simmer. Add leeks and cover. Simmer over medium heat for 20 minutes, or until tender. Drain and cool thoroughly.

2 Preheat oven to 350°F. In a medium bowl, beat eggs and add half-and-half, cheese, and seasonings. Stir in leeks.

3 Generously butter timbale molds or ramekins and pour in leek mixture.

4 Place in a shallow pan of hot water and bake for 20 to 25 minutes, or until puffed. Invert and unmold.

May be prepared up to 4 hours ahead through Step 1 and kept in refrigerator. Bring to room temperature before continuing.

SAUTÉED SWISS CHARD

Serves 4 to 6

Swiss chard is often forgotten with the wide variety of vegetables available to us. A wonderful change from spinach, Swiss chard is available with red branches and leaves as well as with white. It provides a colorful alternative and can accompany most grilled or roasted entrées. This simple version has the addition of rice wine vinegar to provide a slightly sweet yet tart taste. Serve with Roast Chicken Stuffed Under the Skin with Goat Cheese-Leek Filling or Swordfish in Lemon-Ginger Marinade.

1 bunch red or white Swiss chard, rinsed (see Note)	1 teaspoon rice wine vinegar
	¼ teaspoon salt
2 tablespoons unsalted butter	⅛ teaspoon finely ground pepper

1 Separate chard leaves from ribs. Chop red or white ribs into ¼-inch pieces. Immerse ribs in a small pan of boiling water and boil 2 minutes. Drain and set aside.

2 In a medium skillet, melt butter. Add Swiss chard leaves and sauté for 1 minute. Cover pan and steam 3 to 5 minutes over low heat. Mix in cooked ribs. Add vinegar, salt, and pepper. Taste for seasoning and serve immediately.

May be prepared up to 4 hours ahead through Step 1 and kept in refrigerator. Remove from refrigerator ½ hour before continuing.

The effect of the red or white ribs against the green leaves of the chard makes for an unusual and elegant appearance.

STUFFED ZUCCHINI WITH BANANA SQUASH PUREE

Serves 6

Bright yellow-orange banana squash puree is piped into blanched zucchini shells for a colorful addition to simple chicken or meat entrées. Hubbard, acorn, or other winter squash may be used. Serve as an accompaniment to Grilled Squab with Basil Butter, Veal Medallions with Lime-Ginger Sauce, or Whitefish with Tomato Béarnaise Sauce.

3 small zucchini	2 shallots, finely chopped
2 tablespoons unsalted butter	¼ cup whipping cream
1 pound banana squash,	½ teaspoon salt
peeled and cut into 2-inch pieces	Pinch of finely ground white pepper

1 Cut zucchini in halves lengthwise. With a spoon, scoop out center, leaving a ¼-inch border all the way around. Discard centers.

2 Immerse zucchini in a pan of boiling water and boil 2 minutes. Drain and reserve. Cut halves into 3-inch sections; you should have 2 small zucchini sections for each half. Place in a buttered medium baking dish. Melt 1 tablespoon of the butter and brush on zucchini. Set aside.

3 Steam banana squash in a covered steamer above boiling water for 15 to 20 minutes, or until tender. Puree in a food processor.

4 In a medium skillet heat the remaining butter over medium-high heat until foaming. Add shallots and sauté for 2 minutes, or until soft. Add to banana squash with cream, salt, and pepper. Taste for seasoning.

5 Spoon squash mixture into a medium pastry bag fitted with the medium star or plain tip. Pipe banana squash into zucchini shells.

6 Preheat oven to 350°F. Bake for 20 minutes, or until zucchini is tender and squash is bubbling.

ADVANCE PREPARATION:

May be prepared up to 4 hours ahead through Step 5 and kept in refrigerator. Bring to room temperature before baking.

SAUTÉED BABY TOMATOES

Serves 6

Baby tomatoes are suitable for quick sautéing after the skin is removed through blanching. Serve with Sautéed Chicken Breasts with Mustard and Tarragon, or Fillet of Salmon Glazed with Pesto Hollandaise Sauce.

FOR CHIVE BUTTER:

2 tablespoons unsalted butter, softened

2 tablespoons chopped chives

¼ teaspoon salt

⅛ teaspoon finely ground pepper

24 cherry tomatoes

Salt and pepper to taste

FOR GARNISH:

1 tablespoon chopped fresh parsley

1 For chive butter: Cream butter until very smooth. Stir in chives, salt, and pepper. Taste for seasoning.

2 In a large saucepan, bring water to boil. Immerse tomatoes in water for 10 seconds. Drain and remove skins.

3 In a large skillet heat chive butter until foaming. Add tomatoes and sauté for about 2 minutes, or until warmed. To be sure that tomatoes are evenly cooked, continuously roll them around pan by jerking skillet handle back and forth. Season with salt and pepper.

4 Transfer tomatoes to a serving dish. Add chive butter from pan and mix gently. Garnish with chopped parsley and serve immediately.

MUSTARD-BAKED TOMATOES

Serves 8

The taste of red tomatoes is greatly enhanced when they are topped with this blend of mustard, cream, and bread crumbs. Serve with Tenderloin of Beef with Roasted Shallots and Tarragon, or Leg of Lamb, California Style, or Sea Bass with Garlic Mayonnaise.

8 slightly firm small red tomatoes
   (about 2 pounds)
1 cup fine bread crumbs (whole-wheat,
   sourdough, or French)
½ cup sour cream or crème fraîche
   (page 280)

2 tablespoons grainy mustard
2 tablespoons finely chopped
   fresh parsley
1 medium shallot, finely chopped
Pinch of salt
Pinch of finely ground black pepper

1 Preheat oven to 350°F. Cut tops off tomatoes. Remove seeds with a spoon and separate juice from them by passing them through a strainer. Reserve ½ cup juice.

2 In a small mixing bowl combine tomato juice, bread crumbs, sour cream, mustard, parsley, shallot, salt, and pepper. Stir until blended. Taste for seasoning.

3 Spoon enough mixture into each tomato to cover top. Set upright in a buttered baking dish.

4 Bake for about 20 to 25 minutes, or until tomatoes are very hot and filling is bubbly. Serve immediately.

VARIATION:

If small tomatoes are not available, use 4 medium tomatoes cut in half cross-wise. Use ½ tomato per serving.

ADVANCE PREPARATION:

May be prepared up to 4 hours ahead through Step 2 and kept in refrigerator. Remove from refrigerator ½ hour before baking.

Vegetables

SAUTÉ OF JULIENNED GARDEN VEGETABLES

Serves 6

This is a surprisingly versatile vegetable combination, with possibilities for an almost unlimited range of colors and textures. Its taste is conducive to any number of different dishes. Serve with Whitefish with Tomato Béarnaise Sauce, Grilled Squab with Basil Butter, or New York Steaks with Roquefort Sauce.

4 medium carrots, peeled and julienned

4 medium stalks celery, peeled
   and julienned

2 tablespoons unsalted butter

2 tablespoons oil

1 medium red onion, thinly sliced

3 medium zucchini, julienned

1 medium clove garlic, minced

½ teaspoon salt

⅛ teaspoon coarsely cracked pepper

1 tablespoon chopped fresh parsley

1 Immerse carrots in a pan of boiling water and boil 1 minute. Drain and set aside.

2 Immerse celery in a pan of boiling water and boil for 30 seconds. Drain and set aside.

3 Heat butter and oil in a large skillet until hot. Add onion and sauté over medium heat for 3 to 5 minutes, or until soft but not brown. Add carrots and celery and continue sautéing another minute. Add zucchini and sauté for another 2 minutes, or until cooked but not soft. Add garlic, salt, pepper, and parsley. Mix well, taste for seasoning, and serve immediately.

VARIATION:

Other vegetables that may be used include blanched green beans, jicama, summer squash, blanched turnips, red Swiss chard, and red peppers.

ADVANCE PREPARATION:

May be prepared up to 4 hours ahead through Step 2 and kept in refrigerator.

SAUTÉ OF CARROTS AND TURNIPS

Serves 4 to 6

Here is a wintertime recipe with an attractive assortment of shapes and colors. Chicken stock and cream create a glaze as they reduce and bring out the natural sweetness of the two vegetables. Serve with Stuffed Pork with Apples and Prunes or Grilled Squab with Basil Butter.

2 tablespoons unsalted butter	1 cup chicken stock (page 276)
1 tablespoon oil	¼ teaspoon salt
3 to 4 medium carrots, peeled and cut into ¾-inch chunks (about 2 cups)	⅛ teaspoon coarsely cracked pepper
	1 tablespoon whipping cream
6 medium turnips, peeled, quartered, and cut into ¾-inch chunks (about 2 cups)	2 tablespoons finely chopped fresh parsley

1 In a medium skillet, heat butter and oil. Add carrots and turnips and sauté for 3 to 5 minutes.

2 Add chicken stock, salt, and pepper. Cover and simmer 15 minutes over medium heat.

3 Remove cover, raise heat, and add cream. Boil until liquid is cooked down to a glaze. Add chopped parsley. Taste for seasoning and serve immediately.

VARIATION:

Rutabagas or parsnips may be substituted for turnips.

ADVANCE PREPARATION:

May be prepared up to 4 hours ahead through Step 2 and kept in refrigerator. Reheat before continuing.

SAUTÉED SUGAR SNAP PEAS AND RED PEPPERS

Serves 4 to 6

This side dish always makes a pretty presentation. It is crunchy and, with its green and red hues, very colorful. If you cannot find sugar snap peas, substitute Chinese long green beans, French green beans, or snow peas. Serve with Tenderloin of Beef with Roasted Shallots and Tarragon, Grilled Chicken with Basil and Garlic, or Whitefish with Tomato Béarnaise Sauce.

¾ pound sugar snap peas,
   strings removed
2 small red bell peppers, seeded
   and julienned

2 tablespoons unsalted butter
¼ teaspoon salt
Pinch of pepper

FOR GARNISH:

1 teaspoon finely chopped chives
1 teaspoon finely chopped fresh parsley

1 Immerse sugar snap peas and peppers in a pan of boiling water and boil for 1 minute.

2 Pour cold water over vegetables to stop the cooking process. Drain well.

3 Melt butter in a medium skillet. Add vegetables and sauté for 1 minute, or until heated through. Add salt and pepper and taste for seasoning.

4 Garnish with fresh chopped herbs. Serve immediately.

ADVANCE PREPARATION:

May be prepared ahead through Step 2 up to 4 hours ahead. Cover and keep at room temperature.

GRATIN OF VEGETABLES

Serves 6 to 8

Gratin vegetables are browned in a baking dish. In this recipe, silky-textured butternut squash, leeks, and tomatoes are presented in three distinct layers of yellow, white, and red. This ambrosial gratin is excellent as a first course or as a superb main course in a vegetarian meal. Try preparing it in individual ovenproof casseroles for a different presentation.

2 pounds butternut squash or other winter squash

⅓ cup olive oil

1 teaspoon salt

⅓ teaspoon finely ground pepper

3 medium leeks, white and light green parts cleaned

2 pounds tomatoes, peeled, seeded, and chopped

1 teaspoon chopped fresh thyme, or ½ teaspoon dried thyme

1 cup (¼ pound) grated sharp Cheddar cheese or Gruyère

3 tablespoons olive oil

1 Cut peel from squash and cut flesh in ½-inch slices. Place squash slices in a steamer and steam until slightly softened. Check doneness with a fork. Transfer to a medium-sized oiled gratin dish or baking dish. Sprinkle with ¼ teaspoon of the salt and a pinch of pepper.

2 Cut leeks into thin slices. Heat 2 tablespoons oil in a skillet and add leeks, ¼ teaspoon of the salt, and a pinch of pepper. Cook over low heat, stirring often, for about 5 minutes, or until softened. Spoon over squash in gratin dish.

3 Heat the remaining tablespoon of oil in pan used to sauté leeks. Add tomatoes, thyme, the remaining ½ teaspoon salt, and ¼ teaspoon pepper. Cook over medium-high heat, stirring often, about 15 minutes or until soft and thickened. Taste for seasoning.

4 Preheat oven to 425°F. Spoon tomatoes over leeks. Sprinkle cheese over all. Bake for about 15 minutes, or until cheese browns lightly. Serve immediately.

ADVANCE PREPARATION:

May be prepared up to 4 hours ahead through Step 3 and kept in refrigerator. Bring to room temperature before continuing.

RICE AND POTATOES

$\mathcal{T}$HESE RICE AND POTATO DISHES ARE BOTH

SIMPLE AND AESTHETICALLY PLEASING. Each one will provide

variety and a contrast of texture to your main course.

OVEN-ROASTED POTATOES

BAKED POTATO ROSE

ROASTED POTATO FANS

ROSEMARY POTATOES STEAMED IN FOIL

STEAMED NEW POTATOES WITH CHIVE BUTTER

SAUTÉED POTATOES WITH ONION, APPLE, AND MINT

POTATO-LEEK PANCAKE

SWEET POTATO-SHALLOT SAUTÉ

BAKED YAMS WITH SOUR CREAM AND CHIVES

SAFFRON RICE

AUTUMN RICE WITH RED PEPPERS AND PINE NUTS

GREEN VEGETABLE RICE

LEMON RICE WITH CAPERS AND PARSLEY

RICE WITH CLAMS AND CILANTRO BUTTER

RISOTTO WITH FRESH PEAS AND MUSHROOMS

SPICY BROWN RICE WITH EGGPLANT AND TOMATOES

BROWN RICE WITH GINGER AND SHRIMP

WILD RICE WITH PINE NUTS AND CURRANTS

OVEN-ROASTED POTATOES

Serves 6

The sweet Red or White Rose or yellow Finnish potatoes are baked with simple seasonings to a crispy golden brown. These potato varieties remain moist throughout the cooking process. They are versatile and will highlight many main dishes without overpowering them. Serve with Vegetable Frittata, Grilled Chicken with Basil and Garlic, or Stuffed Pork with Apples and Prunes.

2½ pounds small Red or White Rose potatoes or yellow Finnish potatoes	2 teaspoons salt
¼ cup oil	¼ teaspoon paprika
	½ teaspoon finely ground pepper

1 Preheat oven to 425°F. Peel potatoes, rinse, and pat dry. Cut each into eighths or into 2-inch wedges.

2 Combine oil, salt, paprika, and pepper in a bowl and mix well. Add potatoes and toss.

3 Arrange on oiled baking sheet and bake for 45 minutes, turning every 15 minutes, until tender and well browned. Taste for seasoning.

4 Turn into a serving dish and serve immediately.

VARIATIONS:

(1) *Depending on what these will be served with, add 1 teaspoon chopped fresh herbs, such as rosemary, thyme, or oregano, to oil mixture. For a stronger taste, substitute olive oil for vegetable oil.*

(2) *Bake unpeeled, if desired.*

ADVANCE PREPARATION:

May be prepared up to 2 hours ahead and kept at room temperature. Reheat in 350°F oven for 10 to 15 minutes.

BAKED POTATO ROSE

Serves 6

This is a beautiful presentation, suggestive of a rose. The potato slices are arranged to form a large flower when baked. I like them for their crunchy-soft texture contrast and buttery taste. This dish is particularly nice for company, as it may be prepared in advance. Serve with Leg of Lamb, California Style, with Loin of Pork with Rhubarb-Ginger Sauce, or with New York Steaks with Roquefort Sauce.

6 tablespoons (¾ stick) unsalted buter	1 tablespoon oil
1 clove garlic, peeled	1½ teaspoons salt
2 pounds small red potatoes, peeled	¼ teaspoon finely ground white pepper

FOR GARNISH:

1 tablespoon finely chopped parsley

1 Preheat oven to 400°F. Melt butter with garlic clove. To clarify butter, skim off the white milky solids and discard them.

2 Brush a 9- or 10-inch pie plate liberally with clarified butter.

3 Cut off a slice from each end of potato to square it. Slice potatoes in a food processor fitted with the slicer blade, or slice by hand crosswise into ¼-inch-thick slices. Place in cold water for 30 minutes to remove excess starch. Change water when it becomes cloudy.

4 Drain potatoes and dry thoroughly in a kitchen towel. Place potatoes in a medium bowl. Remove garlic clove from butter and pour butter over potatoes. Add oil, salt, and pepper and toss well.

5 Starting at outer edge of pie plate, arrange potato slices in a circle, so that they overlap one another. Begin another circle about 1 inch inward, overlapping the outer circle. Continue placing potato slices in overlapping circles until you reach the center. You will have one layer of potatoes, slightly overlapping. Pour any butter mixture remaining in bowl over potatoes.

6 Bake for 45 to 55 minutes, or until potatoes are tender, brown, and crisp. They will curl slightly to resemble a crisp, brown potato flower. Sprinkle with parsley and serve immediately. Slice with a pizza cutter or serrated knife into wedges.

VARIATION:

These may be cooked in individual shallow 4-inch baking dishes.

ADVANCE PREPARATION:

May be kept up to 2 hours at room temperature. Reheat in 375°F oven for 10 to 15 minutes.

ROASTED POTATO FANS

Serves 6

For this easy to make yet elegant dish, potatoes are sliced crosswise to give a fanned appearance. They are dusted with Parmesan cheese and baked until golden brown. Serve with Sea Bass with Garlic Mayonnaise, Lemon-Herb Chicken, or Tenderloin of Beef with Roasted Shallots and Tarragon.

6 medium baking potatoes
¼ cup (½ stick) unsalted butter,
    melted
½ teaspoon salt

¼ teaspoon finely ground pepper
2 tablespoons freshly grated Parmesan
    cheese

1 Preheat oven to 425°F. Peel potatoes and immerse in cold water to prevent them from darkening.

2 When ready to roast, dry potatoes well. Place potato on a wooden spoon or skewer the potato lengthwise three-quarters of its depth. Beginning ½ inch from each end of the potato, slice crosswise into the potato at intervals of ⅛ inch. The cuts will go only three-quarters of the way through the potato if you use the spoon or skewer as an aid. This will allow the potatoes to resemble fans when baked.

3 Oil a baking dish and arrange potatoes in the baking dish sliced side up. Brush with half the melted butter and sprinkle with salt and pepper. Bake for 30 to 45 minutes.

4 Baste with the remaining butter and dust with Parmesan cheese. Continue roasting 15 to 20 minutes more. The potatoes should be tender and golden brown and should have a fanned appearance. Serve immediately.

ROSEMARY POTATOES STEAMED IN FOIL

Serves 6

I like to serve these foil packages on a separate side dish. The foil is opened immediately and the fragrance of the potatoes fills the air. Serve these moist, flavorful potatoes with Grilled Lemon-Mustard Chicken, Grilled Lobster with Garlic Butter, or Sautéed Lamb Medallions on a Bed of Eggplant with Red Peppers.

18 red new potatoes, unpeeled

2 tablespoons olive oil

Salt and finely ground pepper to taste

2 tablespoons finely chopped fresh
    rosemary sprigs, or 1 tablespoon dried

1 Preheat oven to 450°F. Place 3 potatoes on a 6-by-6-inch piece of aluminum foil. Sprinkle with 1 teaspoon of the oil, the salt, pepper, and rosemary. Wrap securely so no air will escape. Continue with remaining potatoes.

2 Place on a baking sheet and bake for 30 to 45 minutes, depending on size of potatoes. Serve immediately.

VARIATION:

Use other fresh herbs, such as dill, tarragon, or thyme. Or, add 1 medium shallot, finely chopped, to herbs.

STEAMED NEW POTATOES WITH CHIVE BUTTER

Serves 4

These potatoes are an excellent accompaniment to Lamb Stew with Rosemary or Chicken with Pancetta and Zinfandel.

1½ pounds small new potatoes
Salt to taste

FOR CHIVE BUTTER:

2 tablespoons unsalted butter, softened
2 tablespoons chopped chives

¼ teaspoon salt
⅛ teaspoon finely ground pepper

1 Scrub potatoes and peel if desired. Put in steamer rack above a pan of boiling water. Sprinkle potatoes with salt. Cover and steam for about 30 minutes, or until tender.

2 For chive butter: Cream butter until very smooth. Stir in chives, salt, and pepper. Taste for seasoning.

3 Transfer potatoes to a serving dish. Add chive butter and toss or mix gently until potatoes are coated with butter. Serve immediately.

VARIATIONS:
Other flavored butters can be used; see pages 286–287.
ADVANCE PREPARATION:
Chive butter may be kept up to 3 days in refrigerator.

SAUTÉED POTATOES WITH ONION, APPLE, AND MINT

Serves 4 to 6

The New Booneville Hotel in the North Coast region of California prepares a dish similar to this from ingredients harvested in its large backyard garden. A somewhat unusual combination of ingredients brings a sweet, herbal taste to the dish. Make sure to use a skillet and spatula that are amenable to frequent scraping, as this procedure is the key to a successful outcome. Serve these potatoes with Loin of Pork with Rhubarb-Ginger Sauce, Grilled Steaks with Ancho Chile Butter, Grilled Lemon-Mustard Chicken, or Frittata with Zucchini, Sausage, and Red Peppers.

2 pounds White Rose potatoes, peeled

¼ cup (½ stick) unsalted butter

3 tablespoons oil

1 small onion, finely chopped

1 small pippin or other tart apple, peeled, cored, and cut into 1-inch dice

1 teaspoon salt

¼ teaspoon finely ground pepper

2 tablespoons finely chopped fresh mint

1 Immerse potatoes in a large pot of boiling water and simmer for 15 minutes. Drain and cut into 1½-inch dice.

2 Heat 2 tablespoons of the butter and 1 tablespoon of the oil in a large skillet. Add onion and sauté until soft and slightly brown. Remove to a small bowl.

3 Add the remaining butter and oil to skillet and heat. Add potatoes and sauté until brown, about 7 or 8 minutes. Use a large enough skillet to permit even browning, or do this step in 2 separate batches. Scrape up brown bits from the bottom of the skillet with a spatula as you stir.

4 Add onion and chopped apple to skillet. Cover and cook 2 minutes, shaking skillet frequently. Stir potatoes with a wooden spoon, again scraping up brown bits from skillet. Continue cooking for about 7 more minutes, or until vegetables are very tender.

5 Add salt, pepper, and mint. Taste for seasoning and serve immediately.

POTATO-LEEK PANCAKE

Serves 6

After trying different varieties of potatoes, I found that the White Rose works best in this recipe. Less starchy than other potatoes, White Rose potatoes become a crispy pancake flavored with leeks. Serve with Leg of Lamb, California Style, with Fillet of Salmon Glazed with Pesto Hollandaise Sauce, or with Pesto-Stuffed Chicken Breasts.

2 pounds White Rose potatoes

6 tablespoons clarified unsalted butter

2 medium leeks, white part only,
   cleaned and finely chopped

1 teaspoon salt

½ teaspoon finely ground pepper

1 Peel potatoes and soak in cold water for 30 minutes. Change water when it becomes cloudy.

2 Grate potatoes and squeeze out every bit of moisture by wringing in a dry kitchen towel.

3 Heat 2 tablespoons of the clarified butter in a skillet. Add leeks and sauté over medium heat until wilted. Season with salt and pepper.

4 Combine leeks and potatoes and mix well.

5 Heat the remaining butter in a large skillet; if possible, use a 9- or 10-inch nonstick skillet, so it can easily be inverted. Place potato mixture in skillet. Flatten with spatula to a pancake. Cover and steam over medium-high heat for about 3 to 5 minutes. Turn pancake, flatten down, and cover. Cook for 3 to 5 minutes, or until brown and crisp.

6 To serve, invert onto serving platter and slice into wedges with a serrated knife or pizza cutter. Serve immediately.

SWEET POTATO–SHALLOT SAUTÉ

Serves 4 to 6

This is an unusual combination of tastes and textures. Sautéed sweet potatoes are an excellent accompaniment to duck dishes, and the addition of browned, sweet shallots makes for a successful blend. Serve with Barbecued Roast Duck with Red Wine and Black Currants or Turkey Sauté with Lemon, Mushrooms, and Capers.

2 pounds sweet potatoes, peeled

7 tablespoons unsalted butter

8 large shallots, peeled and
    cut into quarters

¼ cup veal stock (page 274) or chicken
    stock (page 276)

Pinch of finely ground white pepper

½ teaspoon salt

FOR GARNISH:

1 tablespoon chopped fresh parsley

1 Cut sweet potatoes in ½-inch slices. Cut each slice into quarters.

2 In a 14-inch skillet, melt 3 tablespoons of the butter over medium-high heat. Add half the potatoes and sauté until lightly brown, 7 to 10 minutes on each side. Make sure all pieces of potatoes touch the bottom of skillet so that they brown evenly. Remove to a bowl. Add 3 tablespoons of the butter to skillet and sauté remaining potatoes. Remove to bowl.

3 Add the remaining tablespoon butter to skillet and melt over medium heat. Add shallots and sauté until light brown. Add stock and simmer, rolling shallot pieces often until cooked and glazed.

4 When ready to serve, increase heat to medium-high and warm shallots. Add sautéed potatoes and cook until heated through and golden brown, about 5 minutes. Use a spatula to turn potatoes while heating them. Season with salt and pepper.

5 Transfer to a serving dish and garnish with chopped parsley. Serve immediately.

ADVANCE PREPARATION:

May be prepared up to 4 hours ahead through Step 3. Cover potatoes in bowl and keep at room temperature. Keep shallots in skillet, covered, at room temperature.

BAKED YAMS WITH SOUR CREAM AND CHIVES

Serves 6 to 8

In this dish, a universal favorite, baked potato and chives, is adapted to the yam. This unusual combination may accompany Sea Bass with Garlic Mayonnaise, Spicy Sautéed Chicken Breasts, or Grilled Steaks with Ancho Chile Butter.

2 pounds evenly sized and shaped yams
2 teaspoons unsalted butter, softened

FOR GARNISH:

¼ cup sour cream
2 teaspoons chopped chives

1 Preheat oven to 400°F. Wash yams and rub lightly with butter.

2 Place yams on baking sheet and bake for 30 minutes. Prick skin of yams and return to oven for 30 minutes more, or until tender.

3 Remove pointed ends of yams and slice crosswise into 1½-inch-thick slices.

4 Lay slices flat on plate and garnish each with 1 teaspoon sour cream and ¼ teaspoon chives. Serve 1 or 2 slices per person, depending on thickness of yam. Serve immediately.

VARIATION:

Substitute leeks for chives. Sauté 2 medium leeks, finely chopped, in 2 table-spoons unsalted butter on medium heat for 5 minutes, or until very soft. Top yams with sour cream and leeks.

SAFFRON RICE

Serves 6

The distinctive flavor of saffron permeates the rice and gives it a golden color. Serve this when a simple rice dish is called for. Saffron is a dominant taste, so select your other courses with care. I find it goes well with Swordfish Brochette, Marinated Roasted Rack of Lamb with Spicy Peanut Sauce, or Turkey Sauté with Lemon, Mushrooms, and Capers.

2 cups chicken stock (page 276)	1 medium onion, chopped
¼ teaspoon saffron threads	1 cup long-grain white rice
1 tablespoon oil	1 teaspoon salt
¼ cup (½ stick) unsalted butter	¼ teaspoon finely ground pepper

1 Heat chicken stock until warm. Remove from heat, add saffron, and leave to soak for 20 minutes.

2 In a medium skillet, heat oil and 1 tablespoon of the butter. Add onion and cook over low heat, stirring occasionally, until soft but not browned. Add rice and cook, stirring occasionally, until rice is lightly browned.

3 Pour in saffron-flavored stock and add salt and pepper. Bring to boil, cover, and simmer over low heat for 20 minutes.

4 Let rice stand, covered, for 10 minutes.

5 Using a large fork, carefully stir in the remaining butter and taste for seasoning. Serve immediately.

ADVANCE PREPARATION:

May be kept up to 2 hours at room temperature. Reheat carefully in the top part of a double boiler over medium heat for 10 minutes.

AUTUMN RICE WITH RED PEPPERS AND PINE NUTS

Serves 6

Red bell peppers are at their peak in the autumn months. This white rice dish is decorated by colorful red bell peppers, celery, parsley, and toasted pine nuts. The peppers are somewhat sweet, while the other ingredients maintain their individual distinctive flavors. Serve with Swordfish in Lemon-Ginger Marinade, Grilled Chicken with Basil and Garlic, or Grilled Veal Chops with Rosemary.

3 tablespoons pine nuts	2 tablespoons oil
2 cups chicken stock (page 276)	1 medium onion, finely chopped
1 cup long-grain white rice	½ cup diced red bell pepper
½ teaspoon salt	(½-inch dice)
⅛ teaspoon finely ground pepper	½ cup diced celery (¼-inch dice)
2 tablespoons unsalted butter	2 tablespoons finely chopped fresh parsley

1 Preheat oven to 350°F. Toast pine nuts on a baking sheet in oven for 5 minutes, or until lightly browned.

2 In a saucepan, bring chicken stock to boil over high heat. Add rice, salt, and pepper and stir with fork. Lower heat, cover, and simmer 20 minutes.

3 In a medium skillet, heat butter and oil over medium heat. Add onion and sauté, stirring occasionally, until soft. Add red pepper and celery and continue sautéing for about 5 minutes. Vegetables should be cooked but slightly crisp.

4 When rice is cooked, add vegetables, pine nuts, and parsley. Toss with a fork, taste for seasoning, and serve immediately.

VARIATION:

Walnuts, pecans, or almonds may be substituted for pine nuts.

ADVANCE PREPARATION:

May be prepared up to 2 hours ahead and kept at room temperature. Reheat carefully in top part of double boiler over medium heat for 10 minutes.

GREEN VEGETABLE RICE

Serves 6

Celery leaves, spinach, parsley, and mild green chiles lend a fresh and slightly spicy touch to white rice. Serve this as an accompaniment to Swordfish Brochette, Seafood Quartet, Spicy Sautéed Chicken Breasts, or Corn and Shrimp Frittata.

1 tablespoon oil

3 tablespoons unsalted butter

1 medium onion, finely chopped

1 cup long-grain white rice

1 tablespoon finely chopped California chiles (see Note)

¼ cup chopped celery leaves

2 medium cloves garlic, minced

1¾ cups chicken stock (page 276)

½ teaspoon salt

½ cup spinach leaves, stems removed

2 tablespoons finely chopped fresh parsley

1 In a medium skillet or sauté pan, heat oil and 1 tablespoon of the butter. Add onion and sauté over low heat, stirring occasionally, until lightly browned. Add rice and cook, stirring occasionally, until lightly browned.

2 Stir in chiles, celery leaves, and garlic. Pour in stock and add salt. Bring to boil, cover, and simmer over low heat for 15 minutes.

3 Thoroughly rinse spinach leaves and chop them. Using a two-pronged fork, carefully stir spinach into rice. Cover and continue to simmer for about 5 minutes, or until rice is tender. Remove from heat. Let stand for 10 minutes.

4 Stir in the remaining butter and the parsley and taste for seasoning. Serve immediately.

ADVANCE PREPARATION:

May be kept up to 2 hours at room temperature. Reheat carefully in top part of double boiler over medium heat for 10 minutes.

NOTE:

When working with chiles always wear rubber gloves. Wash cutting surface and knife immediately afterward.

LEMON RICE WITH CAPERS AND PARSLEY

Serves 6

A refreshing change of pace from plain rice is this mixture of capers and parsley with white rice. The lemon flavoring makes it a good accompaniment to a robust meal. Serve with Sautéed Chicken Breasts with Mustard and Tarragon, with Veal Stew with Baby Onions, Mushrooms, and Spinach, or with Scallops with Fresh Tomatoes, Herbs, and White Wine.

1 cup long-grain white rice

3 tablespoons unsalted butter

½ teaspoon salt

¼ teaspoon finely ground pepper

1 tablespoon freshly squeezed lemon juice

1 tablespoon capers, drained

2 tablespoons chopped fresh parsley

1 Add rice to a large pan of boiling water and cook over high heat for about 15 minutes, or until just tender. Drain, rinse under cold running water, and drain again thoroughly.

2 Heat 1 tablespoon of the butter in a heavy skillet over low heat. Add rice, salt, and pepper and heat, stirring gently with a fork. Stir in lemon juice, capers, and parsley and remove from heat.

3 Stir in the remaining butter and taste for seasoning. Serve immediately.

ADVANCE PREPARATION:

May be kept up to 2 hours at room temperature. Reheat carefully in top part of double boiler over medium heat for 10 minutes.

RICE WITH CLAMS AND CILANTRO BUTTER

Serves 4 to 6

When cilantro butter and clams are mixed with long-grain white rice, a delicious surprise results. The flavor goes well with Sea Bass with Garlic Mayonnaise. Try it as a first course to precede Spicy Sautéed Chicken Breasts and Baked Japanese Eggplant with Herbs.

2 pounds littleneck or other small clams	1 cup long-grain white rice
½ cup dry white wine	1½ cups water
1 tablespoon oil	½ teaspoon salt
1 tablespoon unsalted butter	¼ teaspoon finely ground pepper
1 medium onion, chopped	

FOR CILANTRO BUTTER:

¼ cup (½ stick) unsalted butter,
    softened

1 tablespoon chopped cilantro

1 teaspoon freshly squeezed lemon juice

1 Rinse clams thoroughly. Put them in a large saucepan and add wine. Cover and cook over fairly high heat just until they open. Drain liquid, reserving ½ cup of the clam juice.

2 In a medium skillet, heat oil and butter until foaming. Add onion and sauté over low heat, stirring occasionally, until soft but not browned. Add rice and cook, stirring occasionally, until lightly browned.

3 Pour in reserved clam juice and water and add salt and pepper. Bring to a boil, cover, and simmer over low heat for 20 minutes.

4 For cilantro butter: Mix thoroughly softened butter with cilantro and lemon juice.

5 Shell and dice clams. Using a two-pronged fork, carefully stir clams into rice. Cover and let stand 10 minutes.

6 Stir in cilantro butter and taste for seasoning. Serve immediately.

RISOTTO WITH FRESH PEAS AND MUSHROOMS

Serves 4 to 6

Risotto is borrowed from a northern Italian tradition. This dish is made with arborio, a short-grained rice, found in Italian specialty stores and many supermarkets. Here, combined with fresh peas and mushrooms, the rice becomes an excellent first course before Sautéed Lamb Medallions on a Bed of Eggplant with Red Peppers or an accompaniment to Grilled Veal Chops with Rosemary.

¼ cup (½ stick) unsalted butter	½ teaspoon salt
2 medium shallots, finely chopped	¼ teaspoon finely ground pepper
1 cup arborio rice	3 cups hot chicken stock (page 276)
2 cups shelled fresh peas	¼ pound mushrooms, sliced
(about 2 pounds unshelled)	¼ cup freshly grated Parmesan cheese

1　Heat 2 tablespoons of the butter in a heavy saucepan. Add shallots and cook over low heat until soft but not browned. Stir in rice and sauté lightly without letting it brown.

2　Add peas, ¼ teaspoon of the salt, ⅛ teaspoon of the pepper, and ½ cup of the stock. Simmer over medium heat, stirring often, until stock is absorbed. Continue adding stock ½ cup at a time, cooking until it is absorbed. Stir frequently. Stop adding stock when rice is tender. Total cooking time will be about 20 minutes.

3　Meanwhile, heat 1 tablespoon of the butter in a skillet. Add mushrooms, the remaining salt, and the remaining pepper and sauté over medium-high heat until lightly browned.

4　When rice is done, gently stir in mushrooms, the remaining butter, and the Parmesan cheese with a two-pronged fork. Taste for seasoning. Serve immediately.

SPICY BROWN RICE WITH EGGPLANT AND TOMATOES

Serves 6

Californians enjoy brown rice because of its crunchy taste, healthful characteristics, and wide adaptability to casual menus. Here, brown rice is given a Middle Eastern flavor in combination with cilantro, cumin, tomatoes, and eggplant. Serve with Grilled Lemon-Mustard Chicken or Grilled Steaks with Ancho Chile Butter.

½ cup oil

1 medium onion, chopped

2 medium cloves garlic, minced

1 teaspoon ground cumin

1 cup long-grain brown rice

2 cups water

1 eggplant (about 1 pound)

2 ripe medium tomatoes, peeled, seeded, and diced

½ teaspoon salt

¼ teaspoon finely ground pepper

1 tablespoon chopped fresh parsley

1 tablespoon chopped cilantro

1 In a medium skillet, heat 2 tablespoons of the oil. Add onion and cook over low heat, stirring occasionally, until soft but not browned. Add garlic and cumin and cook for 30 seconds. Add rice and cook, stirring occasionally, until lightly browned.

2 Pour in water and bring to boil. Cover and simmer over low heat for 40 minutes, or until tender.

3 Meanwhile, peel eggplant and cut it into 1-inch cubes. In another medium skillet, heat the remaining oil. Add eggplant cubes and sauté in batches for about 10 minutes, or until very tender. Remove and drain on paper towels. Remove any excess oil from skillet.

4 Add tomatoes to skillet used to cook eggplant and cook over medium heat, stirring, until liquid is completely absorbed.

5 Using a two-pronged fork, carefully stir eggplant and tomatoes into rice. Cover and let stand for 10 minutes.

6 Stir in salt, pepper, parsley, and cilantro and taste for seasoning. Serve immediately.

For a spicier dish, add ¼ to ½ teaspoon chili powder.

May be kept up to 2 hours at room temperature. Reheat carefully in top part of double boiler over medium heat for 10 minutes.

BROWN RICE WITH GINGER AND SHRIMP

Serves 4

This makes a pleasing main course dish with an Asian influence. For a California Cuisine menu, start with Garlic-Vegetable Soup and accompany with Stir-Fried Broccoli.

¼ cup vegetable oil

1 medium onion, chopped

1 cup long-grain brown rice

2 cups water

1 tablespoon chopped fresh ginger

½ pound raw small shrimp,
    shelled and deveined

1 teaspoon freshly squeezed lemon juice

½ teaspoon salt

¼ teaspoon finely ground pepper

2 tablespoons unsalted butter

1 In a medium skillet, heat 2 tablespoons of oil. Add onion and cook over low heat, stirring occasionally, until soft but not browned. Add rice and cook, stirring occasionally, until lightly browned.

2 Pour in water. Bring to boil, cover, and simmer over low heat for 40 minutes, or until tender.

3 In another skillet or a wok, heat the remaining oil. Add ginger and stir-fry over high heat for about 30 seconds. Add shrimp and stir-fry for about 2 minutes, or until shrimp turn pink. Remove from heat and add lemon juice, salt, and pepper.

4 Using a two-pronged fork, carefully stir shrimp mixture into rice. Cover and let stand for 10 minutes.

5 Stir in butter and taste for seasoning. Serve immediately.

༃

WILD RICE WITH PINE NUTS AND CURRANTS

Serves 6

Potter Valley is a beautiful, lush green area in Northern California's Lake County. Farmers here have successfully engineered the cultivation of wild rice. In this recipe, the nutty wild rice is paired with softened sweet black currants and toasted pine nuts. Serve it with Barbecued Roast Duck with Red Wine and Black Currants or Loin of Pork with Rhubarb-Ginger Sauce.

2 tablespoons currants	1 small onion, finely chopped
2 tablespoons pine nuts	1½ quarts water
1 cup wild rice	½ teaspoon salt
1 tablespoon unsalted butter	¼ teaspoon finely ground pepper
1 tablespoon oil	1 tablespoon finely chopped fresh parsley

1 Put currants in a small bowl and pour enough boiling water over them to cover. Allow to soften for at least 30 minutes or up to 2 hours. Drain and reserve.

2 Preheat oven to 350°F. Toast pine nuts on a baking sheet in oven for 5 minutes, or until lightly browned. Reserve.

3 Rinse wild rice thoroughly with cold water in a strainer. Drain.

4 Heat butter and oil until foaming in a small skillet over medium heat. Add onion and sauté for about 3 to 5 minutes, or until softened.

5 Place rice in medium saucepan and cover with 1½ quarts water. Bring to a rapid boil. Reduce heat to simmer and cook uncovered for 30 minutes,

or until grains have opened. The rice should not be too soft. Drain rice in a strainer or colander.

6 Combine rice, onion, currants, pine nuts, salt, pepper, and parsley in a serving bowl. Toss gently, taste for seasoning, and serve immediately.

May be prepared up to 4 hours ahead through Step 4. Cover and keep at room temperature.

DESSERTS

$\mathcal{F}$RUIT DESSERTS ARE OFTEN SERVED IN CALI-

FORNIA BECAUSE OF YEAR-ROUND AVAILABILITY OF A LARGE

VARIETY OF FRESH FRUITS AND THE EMPHASIS ON SIMPLICITY.

A selection of more elaborate recipes is also included in this

chapter to satisfy the most avid dessert lover. From light to

heavy and from simple to complex, these desserts can suit

any menu or occasion.

❧

SLICED ORANGES AND KIWI

BROILED BERRIES AND CREAM

POACHED PEARS IN RED WINE WITH FRESH APPLESAUCE

CARAMEL CUSTARD WITH STRAWBERRIES

APRICOT-CURRANT BREAD CUSTARD

BAKED PERSIMMON PUDDING

COLD LEMON SOUFFLÉ

CHOCOLATE CREAM

FROZEN HONEY-VANILLA MOUSSE WITH
BLACKBERRY SAUCE

CHOCOLATE-HAZELNUT ICE CREAM

KIWI SORBET

BANANA SORBET

STRAWBERRY SORBET

CINNAMON-PECAN COFFEE CAKE

CHEESECAKE SOUFFLÉ

CHOCOLATE MOUSSE CAKE

CHOCOLATE-ALMOND SOUFFLÉ CAKE

PASTRY DOUGH

CHOCOLATE-CARAMEL WALNUT TORTE

LEMON-ORANGE TART

APPLE-ALMOND TART

PUMPKIN-PRALINE PIE

BROWN BUTTER TART WITH FRESH FRUIT

TULIP COOKIE CUPS

❧

SLICED ORANGES AND KIWI

Serves 4 to 6

Originally from China, the kiwi fruit was cultivated at the turn of the century in New Zealand and brought to California in the 1930s. Kiwi fruit is grown all over the world on vines; however, California has the greatest kiwi production in the United States. Kiwi is unique for its emerald green flesh and sweet, tart taste. Here, candied orange rind is interspersed with fresh orange and kiwi slices in a colorful fruit dessert. Serve this light dessert after a meal of several courses.

3 oranges

3 tablespoons sugar

3 tablespoons water

3 kiwis, peeled

1 Use a zester to remove thin outer layer of orange zest in strips and set aside.

2 Remove peel and outer white membrane from oranges with a sharp paring knife. Slice oranges into ¼-inch slices.

3 In a 1-quart saucepan, combine sugar and water and place over moderate heat. Cook, stirring, until sugar dissolves. Boil 1 minute and add orange zest. Simmer for 1 minute. Remove from heat and drain.

4 Peel kiwis and slice in ¼-inch-thick slices.

5 In a medium rectangular serving dish (approximately 12 by 6 inches), arrange overlapping slices, alternating oranges and kiwi. Garnish with cooled sweetened orange zest.

VARIATION:

This may also be presented on individual dessert dishes. Overlap fruit in a circular pattern and garnish with sweetened orange zest.

ADVANCE PREPARATION:

May be kept up to 4 hours in refrigerator.

Desserts

BROILED BERRIES AND CREAM

Serves 6 to 8

Although berries are usually enjoyed cool, this recipe brings out their essence in a warm, light custard. It is a simple dish to make that is elegant both in taste and presentation.

2 cups strawberries, cut into medium
   slices, at room temperature
2 cups raspberries, at room temperature
1 cup whipping cream

2 egg yolks
½ cup powdered sugar
1 teaspoon vanilla extract
1 tablespoon raspberry liqueur

FOR GARNISH:
Powdered sugar (optional)

1 Preheat oven to 400°F.

2 Combine berries in a bowl. Fill 6 to 8 (4- to 6-ounce) ovenproof dishes ⅞ full with berries. Place dishes on a baking sheet.

3 Whip cream in a chilled bowl until soft peaks form. Add egg yolks, sugar, and vanilla. Continue whipping another minute.

4 Sprinkle raspberry liqueur over berries, then pour prepared cream evenly into the dishes. Bake for 3 minutes. Preheat broiler, if necessary. Transfer dishes of berries to broiler and broil until evenly browned, watching carefully. Dust with powdered sugar if desired. Serve immediately.

ADVANCE PREPARATION:
May be prepared up to 3 hours ahead through Step 2 and kept covered at room temperature.

POACHED PEARS IN RED WINE WITH FRESH APPLESAUCE

Serves 8

The best of California's produce and wines are included in this dessert. Serve separately in a large serving bowl or in individual glass bowls with the pears placed atop fresh applesauce. This dessert is delicious either warm or cold.

3 tablespoons chopped walnuts	1½ cups red wine
6 pippin or Golden Delicious apples	¾ cup tawny port
1 tablespoon unsalted butter	2-inch length lemon zest
1 cup sugar	8 Bosc pears
2 cinnamon sticks	¼ cup California brandy

1 Preheat oven to 350°F. Toast walnuts on a baking sheet in oven for about 7 minutes or until lightly browned. Reserve.

2 Peel, core, and coarsely chop apples. Combine apples with butter, ¼ cup of the sugar, and 1 cinnamon stick in a large saucepan and cook over low heat until apples are soft, 20 to 30 minutes. Remove cinnamon and add chopped toasted walnuts.

3 In an enamel casserole, bring the red wine, port, remaining sugar, second cinnamon stick, and lemon zest to boil.

4 Peel pears, leaving stems attached, and add to wine syrup. Cover and poach over low heat until tender, 25 to 35 minutes, depending on size. Turn frequently with 2 spoons to retain even color.

5 Put apple mixture in a serving bowl and arrange pears on top.

6 Boil down the syrup until it is a fine glaze and measures about ¼ cup. Remove cinnamon stick.

7 Add brandy to hot glaze and ignite with a long match, averting your face and making sure the overhead fan is not on. Pour over pears. Serve warm.

ADVANCE PREPARATION:
May be prepared up to 4 hours ahead through Step 3 and kept at room temperature. Reheat before continuing. Finished dessert may be kept up to 1 day in refrigerator and served cold.

CARAMEL CUSTARD WITH STRAWBERRIES

Serves 4 to 6

This California version of Mexican flan is distinctive in two ways. First, the custard is infused with the caramel for an exceptionally rich, deep quality. Second, sweet, seasonal strawberries are spooned over the flan for a colorful and informal presentation. California strawberries have a long season, stretching from February through November, which allows for almost year-round use. Enjoy this light dessert after Mexican Chicken with Raisins and Almonds or Pesto-Stuffed Chicken Breasts.

FOR CUSTARD:

2½ cups half-and-half

1 vanilla bean, or 1 teaspoon
    vanilla extract

FOR CARAMEL:

½ cup granulated sugar

2 tablespoons water

3 whole eggs

3 egg yolks

½ cup granulated sugar

FOR TOPPING:

1 pint sliced strawberries

1 teaspoon powdered sugar

1 Preheat oven to 350°F.

2 For custard: In a small saucepan, combine half-and-half and vanilla bean (if using extract, do not add). Bring to a boil. Turn off heat, cover, and let vanilla infuse in half-and-half for 30 minutes.

3 For caramel: Combine sugar and water in a small heavy saucepan. Do not use a dark-colored pan, as you will not be able to see the color of the

caramel. Dissolve sugar in water over low heat. Turn up heat and continually swirl the pan over the flame. Mixture will be bubbly. If sugar crystals form on sides of pan, cover for 1 minute; this will dissolve them. Boil until mixture reaches a golden brown color. Watch carefully, as caramel can burn easily.

4 When mixture turns golden brown, remove from heat and pour about 1 tablespoon of caramel into hot half-and-half (see Step 2 above). Pour remaining caramel into a 1½-quart porcelain baking dish. Rotate dish rapidly to spread caramel evenly on bottom of dish. (If it is not even, it will distribute itself somewhat during the baking process.)

5 In a 3-quart mixer bowl, beat eggs and egg yolks until frothy. Slowly add sugar and beat until light, thick, and lemon colored.

6 Continue beating while pouring in half-and-half in a thin stream. Stir in vanilla extract if vanilla bean was not used. Strain mixture into caramel-lined mold.

7 Set mold in a larger baking pan. Add enough hot water to reach halfway up sides of mold.

8 Reduce oven temperature to 325°F and put mold in its water bath in bottom third of oven. Be sure to regulate the oven so water in pan never exceeds a simmer; if custard boils, it will not be smooth. Bake for 40 minutes, or until a tester inserted 1 inch from outside edge of custard comes out clean.

9 Cool to room temperature. Refrigerate for at least 2 hours.

10 To unmold, run a knife between custard and edge of mold. Place a serving dish upside down over mold, quickly invert the two, and remove mold from custard.

11 For topping: In a medium bowl, combine strawberries and powdered sugar and mix well. After custard has been refrigerated and unmolded, spoon sliced strawberries over top and around sides. Slice and serve in bowls or dishes.

ADVANCE PREPARATION:

May be prepared up to 1 day in advance through Step 9 and kept in refrigerator.

APRICOT-CURRANT BREAD CUSTARD

Serves 6 to 8

The padres brought apricots to California from Spain for their mission gardens. Nowadays, apricots are harvested during the summer months and then sun-dried to intensify their taste and color, a process that makes them available year-round. Brandied dried apricots and currants accent this silky-textured custard. The toasted bread rises to the top during cooking and is quickly browned under the broiler before serving.

½ cup finely chopped dried apricots
2 tablespoons currants
½ cup California brandy
5 whole eggs
4 egg yolks
1 cup granulated sugar
1 cup whipping cream

1 quart milk
1 vanilla bean
14 small slices French bread,
   ¼ inch thick
Powdered sugar
2½ cups Brandy Sauce
   (optional; page 295)

1 Combine apricots and currants in a small bowl. In a small saucepan, bring brandy to a boil. Pour over apricots and currants and leave for 1 hour. Fruit should be soft. Drain well and save brandy for softening other fruits.

2 In a mixer bowl, beat eggs and egg yolks together until frothy. Slowly add sugar and beat until light, thick, and lemon colored.

3 In a medium saucepan, combine cream, milk, and vanilla bean. Bring to a boil. Turn off heat, cover, and let vanilla infuse mixture for 30 minutes.

4 Pour milk and cream through a strainer and into egg mixture, beating well.

5 Butter French bread generously on one side.

6 Preheat oven to 375°F. Generously butter a 2-quart soufflé dish and arrange bread in it. Sprinkle half of fruit on bread. Pour egg and cream mixture over bread and sprinkle with remaining fruit.

7 Set soufflé dish in a larger pan. Add enough hot water to reach halfway up sides of soufflé dish. Place in oven and bake for 40 to 45 minutes, or until a

cake tester or skewer inserted into custard comes out clean. If custard is to be eaten warm, insert tester 1 inch from center. If custard is to be eaten cold, insert tester 1 inch from outside edge. Remove from hot water.

8 Sprinkle with powdered sugar and put under broiler to caramelize top. Serve immediately, or serve chilled, or at room temperature. Serve accompanied by Brandy Sauce, if desired.

ADVANCE PREPARATION:

May be kept up to 4 hours at room temperature or up to 1 day in refrigerator. Remove from refrigerator ½ hour before serving.

BAKED PERSIMMON PUDDING

Serves 8 to 10

The persimmon tree in winter is a beautiful work of art. I have come across a number of gorgeous persimmon trees in my travels through the Napa Valley region of California. By November most of the leaves fall off, leaving only the branches laden with plump orange fruits hanging symmetrically. Try this dessert on a chilly fall evening. You will find the cool brandy sauce a superb accompaniment to this dense dessert.

2 cups persimmon pulp (see Note)

2 eggs

¾ cup sugar

¼ cup honey

1 ½ cups all-purpose flour

1 teaspoon baking powder

1 teaspoon baking soda

¼ teaspoon salt

2 teaspoons ground cinnamon

1 teaspoon ground ginger

½ teaspoon freshly grated nutmeg

1½ cups half-and-half

1 teaspoon vanilla extract

¼ cup (½ stick) unsalted butter, melted

1 cup dark or golden raisins

2½ cups Brandy Sauce (page 295)

1 Preheat oven to 350°F. Generously butter a 13-by-9-by-2-inch baking dish.

2 Combine persimmon pulp, eggs, sugar, and honey in a large bowl. Stir until well blended.

3 In another bowl, combine flour, baking powder, baking soda, salt, cinnamon, ginger, and nutmeg. Mix well.

4 Stir dry mixture alternately with half-and-half into persimmon mixture. Add vanilla, melted butter, and raisins and mix well.

5 Pour into baking dish and bake for 1 hour, or until puffed and brown.

6 Remove from oven, cut into squares, and serve warm. Pass Brandy Sauce separately.

ADVANCE PREPARATION:

May be kept up to 6 hours ahead at room temperature. Reheat in a 350°F oven for 15 to 20 minutes.

NOTE:

To make pulp, use persimmons that are ripe and slightly soft to the touch. Peel persimmons and remove any seeds. Puree in a food processor fitted with the steel blade or in a blender. Make pulp immediately before using.

❧

COLD LEMON SOUFFLÉ

Serves 4 to 6

Here are two presentations for cold lemon mousse. In the first, a cold soufflé, the mixture is puffed 2 inches higher than the dish with the aid of a waxed paper collar. This is the more traditional presentation, which demands less last-minute work because it is brought to the table whole. In the second presentation, individual inverted molds can be accompanied by a red raspberry sauce and fresh mint leaves. A California touch is provided by the garnish of either California almonds or pistachios.

4 eggs, separated

1 cup sugar

3 tablespoons finely grated lemon zest

½ cup freshly squeezed lemon juice

1½ envelopes or 1½ tablespoons
   unflavored gelatin

¼ cup water

1½ cups whipping cream

½ cup finely chopped almonds
   or pistachios

1 Double a piece of waxed paper and make a 1-inch pleat around the base. Tape the paper around a 1-quart soufflé dish so that it comes 2 inches above the top and forms a collar around dish.

2 In a medium bowl, combine egg yolks, sugar, and lemon zest and beat with an electric mixer until thick. In a small saucepan, heat lemon juice to simmer. Beat into yolk mixture. Continue to beat until mixture becomes very thick and forms a thick ribbon when beater is lifted, about 10 minutes.

3 Combine gelatin and water in saucepan and let stand for 5 minutes, or until it becomes spongy. Dissolve over low heat; do not boil, or it will become stringy. Stir into lemon mixture.

4 Lightly whip 1 cup cream in a chilled bowl until soft peaks form. Set aside.

5 Beat egg whites until they are stiff. Set aside.

6 Put lemon mixture over a bowl of ice water and stir gently until it begins to thicken. Carefully fold in whipped cream and egg whites. Pour into prepared soufflé dish. Mixture should come about 2 inches above rim of dish.

7 Refrigerate for about 2 hours, or until firm.

8 A short time before serving, whip remaining cream in chilled bowl until stiff; refrigerate.

9 To serve, carefully remove paper collar and spread cream over top of soufflé. Spoon remaining cream into a medium pastry bag fitted with the small star tip. Pipe rosettes of cream around edge of soufflé. Press almonds or pistachios around exposed sides of soufflé.

VARIATION:

For lemon mousse, pour lemon soufflé mixture into individual 6-ounce serving dishes or molds. If unmolding, spoon a few tablespoons of Raspberry Sauce (page 294) on serving plate, unmold lemon mousse into sauce, and decorate with fresh mint leaves.

ADVANCE PREPARATION:

May be kept up to 2 days in refrigerator.

CHOCOLATE CREAM

Serves 10 to 12

This variation on a more common mousse dessert will please even the most fanatical chocolate lover. The contrast of the crème fraîche with the chocolate is elegant. Best of all, it's simple to prepare and can be made in advance.

1 pound semisweet chocolate
2 cups milk
6 egg yolks

⅓ cup sugar
Drop of almond extract
Drop of vanilla extract

FOR GARNISH:
Crème fraîche (page 280)
Candied violets

1 In the top part of a double boiler, combine chocolate and milk above hot water over low heat. Leave until melted, stirring occasionally.

2 In a mixing bowl, beat egg yolks until frothy. Slowly add sugar and extracts and beat until light, thick, and lemon colored.

3 Whisk chocolate mixture into egg yolks. Strain into a pitcher and pour into 3- to 5-ounce serving containers. Refrigerate for 4 hours, or until cold.

4 Garnish each with a dollop of crème fraîche and a candied violet.

ADVANCE PREPARATION:
May be kept up to 2 days in refrigerator.

FROZEN HONEY-VANILLA MOUSSE
WITH BLACKBERRY SAUCE

Serves 6

This dessert makes for an elegant presentation, with the honey mousse centered atop a dark blackberry sauce. Garnished with refreshing mint leaves, it is beautiful served on a plain white dish. The mousse is easy to make but requires freezing, so enjoy it when you are preparing other dishes that take more time.

1 cup whipping cream

6 egg yolks

½ cup honey

1 teaspoon vanilla extract

FOR SAUCE:

12 ounces fresh or frozen unsweetened
    blackberries

¼ cup powdered sugar

FOR GARNISH:

Mint sprigs

Fresh blackberries (optional)

1 Whip cream in a chilled bowl until stiff.

2 In a mixing bowl, beat egg yolks until frothy. Add honey and vanilla and beat until light, thick, and pale, about 5 to 10 minutes.

3 Fold in whipped cream. Pour into an 8-by-4-inch rectangular baking dish and freeze for 6 hours, or until serving time.

4 For sauce: If using frozen berries, defrost and drain them. Puree berries in a food processor fitted with the steel blade. Add powdered sugar and process until smooth.

5 Strain puree into a bowl through a nylon strainer, using one spatula to push sauce through and another to push sauce off underside of strainer.

6 To serve, spoon a thin layer of blackberry sauce on the center of each dessert plate, and tip dish to cover it completely with sauce. Slice mousse

into 1-inch-thick slices and place in center of each plate. Garnish with fresh mint sprigs and fresh blackberries, if available.

ADVANCE PREPARATION:

Mousse may be kept in freezer up to 2 weeks covered tightly. Do not thaw before serving. Sauce may be kept up to 5 days in refrigerator.

❧

CHOCOLATE-HAZELNUT ICE CREAM

Yields 1½ quarts

Everyone loves to go out to the ice cream parlor, but with the advent of ice cream makers, Californians are increasingly saving this form of amusement for home. This is a creamy, nutty, rich chocolate ice cream. Hazelnut liqueur is added for a special touch.

1 cup whole milk	5 ounces semisweet chocolate
3 cups whipping cream	1 ounce unsweetened chocolate
4 egg yolks	2½ ounces hazelnuts
½ cup sugar	2 tablespoons hazelnut liqueur

1 In a 3-quart saucepan, combine milk and cream and scald.

2 In a mixing bowl, beat egg yolks until frothy. Slowly add sugar and beat until light, thick, and lemon colored.

3 When milk and cream are scalded, gradually beat 1 cup into yolk mixture. Gradually pour mixture back into milk and cream in saucepan, whisking.

4 Heat slowly over low heat, stirring constantly, until mixture is thick enough to coat a wooden spoon. Be careful not to cook too long, or mixture will curdle. Remove from heat and let cool.

5 Melt 3 ounces of the semisweet chocolate and the unsweetened chocolate in the top part of a double boiler above hot water over low heat, stirring occasionally.

6 Melt the remaining 2 ounces semisweet chocolate in second double boiler and let come to room temperature. Reserve.

7 Preheat oven to 350°F. Toast hazelnuts on a baking sheet in oven for 10 minutes. Remove and rub skins off with kitchen towel. Coarsely chop hazelnuts and set aside.

8 Combine the 4 ounces melted chocolate, custard, and hazelnut liqueur and stir until blended.

9 Pour custard mixture into chilled ice cream machine and churn, following manufacturer's instructions, until ice cream is still soft but thickened. Add the reserved 2 ounces chocolate and hazelnuts while machine is running. Chocolate should harden into chunks.

10 Serve immediately or freeze.

ADVANCE PREPARATION:

May be kept in freezer in a covered container up to 1 week. Remove from freezer 15 minutes before serving to soften.

KIWI SORBET

Yields 3 to 3½ cups

Whether it is teamed with other fruit sorbets or served by itself, kiwi sorbet will be appreciated for its sweet yet slightly tart taste and refreshing light green color.

8 kiwis, peeled
2 tablespoons freshly squeezed lemon juice
⅔ cup Simple Syrup (page 280)

1 Puree kiwis with lemon juice and syrup in a food processor fitted with the steel blade or in a blender.

2 Strain to remove seeds.

3 Pour into chilled electric ice cream machine and churn, following instructions, until mixture is firm, about 15 minutes.

4 Serve immediately or freeze.

VARIATION:

Seeds may be left in if desired for a slightly crunchy texture.

ADVANCE PREPARATION:

May be kept in a covered container in freezer up to 1 week. Remove from freezer 15 minutes before serving to soften.

BANANA SORBET

Yields 1 quart

The creaminess and lush taste of this sorbet is extraordinary. It is easily mistaken for ice cream. Try it placed in the center of a Tulip Cookie Cup, lightly topped with Raspberry Sauce, or on a plate as one of a medley of refreshing sorbets. Garnish with fresh mint leaves.

4 ripe bananas, peeled and cut into 2-inch pieces	3 tablespoons lemon juice ½ cup Simple Syrup (page 280), cooled

1 Puree bananas with lemon juice and syrup in a food processor fitted with the steel blade or in a blender, or mash by hand.

2 Pour into a chilled electric ice cream machine and churn, following manufacturer's instructions, until mixture is semisolid, 15 to 20 minutes (see Note).

3 Serve immediately or freeze.

Lime juice may be substituted for lemon juice. Chopped walnuts or pecans may be added for a different texture.

May be kept in a covered container in freezer up to 1 week. Remove from freezer 15 minutes before serving to soften.

If you do not have an electric ice cream machine, place mixture in a bowl in the freezer. Every 30 minutes, whip it vigorously to soften it and keep it from becoming too icy. It should take 2 to 3 hours for the ingredients to freeze.

STRAWBERRY SORBET

Yields 1 quart

Among an assortment of fresh fruit sorbets, this one will stand out because of its pink color.

2¾ cups pureed fresh strawberries (about 1 quart)

2 tablespoons freshly squeezed lemon juice
⅔ cup Simple Syrup (page 280)

1 Blend strawberries, lemon juice, and syrup together in a food processor fitted with the steel blade or in blender.

2 Strain to remove seeds.

3 Pour into a chilled electric ice cream machine and churn, following manufacturer's instructions, until mixture is firm, about 15 minutes.

4 Serve immediately or freeze.

Seeds may be left in, if desired, for a slightly crunchy texture.

May be kept in a covered container in freezer up to 1 week. Remove from freezer 15 minutes before serving to soften.

CINNAMON-PECAN COFFEE CAKE

Serves 6 to 8

This coffee cake has swirls of cinnamon and pecan throughout. Serve it warm for breakfast or brunch with fresh berries, if in season.

FOR FILLING:

2 cups chopped pecans
2 tablespoons granulated sugar
2 teaspoons ground cinnamon

1 cup (2 sticks) unsalted butter
2 cups granulated sugar
2 eggs
1 cup sour cream

2 teaspoons vanilla extract
2 cups all-purpose flour
1 teaspoon baking powder
¼ teaspoon salt

FOR GARNISH:

Powdered sugar

1 Preheat oven to 350°F. Grease and flour a 9-inch bundt pan or angel food cake pan.

2 For filling: Toast pecans in oven for 5 minutes, or until lightly browned. Combine pecans, sugar, and cinnamon in small bowl and set aside.

3 Cream butter and sugar on high speed of an electric mixer until light and fluffy. Beat in eggs 1 at a time. Stir in sour cream and vanilla by hand.

4 Combine flour, baking powder, and salt and mix well. Fold into butter mixture.

5 Spread ⅓ of batter into prepared pan with a spatula. Sprinkle with half of nut mixture. Spread with ⅓ more batter. Sprinkle with remaining nut mixture. Spread with remaining batter.

6 Bake until tester inserted in center comes out clean, about 1 hour to 1 hour and 15 minutes. Let cool in pan for 5 minutes. Invert onto a cake rack and let cool for about 30 minutes before serving.

7 To decorate, dust generously with powdered sugar.

Toasted walnuts may be substituted for pecans.

The coffee cake may be made up to 2 hours ahead but is best eaten warm, ½ hour out of the oven.

CHEESECAKE SOUFFLÉ

Serves 8

This could also be dubbed the "San Andreas Cheesecake," as it occasionally develops a fault line in the center. Sprinkle powdered sugar over any cracks that develop, and you will have a beautiful presentation. The cake is supremely light, and the raisins, Marsala, and lemon zest give it a nice balance. Serve at room temperature for optimum flavor and texture.

½ cup golden raisins
½ cup California Marsala

FOR PASTRY:

1 cup pastry flour
Pinch of salt
2 tablespoons granulated sugar

½ cup (1 stick) unsalted butter, frozen
   and cut into small pieces
1 egg yolk

FOR FILLING:

1 pound cream cheese,
   at room temperature
1 tablespoon all-purpose flour
½ cup granulated sugar
4 eggs, separated

½ cup sour cream
1 teaspoon vanilla extract
¼ teaspoon salt
2 tablespoons grated lemon zest

FOR GARNISH:

Lemon leaves (optional)
Powdered sugar

1 In a small bowl, combine raisins and Marsala and leave to soften for 2 to 4 hours. Drain.

2 For pastry: Preheat oven to 400°F. Combine flour, salt, and sugar in a food processor fitted with the steel blade. Process a few seconds to blend. Add butter and egg yolk and process until dough is just beginning to come together and will adhere when pinched.

3 Press about half the pastry onto the base of a 9-inch springform pan. Bake base without sides of pan for about 8 minutes, or until pale brown. Cool. Attach springform sides to base and press remaining pastry inside rim halfway up sides. Chill. Reduce oven temperature to 350°F.

4 For filling: With an electric mixer, beat cream cheese until soft in a medium bowl. Add flour and sugar and mix well. Add egg yolks, sour cream, vanilla, and salt and beat well. Stir in lemon zest and raisins.

5 In a separate bowl, beat egg whites until stiff. Gently fold into cheese mixture. Pour into pan. Bake for 45 minutes. Cool to room temperature.

6 To serve, release sides of pan. Place dessert on a cake platter or basket and surround with lemon leaves. Dust with powdered sugar.

ADVANCE PREPARATION:

May be kept up to 8 hours in refrigerator. Bring to room temperature before serving.

ℰ

CHOCOLATE MOUSSE CAKE

Serves 8 to 10

I am always searching for the "best" chocolate cake. This cake, which contains no flour, may be the one, as confirmed by chocoholics who have tried it. The texture is rich, velvety, and smooth.

14 ounces semisweet chocolate

2 ounces unsweetened chocolate

¼ cup strong brewed coffee

6 large eggs

½ cup sugar

1 cup whipping cream

1 teaspoon vanilla extract

FOR CHOCOLATE WHIPPED CREAM:

1 cup whipping cream

1 teaspoon vanilla extract

2 ounces semisweet chocolate,
  melted and cooled

FOR GARNISH:

10 chocolate coffee beans (optional)

1 Preheat oven to 350°F. Butter a 9-inch springform pan.

2 In the top part of a double boiler, combine both types of chocolate and the coffee above hot water over low heat. Leave until melted, stirring occasionally.

3 In a large mixing bowl beat eggs until frothy. Slowly add sugar and beat until light, thick, and lemon colored, about 5 minutes.

4 In a chilled bowl, whip cream until stiff; add vanilla.

5 Place chocolate mixture in a mixing bowl and beat until shiny. Beat chocolate mixture into eggs. Fold in cream until well combined.

6 Pour chocolate cream mixture into prepared springform pan. Set springform in a larger pan. Add enough hot water to reach halfway up side of springform. Bake for 1 hour. Turn off oven and let sit in oven 15 minutes more. Remove from oven and cool for 30 minutes.

7 For chocolate whipped cream: Whip cream in a chilled bowl until soft peaks form. Add vanilla and whip another minute, or until fairly stiff.

8 Fold in cooled chocolate and blend well.

9 Serve cake warm (see Note). Pass chocolate whipped cream separately.

10 If desired, refrigerate cake. Using a pastry bag with the medium star tip, pipe rosettes of chocolate whipped cream on outside of cake. Decorate with chocolate coffee beans. Remove from refrigerator 1 hour before serving.

Cake may be prepared up to 6 hours ahead and kept at room temperature. Chocolate whipped cream may be kept up to 8 hours in refrigerator.

This cake is best served either warm or at room temperature. The texture changes when it is refrigerated.

CHOCOLATE-ALMOND SOUFFLÉ CAKE

Serves 6

In this recipe, ground almonds are a partial substitute for flour, and whipped egg whites are used rather than whole eggs, resulting in a moist, soufflé-like quality. Watch your baking time, as the cake should be underdone in the center. Although this cake is only one layer, it serves six easily.

3 tablespoons blanched almonds	¾ cup sugar
6 ounces semisweet chocolate	3 tablespoons all-purpose flour
¾ cup (1½ sticks) unsalted butter	Pinch of salt
4 eggs, separated	Pinch of cream of tartar

FOR GLAZE:

6 ounces semisweet chocolate	½ teaspoon safflower oil
½ cup (1 stick) unsalted butter	1 tablespoon light corn syrup

FOR GARNISH:

¼ cup blanched almonds

1 Grind almonds in a food processor fitted with the steel blade for 1 minute, or until fine. Preheat oven to 375°F. Cut a round of waxed paper to fit an 8-inch round cake pan. Place paper in bottom of cake pan. Butter and flour the pan.

2 In the top part of a double boiler, combine chocolate and butter above hot water over low heat. Leave until melted, stirring occasionally. Let cool.

3 In a mixing bowl, beat egg yolks until frothy. Slowly add sugar and beat until light, thick, and lemon colored.

4 Add chocolate mixture to yolk mixture and blend well. Stir in flour and almonds.

5 In a medium bowl, beat egg whites with pinch of salt and pinch of cream of tartar until stiff.

6 Blend ⅓ of egg whites into chocolate to lighten the mixture. Fold in remaining egg whites. There should be no white streaks in mixture.

7 Pour mixture into cake pan. Bake for 25 to 30 minutes, until outside is firm and interior is slightly underdone but not runny. A tester should come out slightly wet. Cool in pan, then unmold onto a cake rack. Place cake rack on a baking sheet lined with waxed paper.

8 For glaze: Melt chocolate and butter in the top part of a double boiler above hot water over low heat. Stir until melted and smooth. Stir in oil and syrup. Let cool.

9 Pour glaze over cake. Use a long metal spatula to spread glaze over edges and all over sides of cake.

10 Preheat oven to 350°F. Toast almonds on a baking sheet 7 to 10 minutes, or until lightly browned. Cool.

11 Slide spatula under cake and transfer cake to a cake platter lined with a doily, if desired. Decorate cake with toasted almonds.

ADVANCE PREPARATION:

May be kept up to 8 hours in refrigerator. Remove from refrigerator 1 hour before serving.

PASTRY DOUGH

This is a general method for making pastry by hand. Ingredient amounts are not specified, since they will vary with each recipe.

Flour
Salt
Sugar
Egg yolks
Cold water
Butter (cold but not frozen)

1 Sift flour onto a work surface and make a well in center. Add salt, sugar, and/or egg yolks (if desired), and all but 1 tablespoon of cold water and mix with fingertips.

2 Pound the butter to soften it and cut it into pieces. Add it to the well and using a fork quickly mix with other ingredients in the well until partially mixed.

3 Gradually draw in some of the flour to make coarse crumbs. If dough is too dry to come together, add a little more water.

4 Blend the dough by smearing it on work surface, then gathering it up together again. Repeat twice more until dough is nearly smooth. Form into a ball. Wrap in waxed paper or a plastic bag. Chill at least 1 hour before rolling.

CHOCOLATE-CARAMEL WALNUT TORTE

Serves 10 to 12

This dessert has become a favorite in many California restaurants. I first learned to make it when I studied with James Beard in San Francisco. The combination of a buttery crust enclosing the caramel-walnut center and the glaze of semisweet chocolate is extraordinary. You can prepare it at your leisure, as it can be made one day ahead and refrigerated.

FOR PASTRY:

3 cups sifted all-purpose flour

Pinch of salt

¼ cup sugar

1 cup (2 sticks) unsalted butter,
   frozen and cut into small pieces

½ teaspoon vanilla extract

2 egg yolks

4 to 6 tablespoons cold water

FOR FILLING:

1½ cups sugar

1 cup water

1 cup whipping cream

14 tablespoons (1¾ sticks)
   unsalted butter, softened

⅓ cup honey

4 cups (1 pound) walnuts,
   coarsely chopped

FOR GLAZE:

8 ounces semisweet chocolate

6 tablespoons (¾ stick)
   unsalted butter, softened

2 teaspoons oil

FOR GARNISH:

10 to 12 walnut halves

1 For pastry: Combine flour, salt, and sugar in a food processor fitted with the steel blade. Process a few seconds to blend. Add butter, vanilla, and egg yolks and process until mixture resembles coarse meal, about 5 to 10 seconds.

2 With blades of processor turning, gradually add the cold water until dough is just beginning to come together and will adhere when pinched. Wrap in waxed paper or plastic wrap and refrigerate for 2 to 4 hours.

3 Transfer two-thirds of dough to floured pastry board or work surface. Press into round shape for easy rolling. Roll out into a circle 12½ inches in diameter. Drape circle over rolling pin and fit it either into an 11-inch flan ring that is placed on a baking sheet or into an 11-inch tart pan with a removable bottom. Press pastry with fingers so that it adheres to sides of pan. Be sure that ½ inch of pastry hangs over side of pan. Refrigerate 30 minutes. Refrigerate rest of dough as well.

4 For filling: Combine sugar and water in a large heavy saucepan. Do not use a dark-colored pan, as you will not be able to see the color of the caramel. Dissolve sugar in water over low heat. Turn up heat and bring to a boil. If sugar crystals form on sides of pan, cover for 1 minute; this will dissolve them. Boil until mixture reaches a light caramel color, 10 to 15 minutes. Watch carefully, as caramel can burn easily.

5 Remove from heat and add cream, butter, and honey. The filling may become very sticky, but if it is continually stirred, it will become smooth. Simmer, stirring constantly, for 15 minutes. Stir in walnuts. Filling should be very thick.

6 To assemble: Preheat oven to 400°F. Roll remaining dough to an 11-inch circle on a lightly floured surface.

7 Quickly pour filling into lined pan.

8 Brush overhanging pastry with water. Cover filling with pastry round. Press the edges firmly to seal to bottom round. Trim any excess dough. If using a tart pan with a removable bottom, place pan on a baking sheet.

9 Cut a slit in center of pastry and bake for 30 to 45 minutes, or until golden.

10 Let cool on a baking sheet for at least 2 hours. Release from pan and invert onto a cake rack with a baking sheet underneath.

11 For glaze: Melt chocolate and butter in the top part of a double boiler above hot water over low heat, stirring often. Stir in oil. Cool.

12 Pour glaze onto center of torte and spread evenly with a large spatula to cover top and sides. Garnish with walnut halves. Chill until chocolate is firm. Transfer to a serving platter.

VARIATION:

Pecans can be substituted for walnuts.

ADVANCE PREPARATION:

May be prepared up to 1 day ahead through Step 10 and kept in refrigerator. Bring to room temperature and then glaze.

LEMON-ORANGE TART

Serves 8

This typically Californian dessert captures the essence of citrus. Simple yet elegant, it makes a most exquisite, bright presentation, with lemon sections arranged in the center of the tart to resemble a flower. Serve this any time of year.

FOR PASTRY:

1 1/4 cups pastry flour

Pinch of salt

2 tablespoons powdered sugar

1/2 cup (1 stick) unsalted butter, frozen
   and cut into small pieces

1 egg yolk

1/4 cup cold water

FOR FILLING:

4 eggs

2 tablespoons unsalted butter, softened

1 cup granulated sugar

1 tablespoon finely chopped orange zest

1 1/2 teaspoons finely chopped lemon zest

2 tablespoons whipping cream

1/2 cup freshly squeezed lemon juice

1/2 cup freshly squeezed orange juice

FOR GARNISH:

1 1/2 tablespoons powdered sugar

1 lemon, peeled and sectioned

1 cup fresh whipped cream

1 For pastry: Combine flour, salt, and powdered sugar in a food processor fitted with the steel blade. Process for a few seconds to blend. Add butter and egg yolk and process until mixture resembles coarse meal, about 5 to 10 seconds.

2 With blades of processor turning, gradually add the cold water until dough is just beginning to come together and will adhere when pinched.

3 Transfer to floured pastry board or work surface. Press into a round shape for easy rolling. Roll out into a circle large enough to fit an 11-inch tart pan with removable bottom or a flan ring that has been placed on a baking sheet. Drape circle over a rolling pin and fit it into pan. Roll rolling pin over tart pan or flan ring with moderate pressure to remove excess overlapping dough.

4 Press pastry with fingers so that it adheres to sides of pan. If using tart pan with straight edges, raise edges of pastry ¼- to ½-inch above top of pan by squeezing dough from both sides with index fingers.

5 Preheat oven to 375°F. Place tart pan on a baking sheet. Cover pastry in pan with a sheet of parchment paper or aluminum foil and press to fit sides. Pour baking beads, beans, or rice into center of paper and distribute evenly. Bake crust for 15 minutes.

6 Remove baking beads and paper and prick crust with a fork. Return to oven and bake until light brown, approximately 5 to 7 minutes more. Remove from oven.

7 For filling: In a mixing bowl, beat eggs until frothy. Add butter and sugar and beat until thick and lemon colored. Add orange and lemon zest, cream, and juices. Mix well.

8 Pour filling into pie crust and bake for 10 minutes. Reduce oven temperature to 350°F and bake an additional 12 to 15 minutes, until filling is slightly brown, set in the center, and moves just slightly when pan is moved. Remove from oven.

9 Preheat broiler if necessary. Sprinkle tart with powdered sugar through a strainer so that top is uniform. Place lemon sections in center of tart in a spokelike fashion to resemble a flower. Broil, checking carefully, for 1 to 1½ minutes. Tart should be completely brown around lemon flower.

10 Serve at room temperature. Pass whipped cream separately.

ADVANCE PREPARATION:

May be kept up to 8 hours at room temperature. May be prepared up to 1 day ahead through Step 3 and kept in refrigerator.

APPLE-ALMOND TART

Serves 8 to 10

This dessert is an all-time favorite of my students. They are always surprised by the accolades they receive for its delicious taste and professional presentation. The pastry is flaky and the intense almond filling is balanced by the mild Golden Delicious apples.

FOR PASTRY:

1 cup pastry flour

Pinch of salt

6 tablespoons (¾ stick) unsalted butter, frozen and cut into small pieces

¼ cup ice water

FOR ALMOND FILLING:

1½ cups blanched almonds

¾ cup sugar

¼ cup (½ stick) unsalted butter

2 tablespoons all-purpose flour

¼ cup Amaretto

2 eggs

FOR APPLE TOPPING:

8 medium Golden Delicious apples, peeled, cored, and halved

3 tablespoons unsalted butter

3 tablespoons sugar

FOR GARNISH:

1 cup Apricot Glaze (page 295)

2 tablespoons chopped pistachios

1 For pastry: Combine flour and salt in a food processor fitted with the steel blade. Process for a few seconds to blend. Add butter and process until mixture resembles coarse meal, about 5 to 10 seconds.

2 With blades of processor turning, gradually add water until dough is just beginning to come together and will adhere when pinched.

3 Transfer dough to floured pastry board or work surface. Press into round shape for easy rolling. Roll out into a circle large enough to fit a 10-inch tart pan with a removable bottom. Drape pastry circle over rolling pin and fit it into pan. Roll rolling pin over tart pan with moderate pressure to remove excess overlapping dough. Place tart on baking sheet. Preheat oven to 400°F.

④ Press pastry with fingers so that it adheres to sides of pan. If using tart pan with straight edges, raise edges of pastry ¼- to ½-inch above top of pan by squeezing dough from both sides using index fingers.

⑤ For almond filling: Grind almonds in a food processor fitted with the steel blade until they are fine.

⑥ Add sugar, butter, flour, and Amaretto. Pulse machine repeatedly until a meal-like paste is formed. Add eggs and process for 10 seconds to incorporate.

⑦ Spread mixture in lined pan to make an even layer.

⑧ For apple topping: Slice apple halves in a food processor fitted with the slicing disk. Arrange apple slices, overlapping them in concentric circles; be sure to fit them tightly together. Arrange 2 rows of apple slices in center of tart.

⑨ Dot apples with butter and sugar and bake 1 hour to 1 hour and 15 minutes, until tart is brown on top. Remove from oven and let cool.

⑩ Bring glaze to boil in a saucepan and spoon over tart. Let cool and decorate with chopped pistachios.

ADVANCE PREPARATION:

May be prepared through Step 6 and refrigerated 8 hours, or overnight. The finished tart may be kept up to 6 hours in refrigerator. Remove from refrigerator 1 hour before serving. Tart is best served at room temperature.

PUMPKIN-PRALINE PIE

Serves 6 to 8

A slightly nutty taste complements the custard in this variation of pumpkin pie. The praline topping is distinctive both in flavor and presentation. I recommend using a tart pan with a removable bottom for an elegant appearance. This dessert is especially good for holiday meals.

1½ cups pastry flour

Pinch of salt

1 tablespoon coarsely chopped pecans

1 tablespoon powdered sugar

9 tablespoons unsalted butter, frozen
and cut into small pieces

¼ cup cold water

3 eggs

⅔ cup granulated sugar

2 cups fresh or canned pumpkin puree

½ teaspoon freshly grated nutmeg

½ teaspoon ground ginger

½ teaspoon allspice

Pinch of salt

1 ¼ cups half-and-half

3 tablespoons bourbon

¾ cup light brown sugar

¼ cup (½ stick) unsalted butter,
melted

2 tablespoons whipping cream

⅔ cup pecans, coarsely chopped

½ cup pecan halves

½ cup whipping cream

1 teaspoon vanilla extract

1 For pastry: Combine flour, salt, pecans, and powdered sugar in a food processor fitted with the steel blade. Process for a few seconds to blend. Add butter and process until mixture resembles coarse meal, about 5 to 10 seconds.

2 With blades of processor turning, gradually add the cold water until dough is just beginning to come together and will adhere when pinched.

3 Transfer dough to a floured pastry board or work surface. Press into a round shape for easy rolling. Roll out dough to a circle large enough to fit an 11-inch flan ring placed on a baking sheet, an 11-inch tart pan with a removable bottom, or a 9-inch pie pan. Drape circle over rolling pin and fit it into pan. Roll rolling pin over tart pan or flan ring with moderate pressure to remove excess overlapping dough. If using pie pan, cut off excess dough with knife.

4 Place tart pan or pie pan on a baking sheet. Press pastry with fingers so that it adheres to sides of pan. If using tart pan with straight edges, raise edges of pastry ¼- to ½-inch above top of pan by squeezing dough from both sides with index fingers. Preheat oven to 400°F.

5 Cover pastry in pan with sheet of parchment paper or aluminum foil and press to fit sides. Pour baking beads, beans, or rice into center of paper and distribute evenly. Bake crust for 8 minutes.

6 Remove crust from oven and remove beans and paper. Prick pastry and return to oven for 5 minutes. Remove from oven and let cool 15 minutes.

7 For filling: Using an electric mixer or a food processor fitted with the steel blade, beat eggs and sugar until light, thick, and lemon colored, about 3 minutes. Add remaining ingredients and mix well. Pour into pie shell.

8 Bake for 15 minutes. Reduce oven temperature to 350°F and bake an additional 35 to 45 minutes, or until set. Remove from oven and let cool to room temperature.

9 For topping: Combine all ingredients and mix well. Spread evenly over pie. Garnish with pecan halves.

10 Preheat broiler if necessary. Place pie under broiler, rotating until topping browns; make sure it does not burn.

11 Whip cream with vanilla in chilled bowl until fairly stiff. Serve pie warm. Pass whipped cream separately.

ADVANCE PREPARATION:

May be prepared up to 8 hours ahead through Step 9 and kept in refrigerator. Bring to room temperature before continuing. Heat before serving.

❧

BROWN BUTTER TART WITH FRESH FRUIT

Serves 6

Mangia restaurant in Los Angeles has a tart similar to this as the specialty of the house. The brown butter filling is baked and takes on a taste reminiscent of almonds. Any fresh seasonal fruit may be placed on top before glazing.

1 cup pastry flour

Pinch of salt

1 tablespoon powdered sugar

6 tablespoons (¾ stick) unsalted butter,
   frozen and cut into small pieces

1 egg yolk

2 tablespoons ice water

¾ cup (1½ sticks) unsalted butter

3 eggs

1 cup granulated sugar

3 tablespoons all-purpose flour

1 cup Apricot Glaze (page 295)

3 medium kiwi

14 medium strawberries, stems removed

1 For pastry: Combine flour, salt, and powdered sugar in a food processor fitted with the steel blade. Process for a few seconds to blend. Add butter and egg yolk and process until mixture resembles coarse meal, about 5 to 10 seconds.

2 With blades turning, gradually add water until dough is just beginning to come together and will adhere when pinched.

3 Transfer to floured pastry board or work surface. Press into round shape for easy rolling. Roll out into a circle large enough to fit a 9-inch tart pan with removable bottom or a flan ring that is placed on a baking sheet. Drape circle over rolling pin and fit it into tart pan or flan ring. Roll rolling pin over tart pan or flan ring with moderate pressure to remove excess overlapping dough. If using a pie pan, cut off excess with a knife.

4 Preheat oven to 375°F. Press pastry with fingers so that it adheres to sides of pan. If using tart pan with straight edges, raise edges of pastry ¼ to ½ inch above top of pan by squeezing dough from both sides with index fingers.

5 Place tart or pie pan on baking sheet before placing in oven. Cover pastry in pan with a sheet of parchment paper or aluminum foil and press to fit sides. Pour baking beads, beans, or rice into center of paper and distribute evenly. Bake for 15 minutes. Remove baking beads and paper and prick dough with fork. Return to oven and bake until light brown, approximately 5 to 7 minutes more. Remove from oven.

6 For filling: Place butter in a small saucepan and melt over high heat. Watch carefully and cook until butter is dark brown. Remove immediately from heat. Strain through a strainer lined with a double thickness of cheese-cloth into a small saucepan. Keep warm. There should be no black specks in the butter.

7 In a medium mixing bowl, beat eggs until frothy. Beat in sugar until smooth. Sprinkle in the flour and whisk until smooth and without lumps. Gradually whisk in warm burnt butter.

8 Reduce oven temperature to 350°F. Place pie shell on baking sheet in oven and pour filling into crust. Bake for 20 to 25 minutes, or until filling is dark brown, set in the center, and moves only slightly when pan is moved. Remove from oven and let cool.

9 Bring glaze to boil in a saucepan and brush over tart, reserving some to glaze fruit.

10 Peel and slice kiwis and arrange decoratively along outside rim of tart shell. Arrange whole strawberries in center, stem side down, so that tart is completely covered. Brush remaining glaze on fruit. Refrigerate until serving.

ADVANCE PREPARATION:

May be kept up to 8 hours in refrigerator. Remove from refrigerator ½ hour before serving.

TULIP COOKIE CUPS

Yields approximately 16 cookie cups

This delicious buttery cookie resembles a flower. Tulip Cookie Cups make attractive containers for fresh fruit, sorbet, or ice cream. In these suggested presentations, like an ice cream cone, the containers are crunchy while the ingredients inside are soft. The extra batter can be piped onto a buttered baking sheet to make regular, flat cookies. Serve them at lunch or with tea.

5½ tablespoons unsalted butter, softened

½ cup sugar

Pinch of salt

½ teaspoon vanilla extract

3 egg whites

½ cup plus 2 tablespoons all-purpose flour

½ teaspoon cornstarch

1 Preheat oven to 375°F. Generously butter and flour 2 baking sheets. Using a 6- or 7-inch mold, mark 2 circles onto each floured baking sheet.

2 Cream butter with sugar, salt, and vanilla on high speed of an electric mixer until light and fluffy.

3 Add egg whites slowly. Mixture will look slightly curdled.

4 Fold in flour and cornstarch until batter is smooth.

5 Place a tablespoon of batter in center of circle. With a long spatula, spread batter into a thin 6- or 7-inch circle.

6 Bake for about 5 to 7 minutes, or until light brown. Remove each cookie with a long metal spatula and place over a cup that has no handle or over a small glass ramekin. Invert another cup over the top to press cookie into a tulip shape. Leave for 20 seconds. Remove molds and set cookie cups aside.

7 Repeat with remaining batter.

ADVANCE PREPARATION:

Cookies or cups may be kept crisp up to 2 days in an airtight container.

NOTE:

To make small flat cookies, use a small plain pastry tip and pipe out 3-inch-long cookies on a buttered and floured baking sheet. Bake for 10 minutes, or until brown.

BASICS

VEAL STOCK

DUCK STOCK

CHICKEN STOCK

FISH STOCK

MARINARA SAUCE

RAW TOMATO-BASIL SAUCE

HOT PEPPER OIL

CRÈME FRAÎCHE

SIMPLE SYRUP

BASIC VINAIGRETTE

BALSAMIC VINAIGRETTE

SPICY RED SALSA

GREEN CHILE SALSA

HOLLANDAISE SAUCE

TOMATO BÉARNAISE SAUCE

WHITE WINE BUTTER SAUCE

ANCHO CHILE BUTTER

FRESH GARLIC MAYONNAISE

SPICY GARLIC MAYONNAISE

PESTO SAUCE

SPINACH-WATERCRESS SAUCE

FENNEL SAUCE

CUCUMBER-MUSTARD DILL SAUCE

LEMON-CHIVE SABAYON SAUCE

RASPBERRY SAUCE

BRANDY SAUCE

APRICOT GLAZE

VEAL STOCK

Yields 3½ quarts

It has become very important in California cooking to have a ready supply of veal stock on hand. Although it has a meaty richness, this stock is not as heavy and overpowering as beef stock. Prepare it in large quantity and divide into small containers to keep in your freezer for convenient use. It is primarily used in sauces and reductions.

2 pounds veal necks

1 pound veal bones

2 large carrots, peeled and cut
   into 2-inch slices

1 large onion, cut into 2-inch slices

2 leeks, cleaned and sliced
   into 2-inch chunks

Bouquet garni (see Note)

1 Preheat oven to 425°F. Place necks and bones in a large roasting pan. Roast in oven until browned, about 1½ hours.

2 Remove pan from oven and place on top of burner. Remove bones and place in a 6-quart stockpot.

3 Add about 3 cups water to roasting pan over medium-high heat. Stir and scrape bits from bottom of pan. The water should become a rich brown color. Bring water to boil.

4 Pour water from roasting pan into stockpot and add enough water to nearly cover bones. Add vegetables and bouquet garni.

5 Bring mixture to boil over medium heat, then turn down heat to lowest setting. Simmer, uncovered, for 8 to 10 hours, or overnight. Skim occasionally.

6 Turn off heat and let cool. Remove bones and pour stock through a fine-meshed strainer into a large bowl (a conical strainer is excellent for this purpose). Let cool to room temperature. Cover and refrigerate 2 hours.

7 With a large spoon, remove fat from surface of stock and discard. The stock should be clear.

8 Line the strainer with cheesecloth, then pour stock through again to make sure stock is fat-free. If not using immediately, pour into containers and refrigerate.

VARIATION:

For beef stock, substitute beef bones for veal bones.

ADVANCE PREPARATION:

If not used within 3 days, stock should be frozen and then reboiled before using. Freeze in small containers for convenient use.

NOTE:

To make a bouquet garni, wrap a parsley stem, bay leaf, and a sprig of fresh thyme in cheesecloth and tie with string.

DUCK STOCK

Yields 1 quart

1 tablespoon oil	1 medium carrot, peeled and sliced
Giblets (except liver), neck, and	5 cups chicken stock (page 276)
wing tips from 1 duck	or veal stock (page 274)
1 medium onion, sliced	Bouquet garni (see Note)

1 Heat oil in a stockpot. Add giblets, neck, and wing tips and brown them on all sides over medium-high heat, about 5 minutes.

2 Add onion and carrot and cook until browned. Add stock and bouquet garni.

3 Partially cover and bring to boil over medium heat. Reduce heat to simmer for 1 hour, skimming occasionally. Strain stock into a bowl through a fine strainer and let cool.

4 Chill stock for at least 2 hours. With a large spoon, remove fat from surface and discard.

5 If not using immediately, pour into containers and refrigerate.

ADVANCE PREPARATION:

If not used within 3 days, stock should be frozen and then reboiled before using. Freeze in small containers for convenient use.

NOTE:

To make a bouquet garni, wrap a parsley stem, bay leaf, and a sprig of fresh thyme in cheesecloth and tie with string.

CHICKEN STOCK

Yields 3 quarts

4 pounds chicken necks and backs

3 stalks celery

3 medium carrots, peeled

2 medium onions, root end cut off,
    cut into halves

2 medium leeks, green and white parts,
    cleaned and sliced

Bouquet garni (see Note)

2 teaspoons salt

1 Combine all ingredients except salt in a 6-quart stockpot. Add enough cold water to fill the pot three-quarters full. Bring slowly to boil over medium heat, uncovered.

2 Turn down heat to lowest setting and simmer for 3 hours. Add salt. Taste for seasoning. Strain stock into a bowl through a colander or a strainer lined with cheesecloth and let cool.

3 Chill stock for at least 2 hours. With a large spoon, remove fat from surface and discard.

4 If not using immediately, pour into containers and refrigerate.

ADVANCE PREPARATION:

If not used within 3 days, stock should be frozen and then reboiled before using. Freeze in small containers for convenient use.

NOTE:

To make a bouquet garni, wrap a parsley stem, bay leaf, and a sprig of fresh thyme in cheesecloth and tie with string.

FISH STOCK

Yields about 1 gallon

2 tablespoons vegetable oil

2 pounds heads, skin, bones,
   and flesh of fresh fish

1 medium onion, thinly sliced

2 medium carrots, unpeeled and cut
   into 2-inch pieces

6 parsley stems

2 stalks celery, with leaves,
   cut into 2-inch pieces

1 bay leaf

10 white peppercorns

5 sprigs fresh dill

1 lemon, thinly sliced, with peel

1 In a 6-quart stockpot, heat oil and sauté fish for 2 to 3 minutes on low heat. Do not brown.

2 Add remaining ingredients to pot and enough water to nearly cover them. Bring to boil over medium heat. Reduce heat and simmer, uncovered, for 45 minutes. Strain stock into a bowl through a colander or strainer lined with cheesecloth and let cool.

3 Chill stock for at least 2 hours. With a large spoon, remove fat from surface and discard.

4 If not using immediately, pour into containers and refrigerate.

ADVANCE PREPARATION:

If not used within 2 days, stock should be frozen and then reboiled before using. Freeze in small containers for convenient use.

MARINARA SAUCE

Yields about 1½ quarts

This sauce is a basic one that is used in recipes to provide color and texture. It is versatile but should be used in moderation. If used excessively it can mask rather than enhance food. Use as a sauce for pasta, eggs, or chicken.

2 tablespoons olive oil

1 medium onion, finely chopped

2 pounds tomatoes, peeled and coarsely
    chopped (about 4 cups), or 1
    (28-ounce) can Italian plum tomatoes,
    drained and coarsely chopped

1 (15-ounce) can tomato puree

2 cups water

1 bay leaf

3 tablespoons chopped fresh basil,
    or 1 tablespoon dried basil

2 tablespoons chopped fresh thyme,
    or 2 teaspoons dried thyme

2 medium cloves garlic, finely minced

1 teaspoon salt

Pinch of finely ground pepper to taste

1 In a medium enamel or stainless-steel saucepan, heat oil. Add onion and sauté over medium heat until soft.

2 Add remaining ingredients, partially cover, and simmer for 1 hour, stirring occasionally. Remove bay leaf and taste for seasoning.

ADVANCE PREPARATION:
May be kept up to 5 days in refrigerator.

RAW TOMATO-BASIL SAUCE

Yields about 1½ cups

This is an excellent sauce to accompany Celery Root Terrine or Spinach-Carrot Terrine. Make sure your tomatoes are fresh and fully ripened.

4 medium tomatoes, peeled, seeded, and coarsely chopped

1 medium red onion, finely chopped

2 medium cloves garlic, minced

3 tablespoons finely chopped fresh basil

3 tablespoons finely chopped Italian parsley

2 tablespoons olive oil

3/4 teaspoon salt

1/4 teaspoon finely ground pepper

1 Combine all ingredients in a medium bowl. Taste for seasoning. Refrigerate until needed.

2 Serve cold.

ADVANCE PREPARATION:

May be kept up to 1 day in refrigerator.

HOT PEPPER OIL

Yields 1 cup

Use this as a seasoning and flavoring ingredient. You will find that it will enliven many recipes.

1/4 cup hot red pepper flakes

1 cup oil

1 Combine pepper flakes and oil in a small saucepan over medium heat. Bring oil to a boil, then immediately turn off heat. Let cool.

2 Strain into a small glass container that can be sealed. Refrigerate.

VARIATION:

Leave pepper flakes in oil. They will fall to the bottom, and the oil can be used in seasoning. The oil will become hotter as it stands.

ADVANCE PREPARATION:

This oil can last indefinitely refrigerated.

CRÈME FRAÎCHE

Yields 1 cup

Crème Fraîche is a versatile substitute for whipping cream in sauces and desserts. You may wish to sweeten it when serving with fresh fruit.

1 cup whipping cream (preferably not
    ultrapasteurized)
2 tablespoons buttermilk

1 Combine cream and buttermilk in a glass jar or crockery bowl (a non-metallic container) and whisk until well blended. Loosely cover jar or bowl with aluminum foil, letting some air in. Leave in a warm place for at least 12 hours and up to 24 hours. The cream will become thick enough for a spoon to stand up in it and will have a sour, nutty taste.

2 Stir cream when thickened. Cover and refrigerate until ready to use.

ADVANCE PREPARATION:
May be kept up to 1 week in refrigerator.

SIMPLE SYRUP

Yields 2 cups

If you are going to make sorbets, prepare this syrup and keep it on hand for your convenience. Make sure that the syrup is very cold before using.

2 cups water
2 cups sugar

1 Place water and sugar in a small saucepan. Bring to simmer, stirring until sugar is dissolved.

2 Cool to room temperature. Refrigerate in a sealed jar.

ADVANCE PREPARATION:

May be kept up to 1 month in refrigerator.

BASIC VINAIGRETTE

Yields 1 cup

A basic dressing with any tossed green salad, vinaigrette is also good with some pasta salads.

¼ cup red wine vinegar

1 teaspoon Dijon mustard

1 medium shallot, finely chopped

½ cup vegetable oil

¼ cup olive oil

½ teaspoon salt

⅛ teaspoon finely ground black pepper

1 In a medium bowl, combine vinegar, mustard, and shallot. Whisk until blended.

2 Slowly pour both oils into bowl, whisking continually until mixture is well blended. Add salt and pepper and taste for seasoning.

ADVANCE PREPARATION:

May be kept up to 1 week in refrigerator. Whisk before using.

BALSAMIC VINAIGRETTE

Yields ½ cup

I like to use this on simple salads when the dressing will be the predominant taste. It is also excellent on sliced ripe tomatoes.

1 small shallot, finely chopped	6 tablespoons light olive oil
1 teaspoon Dijon mustard	¼ teaspoon salt
2 tablespoons balsamic vinegar	Pinch of finely ground pepper

1 Combine shallot, mustard, and vinegar in a small bowl. Whisk until completely blended.

2 Slowly add oil in steady stream, whisking continually. When all oil has been added, add salt and pepper. Taste for seasoning. If not using immediately, refrigerate.

VARIATION:

Substitute walnut oil for the olive oil.

ADVANCE PREPARATION:

May be kept up to 1 week in refrigerator. Remove from refrigerator 1 hour before using and whisk thoroughly to make sure dressing is emulsified.

SPICY RED SALSA

Yields about 1 quart

This spicy salsa is wonderful to have around for use as a condiment. The hotness may be controlled by the number of chiles included. For a spicier salsa, increase the amount of chiles to 2 tablespoons. Cilantro gives this salsa a delightful contrast in color and taste.

4 large fresh tomatoes, peeled, seeded, and finely chopped

1 tablespoon seeded, finely chopped fresh jalapeño chiles (see Note)

2 tablespoons finely chopped cilantro

1 small red onion, finely chopped

1 medium clove garlic, minced

1 teaspoon red wine vinegar or freshly squeezed lemon juice

1 teaspoon salt

Combine all ingredients in a medium bowl and mix well. Taste for seasoning. Cover and refrigerate.

VARIATION:

Canned jalapeños may be used if fresh are not available. Do not add vinegar or lemon juice if using canned chiles.

ADVANCE PREPARATION:

May be kept up to 3 days in refrigerator. Remove from refrigerator ½ hour before serving.

NOTE:

When working with chiles always wear rubber gloves. Wash cutting surface and knife immediately afterward.

GREEN CHILE SALSA

Yields about 2½ cups

This is an alternative to Spicy Red Salsa. Less hot and delicious in its own right, Green Chile Salsa goes well with Mexican Chicken with Raisins and Almonds, tacos, eggs, frittatas, and fish. The green tomatillo is a ripe, slightly sweet green tomato. If fresh tomatillos (green Mexican tomatoes) are unavailable, you may substitute the contents of a 12-ounce can of tomatillos.

3/4 pound tomatillos

1/2 small onion, finely chopped

1 Serrano chile, finely chopped
 (see Note)

1 small yellow chile, finely chopped
 (see Note)

2 teaspoons freshly squeezed lemon juice

2 medium cloves garlic, minced

2 tablespoons chopped cilantro

1/2 teaspoon salt

1 Put tomatillos into a pan with water to cover and bring to boil. Simmer gently for 10 minutes. Drain, cool, and core.

2 Cut tomatillos into small dice or finely chop in a food processor fitted with the steel blade. Place in bowl.

3 Add remaining ingredients and mix well. Cover and refrigerate.

ADVANCE PREPARATION:

May be kept up to 3 days in refrigerator. Remove from refrigerator 1/2 hour before serving.

NOTE:

When working with chiles always wear rubber gloves. Wash cutting surface and knife immediately afterward. You may use Serrano chiles only, and more or less depending on strength desired. Serrano chiles are hotter than yellow chiles.

HOLLANDAISE SAUCE

Yields 3/4 cup

Here is a quick and successful technique for making Hollandaise Sauce with the food processor. If you do not use the sauce immediately, place it in a small thermos that has been heated. This will keep it warm for up to 30 minutes. Hollandaise Sauce is delicious with eggs, vegetables, and fish.

3 egg yolks

2 tablespoons freshly squeezed
 lemon juice

1/2 teaspoon salt

Pinch of finely ground white pepper

1/2 cup (1 stick) unsalted butter

1. Pour boiling water into a 1-pint, wide-necked thermos to warm it.

2. In a food processor fitted with the steel blade or a blender, combine yolks, lemon juice, salt, and white pepper. Blend 10 seconds.

3. Heat butter in a small saucepan until sizzling hot but not browned. (This is important to enable the sauce to thicken properly.)

4. Slowly pour hot butter into blender or food processor in a thin stream while the motor is on. Taste for seasoning. Serve warm.

5. Drain and dry the thermos jar and immediately pour the hot sauce into it. This will keep the sauce hot for up to 30 minutes.

VARIATION:

Add 2 teaspoons Dijon mustard to finished sauce for mustard hollandaise sauce.

TOMATO BÉARNAISE SAUCE

Yields 1½ cups

This sauce is particularly good on fish, steaks, chicken, and poached eggs. It is quite easy to prepare.

2 tablespoons white wine vinegar	4 egg yolks
2 tablespoons dry white wine	½ teaspoon salt
2 teaspoons chopped fresh tarragon,	½ teaspoon coarsely cracked pepper
or 1 teaspoon dried tarragon	1 tablespoon tomato paste
2 medium shallots, finely chopped	1 cup (2 sticks) unsalted butter

1. Pour boiling water into a 1-pint wide-necked thermos jar to warm it.

2. In a small saucepan, heat the first four ingredients until almost all liquid is absorbed.

3 Place shallot mixture in a blender or a food processor fitted with the steel blade. Add egg yolks, salt, pepper, and tomato paste and blend 20 seconds.

4 Heat butter in same pan until sizzling hot but not browned. (This is important to enable sauce to thicken properly.)

5 Slowly pour hot butter into blender or food processor in a thin stream while the motor is on. Taste for seasoning.

6 Drain and dry thermos jar and immediately pour the hot sauce into it. This will keep the sauce hot for up to 30 minutes. Serve warm.

WHITE WINE BUTTER SAUCE

Yields 1 cup

This sauce is used on fish or shellfish for a light and delicate result. It is particularly delicious on steamed fish.

¼ cup dry white wine

2 tablespoons white wine vinegar

3 medium shallots, minced

½ teaspoon salt

¼ teaspoon finely ground white pepper

1 cup (2 sticks) unsalted butter, chilled
    and cut into cubes

1 In a small heavy saucepan, boil wine, vinegar, and shallots until about 2 tablespoons liquid remain. Add salt and white pepper.

2 Over low heat begin adding cubes of butter to shallot mixture, whisking constantly; add them 1 or 2 at a time and wait until they are absorbed before adding more. Sauce should thicken but the butter should not melt. If pan begins to get very hot, remove it from heat and add some of the butter cubes off heat to cool sauce slightly. Remove from heat as soon as last butter cube is added.

3 Strain sauce if a smoother consistency is desired. Taste for seasoning. Serve as soon as possible.

ADVANCE PREPARATION:
Sauce may be kept warm in a thermos for up to 30 minutes.

ANCHO CHILE BUTTER

Yields ½ cup

This butter is unusual and very rich in taste. Garlic and the ancho chile are toasted, which is a Mexican technique for releasing their flavors. The chile is then softened and finally pureed into a delicious compound butter. Try it on eggs, meat, or potatoes.

2 cloves garlic, unpeeled

1 large ancho chile (see Note)

6 tablespoons (¾ stick) unsalted butter

¼ teaspoon salt

1 Place garlic in a small skillet over medium-high heat. Toast garlic by heating cloves and turning as they begin to brown. When light brown in color, remove from heat. Peel garlic.

2 In same skillet, heat chile over medium heat until it begins to expand and flesh is soft. It should smell rich but should not be charred. Remove from heat.

3 Slit chile open. Remove seeds and any veins. Place chile in a small bowl. Pour boiling water over chile to cover and let soften for 30 minutes. Remove from water.

4 In a food processor fitted with the steel blade, puree chile and garlic. Add butter and salt and process until combined. Taste for seasoning.

5 Spoon onto piece of waxed paper and roll up in form of a log. Refrigerate for at least 2 hours.

6 To serve, slice cold butter and place slices on top of food. Serve immediately.

ADVANCE PREPARATION:

May be kept up to 3 days in refrigerator.

NOTE:

When working with chiles always wear rubber gloves. Wash cutting surface and knife immediately afterward.

FRESH GARLIC MAYONNAISE

Yields about 1½ cups

This basic sauce is used as an enrichment to soups, as a sauce for dipping vegetables, and as a glaze for fish.

4 large cloves garlic

2 egg yolks

1 teaspoon freshly squeezed lemon juice

¼ teaspoon dry mustard

¼ teaspoon finely ground white pepper

½ teaspoon salt

1 to 1½ cups olive oil

1 While motor is running, add garlic cloves to a food processor fitted with the steel blade. Process until pureed.

2 Add egg yolks, lemon juice, and seasonings and process to blend.

3 With blades turning, slowly pour in oil in a fine stream until mayonnaise is thick and smooth and all oil is added. Taste for seasoning. Refrigerate in a tightly covered container until ready to use.

4 Serve cold.

VARIATION:

For plain mayonnaise, omit garlic, use vegetable oil or olive oil, and increase lemon juice to 2 tablespoons or to taste.

ADVANCE PREPARATION:

May be kept up to 3 days in refrigerator.

SPICY GARLIC MAYONNAISE

Yields about 1 cup

Spicy and colorful, this sauce differs from Fresh Garlic Mayonnaise by the addition of pimiento or red bell pepper and cayenne pepper.

½ fresh pimiento or red bell pepper, seeded and coarsely chopped

4 medium cloves garlic

3 egg yolks

1 cup olive oil

1 teaspoon salt

¼ teaspoon finely ground pepper

Pinch of cayenne pepper (optional)

1 Immerse pimiento or red pepper in a pan of boiling water and boil 2 minutes. Remove from water with a slotted spoon. Reserve.

2 While motor is running, add garlic cloves to a food processor fitted with the steel blade. Process until pureed. Add pimiento or red pepper and process until blended. Add egg yolks and blend.

3 With blades turning, slowly pour in olive oil in a fine, steady stream until sauce is thick and smooth and all oil is added. Add salt, pepper, and cayenne. Taste for seasoning. Refrigerate in a tightly covered container until ready to use.

4 Serve cold.

ADVANCE PREPARATION:

May be kept up to 5 days in refrigerator.

PESTO SAUCE

Yields about 1⅓ cups

Fresh basil is a must for this basic sauce, which can be used in many different ways. Try substituting walnuts for the pine nuts for a completely different taste. In addition to its use in the standard pasta dishes, pesto sauce can serve as an enrichment to soups or other sauces. Add the cheese immediately before serving for the freshest taste.

2 medium cloves garlic

2 cups medium-packed fresh basil leaves
    (about 2 medium bunches)

½ cup medium-packed fresh
    parsley leaves

2 tablespoons pine nuts

½ cup olive oil

¾ cup freshly grated Parmesan cheese
    (see Note)

1 While motor is running, add garlic to a food processor fitted with the steel blade. Process until pureed.

2 Add basil and parsley and process just until finely chopped. Add pine nuts and finely chop.

3 With blades turning, slowly pour in olive oil in a fine stream.

4 Just before serving, add the cheese and process until well blended.

5 Refrigerate in a tightly covered container until ready to use.

ADVANCE PREPARATION:

May be prepared through Step 3 and kept up to 1 week in refrigerator.

NOTE:

You may make the pesto without the cheese and refrigerate it. It is used in pesto hollandaise sauce in this form. Serve cold.

SPINACH-WATERCRESS SAUCE

Yields 1 quart

This refreshing blend of spinach, parsley, green onions, chives, and watercress is good with raw vegetables, fish, or chicken.

1 bunch spinach (about ½ pound)

2 tablespoons chopped fresh parsley

3 tablespoons chopped green onion

2 tablespoons chopped chives

1 bunch watercress, leaves only

2 teaspoons Dijon mustard

2 tablespoons chopped fresh dill,
    or 2 teaspoons dried dill

2 tablespoons chopped fresh tarragon,
    or 2 teaspoons dried tarragon

2 tablespoons chopped fresh basil,
    or 2 teaspoons dried basil

1 teaspoon anchovy paste

2 cups mayonnaise

1 cup sour cream

2 tablespoons freshly squeezed
    lemon juice

⅛ teaspoon Tabasco sauce

Finely ground pepper to taste

1 Remove spinach stems and rinse leaves thoroughly. Immerse spinach in a pan of boiling water and boil 2 minutes. Drain and rinse under cold water. Squeeze out excess water. Coarsely chop spinach with a knife or in a food processor fitted with the steel blade. Reserve.

2 Combine all ingredients except spinach in blender or food processor and process until well blended. Add spinach and process 10 seconds more. Taste for seasoning. Refrigerate.

3 Serve cold.

ADVANCE PREPARATION:

May be kept up to 3 days in refrigerator.

NOTE:

Other herbs, such as oregano or rosemary, may be included to vary the taste.

Basics

FENNEL SAUCE

Yields 1½ cups

This versatile sauce can be used as a dip for vegetables, as an accompaniment to cured salmon, or as a sauce for grilled fish.

½ cup coarsely chopped peeled fennel
    bulb (white part)
1 tablespoon finely chopped fennel sprigs
1 cup sour cream

⅛ teaspoon Pernod
2 teaspoons freshly squeezed lime juice
¼ teaspoon salt
⅛ teaspoon coarsely cracked pepper

1 Immerse chopped fennel bulb in a pan of boiling water and boil until soft, about 3 minutes. Drain and remove to a food processor fitted with the steel blade.

2 Puree cooked fennel. Add remaining ingredients and process until well combined. Taste for seasoning. Refrigerate until ready to use.

3 Serve cold.

ADVANCE PREPARATION:
May be prepared 1 day ahead and refrigerated.

CUCUMBER-MUSTARD DILL SAUCE

Yields 1¼ cups

This extraordinary sauce goes well with fish or artichokes. It is also excellent as a dip with raw vegetables.

½ cup sour cream

½ cup mayonnaise

1 tablespoon freshly squeezed
lemon juice

2 teaspoons Dijon mustard

1 tablespoon finely chopped fresh dill,
or 1 teaspoon dried dill

1 tablespoon finely chopped fresh parsley

¼ cup peeled, coarsely chopped
cucumber

½ teaspoon salt

Pinch of finely ground white pepper

1 Combine all ingredients in a medium bowl and stir until well blended. Taste for seasoning. Refrigerate until ready to serve.

2 Serve cold.

ADVANCE PREPARATION:

May be kept up to 2 days in refrigerator.

LEMON-CHIVE SABAYON SAUCE

Yields 1 cup

This light and piquant yellow sauce is delicious with fish or vegetables.

4 egg yolks

1½ tablespoons freshly squeezed
lemon juice

¼ teaspoon salt

Pinch of finely ground pepper

2 tablespoons water

1 tablespoon finely chopped chives

1 Place egg yolks in a double boiler over simmering water. Whisk until thickened and doubled in volume.

2 Beat in lemon juice, salt, pepper, and water and continue whisking until sauce again begins to thicken. It should be thick enough to coat a wooden spoon. Add chives and taste for seasoning. Serve as soon as possible.

May be prepared up to 1 hour ahead and kept at room temperature. To reheat, whisk over very low heat in a saucepan or double boiler.

RASPBERRY SAUCE

Yields 1 cup

This colorful sauce highlights the flavors of sorbets, ice cream, and lemon mousse.

12 ounces fresh or frozen unsweetened raspberries	1½ tablespoons freshly squeezed lemon juice
	2 tablespoons powdered sugar

1 If using frozen raspberries, defrost and drain them. Puree berries in a food processor fitted with the steel blade. Add lemon juice and sugar and process until smooth.

2 Strain puree into a bowl through a nylon strainer, using one spatula to push sauce through and another to push sauce off underside of strainer.

3 Refrigerate until needed.

ADVANCE PREPARATION:

May be kept up to 5 days in refrigerator. Remove from refrigerator ½ hour before serving.

BRANDY SAUCE

Yields about 2½ cups

This is excellent with Baked Persimmon Pudding or Apricot-Currant Bread Custard.

3 egg yolks

¾ cup sugar

2 tablespoons unsalted butter, softened

1 cup whipping cream

3 egg whites

1 teaspoon vanilla extract

3 tablespoons California brandy

① In a medium bowl, whip egg yolks and sugar together until thick and lemon colored. Whip butter into mixture.

② In a small mixing bowl, whip cream until stiff.

③ In another small mixing bowl, whip egg whites until stiff.

④ Fold egg whites and cream alternately into egg yolk mixture until no streaks remain. Fold in vanilla and brandy. Serve immediately.

ADVANCE PREPARATION:

May be kept up to 2 hours in refrigerator. Serve cold.

❧

APRICOT GLAZE

Yields 1½ cups

Use this sweet sauce for glazing fruits or tarts, such as Apple-Almond Tart and Brown Butter Tart with Fresh Fruit.

1 (12-ounce) jar apricot preserves

2 tablespoons freshly squeezed lemon juice

1. In a small saucepan, bring preserves and lemon juice to boil.

2. Strain into a bowl through a fine-meshed strainer.

3. When ready to use, heat glaze just to the boil again. Brush on fruit.

VARIATION:

Add 1 tablespoon Grand Marnier or kirsch to glaze when reheating.

ADVANCE PREPARATION:

May be prepared ahead through Step 2 and kept in a tightly sealed jar. Glaze will last indefinitely refrigerated.

suggested menus

BRUNCH

Vegetable Frittata
Veal and Chicken Sausages with Chiles and Cilantro
Spicy Red Salsa
Oven-Roasted Potatoes
Orange, Kiwi, and Jicama Salad with Lime Dressing
Cinnamon-Pecan Coffee Cake

BUFFET OR LUNCHEON

Oriental-Style Chicken Salad
Braised Spicy Eggplant
Stir-Fried Chinese Vegetable Salad
Cold Chinese Noodles in Peanut-Sesame Sauce
Fresh Fruit

◆

Veal and Pork Pâté with Pistachios and Prunes
Celery Root Terrine, Raw Tomato-Basil Sauce
Tricolor Vegetable Salad with Mustard Vinaigrette
Marinated Mushrooms
Chicken Pasta Salad with Spicy Mayonnaise
Walnut Bread
Fruit and Cheese

Three-Lettuce Salad
Barbecued Roast Duck with Red Wine and Black Currants
Sweet Potato–Shallot Sauté
Banana Sorbet with Raspberry Sauce in Tulip Cookie Cups

Marinated Golden and Red Peppers
Pasta with Fresh Mushroom Sauce
Grilled Veal Chops with Rosemary
Baked Japanese Eggplant with Herbs
Cheesecake Soufflé

Baked Sonoma Goat Cheese with Emerald Sauce
Swordfish in Lemon-Ginger Marinade
Autumn Rice with Red Peppers and Pine Nuts
Sautéed Swiss Chard
Chocolate-Caramel Walnut Torte

Sliced Vegetable Salad with Fennel and Gorgonzola
Chicken with Pancetta and Zinfandel
Steamed New Potatoes with Chive Butter
Apricot-Currant Bread Custard

Baby Red Potatoes with Caviar
Beet and Walnut Salad with Blue Cheese
Tenderloin of Beef with Roasted Shallots and Tarragon
Stuffed Zucchini with Banana Squash Puree
Poached Pears in Red Wine with Fresh Applesauce

Smoked Whitefish Mousse
Garlic-Vegetable Soup
Roast Chicken Stuffed Under the Skin with Goat Cheese-Leek Filling
Sautéed Sugar Snap Peas and Red Peppers
Apple-Almond Tart

Spinach-Carrot Terrine
Leg of Lamb, California Style
Oven-Roasted Potatoes
Mustard-Baked Tomatoes
Lemon-Orange Tart

Sautéed Red Cabbage Salad with Pancetta and Broiled Goat Cheese
Grilled Lemon-Mustard Chicken
Sauté of Julienned Garden Vegetables
Chocolate Mousse Cake

Zucchini-Fresh Oregano Soup
Fresh Tuna with Sautéed Peppers and Garlic in Parchment
Green Vegetable Rice
Brown Butter Tart with Fresh Fruit

Chilled Cucumber-Avocado Soup
Cold Poached Salmon with Tomato-Basil Vinaigrette
Country Garden Pasta Salad
Green Bean-Jicama Salad
Cold Lemon Soufflé

Tomatoes with Fresh Mozzarella and Basil
Seafood Quartet
Saffron Rice or Steamed Rice
Broiled Berries and Cream

special ingredients

CALIFORNIA leads the country in agriculture and enjoys an extraordinary variety of foods, many of which are now available nationwide. In the past few years, our introduction to new ingredients from Europe, China, and Japan has stimulated local cultivation of such items as shiitake mushrooms and arugula. These special ingredients are very important in California cooking.

The following list provides descriptive information on what each ingredient is, where and when it is available, and its best uses. Note that when an ingredient is not available, buying a canned variety as a substitute often will not suffice. It is preferable either to alter your menu or to substitute within the recipe, so that you have the best of what is seasonally and locally available. Substitutes are suggested when appropriate.

Cheese

BUFFALO MOZZARELLA. Made in Italy from the milk of water buffalos, buffalo mozzarella is found in Italian specialty food stores. If unavailable, you may substitute whole cow's milk mozzarella, which is produced domestically. While the taste is inferior, the texture is similar. In California cooking, buffalo or cow's milk mozzarella is used in salads and in pizza toppings. A domestic part-skim mozzarella is available, but it has very little flavor, and its texture is extremely rubbery.

ITALIAN FONTINA. Fontina is firm-textured and has a buttery flavor that combines Swiss cheese characteristics with the mild taste of Port Salut to create a distinctive taste. Make sure it is Fontina d'Aosta, as other Fontinas do not compare. It can be used on pizza and in calzone.

GOAT CHEESE. California is producing its own goat cheese, a breakthrough that has received national and international attention. Ours is slightly milder than the French and European goat cheeses. It is used in appetizers, salads, toppings for pizza, and fillings for calzone. California goat cheese is sold relatively fresh and has a soft texture, almost like cream cheese. As goat cheese ages, it becomes stronger, and its character becomes more pronounced. When California's Sonoma goat cheese is unavailable, a good French goat cheese in a log shape is recommended.

JACK. Commonly called Monterey jack and made in California, this cheese is cured from 3 to 6 weeks and is semisoft. With its high moisture content, it is a good ingredient for egg or pizza dishes.

PARMESAN. There is no American counterpart to the Italian Parmesan cheese. There are many types of Parmesan, but Parmigiano Reggiano is the best available. It is produced in the Parma region of Italy during the spring and summer months in a small, restricted area, where the milk used in making the cheese is kept strictly uniform. Because of this, the cheese is consistently excellent. It is made from cow's milk and is aged for at least 2 years. Its color is a straw yellow and it has a mellow, slightly salty taste. Be certain that when you buy Parmigiano Reggiano, its name is stamped on the outside for proper identification. This cheese is quite expensive and should be purchased in small quantities and freshly grated only when required. If you have any left over, wrap it in layers of damp cheesecloth and then in aluminum foil, so that it will be moist when needed.

If Parmigiano Reggiano is not available, substitute Granna Padano or an equivalent brand. Granna Padano is produced throughout northern Italy, from Turin to Verona. The milk differs in quality among producers, and therefore the cheese does not always have the same character.

Cured Meats

PANCETTA. Pancetta is used often in contemporary California cooking because its taste is more delicate than that of bacon. Pancetta comes from the same cut as bacon, but is salted, lightly spiced, and then cured, rather than smoked. It has a rolled-up salami shape and is suitable for slicing. Most commonly available at Italian specialty delicatessens or in other specialty food stores, it can be ordered cut in any manner, so check your recipe before purchasing; for example, it can be cubed or sliced either thick or thin. The closest substitute to pancetta is bacon. In order to approximate the taste of pancetta, bacon must be immersed in boiling water and boiled for 2 minutes to rid it of its heavy smoked flavor.

PROSCIUTTO. Prosciutto is a salt-cured ham that is neither cooked nor smoked. Domestic prosciutto is available at most Italian specialty delicatessens; ask for "Italian-style" prosciutto. It should not be sliced paper-thin for cooking, or it will fall apart easily. Have it sliced about 1/16 to 1/8 inch thick.

Flour and Grain

PASTRY FLOUR. For many pastry shells, use enriched, unbleached, white pastry flour. The pastry comes out flakier because the flour has a lower gluten content. El Molino pastry flour, which is available at many supermarkets as well as at health food stores, is excellent.

WILD RICE. Wild rice is now indigenous to the Northern California areas of Sacramento Valley and Potter Valley. Not really a rice, it is the seed of a watergrass that has a taste similar to that of rice but distinguished by a rich, nutty flavor. Wild rice was previously grown only in Wisconsin and Minnesota, where water is more plentiful, because an ample water supply is necessary for cultivation of the grain. In California Cuisine, wild rice can be served alone or mixed with other kinds of rice.

Fruits

AVOCADO. California grows more than 80 percent of the avocados consumed in the United States. The two leading types of avocado are the pebbly, black-skinned Haas, available from April to November, and the green, smooth-skinned Fuerte, available from October to March. We are fortunate to have avocados all year. Avocados vary widely in weight, texture, shape, and thickness of skin. Avoid those that have soft dark spots on the surface or that appear badly bruised. Ready-to-eat avocados feel slightly soft to the touch. They can be purchased underripened and allowed to ripen at room temperature for 2 to 5 days. Peel just a short time before serving, because peeled avocados discolor rapidly.

KIWI. Grown in California very successfully, kiwi is used frequently in California cooking because of its intriguing characteristics. It has a dark brown, slightly fuzzy skin and an emerald green pulp that is uniquely sweet and delicate in taste. Due to its production in New Zealand and California, kiwi is available almost year-round. When shopping for kiwis, choose those that yield to gentle fingertip pressure. If the fruit is firm to the touch, it will have to be ripened at home. Kiwis should only be served when soft to the touch. They can be peeled, thinly sliced, and added to salads or used in a wide variety of desserts.

Herbs and Spices

The use of fresh herbs in California cooking is extremely important. Because of the advances being made in agriculture and hydroponic technology, many herbs that were only seasonal before are now available year-round. If possible, use only fresh herbs for the best enhancement of taste. You can grow many herbs in your own garden.

BASIL. Sweet basil is aromatic, fragrant, and has a warm, mildly pungent but sweet taste. In the past, the flowering of basil used to signal the beginning of spring, but now it is available almost year-round. Try to buy leaves that are medium in size. Cut the basil immediately before serving, as it tends to blacken very rapidly. You may also use scissors to shred it instead of chopping it. Basil is an exquisite addition to soups, salads, and sauces.

CHIVES. Available year-round. The long, thin reeds impart a mild onion flavor to soups and salads. When thinly sliced, they are an excellent garnish. Choose chives with dark green, thin leaves.

CILANTRO. The parsleylike leaf of the coriander plant, cilantro is often called fresh coriander and is less frequently referred to as Chinese parsley. It is short-stemmed, with thin, round, lightly fringed leaves. Both the smell and taste are quite pungent. The leaves are much more tender than those of parsley. It is available year-round and is often used in dishes with Mexican or Oriental influence. When selecting cilantro look for good green color and fresh, unwilted leaves.

DILL. Dillweed is particularly suited to dishes using fish or cucumber and serves as an accent herb on soups or salads as well. The edible portion of dillweed consists of hundreds of tiny leaves. When fresh, it is far superior to the dried version found in the supermarket. Fresh dillweed is available most of the year.

GINGER. Fresh ginger, or gingerroot, is used in many recipes in California cooking because of California's strong Chinese and Japanese influences. It is available year-round. Choose tubers that are fresh and firm. Ginger should be peeled first; then it may be shredded, grated, or cut into julienne strips. It enhances the character of many different dishes, including vegetables, meats, and even desserts. Do not substitute dried ground ginger for fresh.

MINT. An accent herb that adds a refreshing taste to many dishes, mint is also used frequently in California cooking as a predominant flavoring and makes a good garnish for desserts.

OREGANO. Because of its distinctive pungent taste, oregano should be used in moderation. It is particularly good with soups, vegetables, and sauces, and should be used fresh if at all possible.

PARSLEY. Parsley, in the familiar curly variety, is the most frequently used herb. It has an acid-sweet pungency and is highly nutritious as well. A less common variety, Italian flat-leaf parsley, offers a more distinctive taste and is preferred in certain dishes where a full flavor is required. When shopping for parsley, look for fresh, green, unwilted leaves. Italian parsley has larger, dark green leaves.

Parsley seems to go with just about every herb and always makes a dish taste fresher. Finely chopped, it finishes a simple and attractive presentation perfectly. Parsley bunches also make an interesting garnish for a platter.

PEPPER. Always use freshly ground pepper, whether a recipe calls for this ingredient coarsely cracked or finely ground. Sometimes white peppercorns are preferred, especially with light-colored sauces. Their tastes are different: black peppercorns are sharper in taste; the white peppercorn is a more mature seed whose outer layer has been removed.

ROSEMARY. Often associated with Italian cooking, rosemary has become an important herb in California cooking. It is available almost year-round. Aromatic and pungent, with a hint of pine, it has been described as a cross between sage and lavender, with a touch of ginger. Because of its very strong flavor, it should be used in moderation. It is delicious with a simple veal chop grilled on a barbecue (see Grilled Veal Chops with Rosemary, on page 174). Rosemary also goes well as a flavoring for soups, chicken, pork, and lamb.

SAFFRON. This herb consists of the dried stigmata—threadlike strands—of the purple autumn crocus. The crocus blossoms are picked by hand and stripped of their orange-red stigmata. The flavor of saffron is highly distinctive—it is delicate, bittersweet, and resembles iodine slightly; thus, it should be used sparingly. It goes well with soups, seafood, chicken, and rice. The whole stigmata are preferred over the powdered form. Store in a cool, dark place.

TARRAGON. French tarragon is superior in flavor and is available in spring and summer. It has a pungent taste with a hint of anise and is slightly tart yet sweet. It goes well with sauces and poultry.

THYME. A strong-flavored herb that is used in soups, stews, marinades, sauces, and pâtés. It is also a common component of a bouquet garni. It is available year-round.

Oils, Vinegars, and Mustards

OILS

Use safflower oil for general purposes. When stir-frying, use peanut oil. While the variety of oils now on the market can be confusing, it is helpful to remember that the taste of the oil shouldn't overwhelm the final dish. This is often what happens when you use olive oils.

HAZELNUT OIL. This oil is imported from France and has the strong flavor and aroma of roasted hazelnuts. It should be used in moderation and in combination with other oils when a large amount is required. Use it in salad dressings and in vegetable dishes where vinaigrette is the predominant component. It is available in specialty markets. Refrigerate shortly after opening to retain the flavor.

OLIVE OIL. The best-quality olive oils come from the South of France and Italy, although California is now making a good-quality virgin olive oil. There are many different varieties of olive oil on the market, and each one has its own particular taste. Use extra virgin olive oil when you want the taste of the oil to be intense and have the flavor of green olives, or when a fruity olive oil is called for. Virgin olive oil, although not derived from a first pressing, has the distinctive taste of olive oil without an overwhelming fruitiness and is good for sautéing.

When storing olive oil, refrigerate it after it has been opened one week. It will become cloudy, but when returned to room temperature it will become clear again. Use it for vegetables and salad dressing.

DARK SESAME OIL. Sesame oil is rich and amber colored and tastes like toasted sesame seeds. It is full-bodied and good for salad dressings with an Asian flair. It can be added after stir-frying for extra flavor. It is available in Asian and specialty markets. Do not substitute sesame seed oil, which is cold-pressed. That oil does not have the full-bodied, toasted taste of dark sesame oil.

WALNUT OIL. While California produces a walnut oil, it is not processed to bring out the full flavor. Therefore, French walnut oil is preferred. It has the distinctive taste of toasted, full-flavored walnuts. Although it is delicate, it should be used in moderation because of its strength of flavor. Refrigerate shortly after opening to retain the flavor. Walnut oil is available in specialty stores.

VINEGARS

Nowhere are the changing cooking habits of Californians more evident than at the vinegar counter of our local markets. Ten years ago, there were two or three types of vinegar; today, there are almost endless possibilities.

BALSAMIC VINEGAR. This wine vinegar, often used in California cooking, is an imported one. It is produced in Italy from special grapes with a high sugar content and is aged for many years in kegs of juniper, mulberry, and chestnut wood. This brings out its delicate and gently perfumed flavor. It has a dark brownish-red color and is slightly thicker than the usual vinegar. Balsamic vinegar is used in salad dressings and can be used as well in sauces or as a flavor enhancer for vegetables.

RASPBERRY VINEGAR. Originally influenced by France's raspberry vinegars, Californians have created a number of their own brands. This type of vinegar can be used in salad dressings, with vegetables, and in sauces for fish and chicken. Because of its intense taste and fragrance, it should be used sparingly.

RICE WINE VINEGAR. A Japanese vinegar that is naturally sweet and mild, it may be found either in the vinegar section or in the Asian specialty-food section of supermarkets. It is delicious in salad dressings, in marinades, or as a seasoning agent with vegetables.

WINE VINEGAR. This type of vinegar is made by fermenting wine until it becomes acidic. Varieties include those made from red wine, from white wine, and from sherry. California produces its own special wine vinegars from Chardonnay (white wine vinegar) and Cabernet Sauvignon (red wine vinegar) grapes.

MUSTARDS

As a seasoning agent in cooking, mustard's versatility is unmatched. It can be added to a dip, sauce, salad dressing, or marinade, or used as a coating for meat, fish, or chicken. As a condiment, mustard is a good partner for cheeses, pâtés, meats, chicken, breads, and vegetables.

As with vinegars, there is a new awareness of the possibilities that mustards offer. The garden-variety American standbys have now been replaced with exotic mustards, such as chutney mustard and white wine mustard laced with basil and olives. Every mustard company has its own coveted recipe. The basic formula mixes sieved and milled mustard seeds with some form of liquid into a pasty consistency. In California cooking, the Dijon-style mustard and grainy mustards are used most frequently.

DIJON MUSTARD. This mustard is made by mixing ground mustard seeds, white wine, the sour juice of freshly squeezed green grapes, vinegar, and spices. Typically, "flavored" mustards are Dijon-style mustards with herbs or other flavorings added. Some of the more common types are tarragon, green peppercorn, shallot, and lemon. These mustards are delicious as condiments or as seasonings. You can create your own variation by selecting an herb or another particular flavor and adding it to unflavored Dijon-style mustard.

GRAINY MUSTARDS. Grainy mustards are of ancient origin. The hull of the mustard seed is not removed, so that a coarse texture is retained. The taste is quite predominant, as the entire hull contains a strong enzyme that, when released, makes the flavor more piquant. Grainy mustards vary in strength, depending on whether or not the seeds have been soaked in vinegar. This type of mustard is an excellent accompaniment to meats, chicken, and fish, as well as a flavor and texture enhancer in cooking.

Nuts

HAZELNUT. Also called filberts, hazelnuts are used often, although the United States produces only a small crop. The brown nuts are round or oval, with a flat end that corresponds to the spot where they were fastened to the tree. The meat of the hazelnut is sweet, firm, and quite distinctive. It is used in salads, with vegetables, and in desserts.

PINE NUT. Although pine nuts are grown in several European countries and in South America, they also grow well in the Southwest. Those grown here are smaller than their European or South American counterparts. The pine nuts (also called Indian nuts or piñons) have a cream color and a rich nutty taste when toasted. They add a unique flavor to many California-style dishes and are called for in salads, rice, and other grain dishes. Pine nuts may be more difficult to find than other types of nuts, so check with your specialty food store if they aren't in the supermarket. Be sure to use pine nuts fresh, as they become stale faster than other nuts.

PISTACHIO. California is the chief domestic supplier of pistachios. The natural color of the shell is a grayish white, and they may be found at your market in the pure form. Sometimes you will find pistachios dyed red, but this is purely cosmetic and not preferred. Californians love pistachios and use them primarily as garnishes for vegetable and rice dishes and in desserts. Use raw, unsalted shelled pistachios for the recipes in this book.

Vegetables

ARUGULA. Arugula, or rocket, is a leafy green plant from the mustard family and is considered an Italian salad green. It has a meaty, slightly bitter and peppery taste that mixes well with other salad greens. Arugula leaves are sold with roots on. This is a very perishable item, so use it as soon as possible after purchase. Substitute dandelion greens or other bitter leafy greens if arugula is not available.

ARTICHOKE. Ninety percent of the artichokes grown in America come from Castroville, California, sometimes called "The Artichoke Capital of the World." Located in the central coastal valley, Castroville has the rich soil, mild, damp winters, moderate summers, and coastal fog that artichokes thrive upon.

Green globe is the type of artichoke grown in California. It is tender, has compact leaves, and comes in several different sizes. A common misconception is that larger artichokes are better for most cooking.

Baby green globe artichokes are about 3 inches in height and extremely delicate. The peak season for artichokes is in the spring, although they are available almost year round.

BELGIAN ENDIVE. Belgian endive has been available in America for many years and has become a common type of green in California salads. Fresh endive is available September through May, with the height of the season being December through February. When buying endive look for stalks that are creamy white, shading to pale yellow at the tips. The stalks should be very tight and the leaves free of blemishes.

To prepare endive, always wipe leaves carefully. Do not wash, or leaves will turn brown. Endive is also good as a dipping vegetable in a raw vegetable basket (see Garden Vegetable Basket, page 12).

CELERY ROOT. Celery root, or celeriac, is a winter vegetable that is common in Europe and is gaining popularity in the United States. Its season is October through April. Look for a medium-size firm brownish root with fresh green tops. Avoid the larger roots, which may have soft centers. Celery root may be shredded and mixed with mayonnaise for a salad, or cooked and used as a vegetable puree base for Celery Root Terrine (page 22).

CHILE PEPPERS

Because of the significant Mexican influence on California cooking, chiles are an important fresh ingredient. Chiles are used in many unusual combinations, such as Ancho Chile Butter or Veal and Chicken Sausages with Chiles and Cilantro. They are used to accentuate food, not to overpower it.

FRESH CHILES. Mild California chiles, also called Anaheim chiles or mild New Mexico chiles, are bright green, 4 to 8 inches long, and are widely available fresh during the summer and fall months. These mild green chiles are also canned in whole or diced form. The poblano chile, a darker green and richer-tasting chile, is sometimes available fresh but is mostly purchased in dried form. Small jalapeño chiles are bright to dark green and extremely hot. They are approximately 2 inches long and ¾ inch wide and are available in supermarkets nationally. Canned jalapeños may be used when fresh ones are unavailable. Serrano chiles are slightly smaller than the jalapeño. These bright green chiles that turn red as they ripen are excellent, with a rich and very hot taste. Both the jalapeño and Serrano chile may be used when hot chiles are recommended in a recipe.

To peel and seed fresh chiles, place on broiler pan and broil approximately 6 inches from heat until blackened on all sides. Use tongs to turn. Put chiles in a plastic bag and close tightly. Let rest 10 minutes. Remove from the bag and drain. Core chiles and peel off skin, using your fingertips. Make a slit in each chile, open it up, and scrape off seeds and ribs.

When working with chiles always wear rubber or latex gloves and wash the cutting surface and knife immediately afterward. Some people are extremely sensitive to chiles and will feel a burning sensation on their skin after direct contact with them.

DRIED CHILES. Ancho chiles are large and have a wrinkled appearance, a triangular shape, and a mahogany red color. They are moderately hot. They are the dried form of the poblano chile and are available in Mexican specialty stores or in the specialty departments of supermarkets, labeled "ancho chiles." They are sometimes mistakenly labeled "pasilla chiles." The real pasilla chile is black, long, and thin and is sometimes labeled "chile negro."

CRUSHED RED PEPPER. Used as a seasoning agent in various recipes, this is a hot dry pepper that has been crushed with the seeds included, so that the final product is very hot—use it sparingly.

CHILE PASTE WITH GARLIC. A thin paste made up of hot red chiles, garlic, and salt, it is used in Asian-influenced recipes to add a spicy taste. It is available in the specialty department of your supermarket or at Asian grocery stores.

EUROPEAN CUCUMBER. This is a cucumber that has been hydroponically grown in a greenhouse. It is much longer than a regular cucumber. Although more expensive than field cucumbers, there is no waste, as they are seedless and do not require peeling. They are available year-round and uniformly packaged. Keep them in their tight plastic wrapper in the refrigerator. Use in salads or soups, or sauté them briefly.

FENNEL. Sometimes called anise or finocchio, fennel is similar in appearance to celery but has a faint licorice flavor. Fennel is at the height of its season in late fall and remains available throughout the winter months. The stalk should be fresh, crisp, and solid. The feathery leaves on the stalks are excellent as a garnish and for flavoring soups or salads.

The fennel bulb can be sliced and eaten raw, or it can be braised, steamed, or cooked in any other way that is appropriate for celery. Cut the stalks off about 2 inches from the fennel bulb and use only the bulb in cooking.

FINNISH POTATOES. These are yellow, all-purpose potatoes used often in California cooking and are suitable for baking, boiling, frying, mashing, and salads. Growers on the West Coast are conscious of the large demand and have increased their production to meet it. Their flesh has an attractive light golden color that gives the appearance of having already been buttered. As a result they are sometimes called butter potatoes. This type of potato can be used in any recipe that calls for white potatoes.

FRENCH GREEN BEANS (HARICOTS VERTS). This thin, delicious green bean was developed by a Southern California produce distributing company and is now widely available in the United States. Although much of the crop goes to restaurateurs, these beans can be found in specialty markets. Their major advantage is their delicate taste and small size. Haricots verts are available from March through October.

To prepare them for cooking, remove the ends. They cook very quickly and should be slightly crisp. When unavailable, large Kentucky or other green beans can be sliced and julienned to approximate French green beans in size.

GARLIC. Available year-round, garlic is used in great quantities in California cooking, both raw and cooked. It has been growing in California for only sixty years; before that it was imported from Italy. Gilroy, California, near the Salinas Valley, has been called "The Garlic Capital of the World." When the climate in Gilroy was discovered to produce high-quality garlic, a thriving industry soon became established. Garlic is also grown in the Imperial Valley and San Joaquin Valley regions of California.

Many supermarkets sell garlic in small packages so that you cannot touch it. This makes it more difficult to test for freshness and can usually be taken as a bad omen. Fresh garlic should be creamy white or have a purplish red cast and should be plump and firm, with its paperlike covering attached rather than shriveled. It should be stored in a cool, dry place with adequate ventilation. Refrigeration is not recommended.

Another type of garlic that has been introduced in California is called elephant garlic, so named because of the huge size of its cloves. It is used somewhat differently from regular garlic. Its flavor is milder, and it can be thinly sliced and eaten raw. Elephant garlic should be stored in a place with good ventilation, not refrigerated. It is more difficult to find than regular garlic but well worth trying, when available. Use one large clove of elephant garlic to equal one medium clove of regular garlic, as it is much milder.

JAPANESE EGGPLANT. Available year-round, with spring and summer being the height of their season, Japanese eggplants have the advantage of being small enough for individual servings (one Japanese eggplant serves one or two). Its flavor is similar to but more delicate than that of a large eggplant.

Japanese eggplant is usually cut in half for cooking, and it is not necessary to peel it since the skin adds color. Large eggplants may be substituted in recipes calling for Japanese eggplants. Cut the large ones into ¾-inch slices when recipes call for halved Japanese eggplants.

JERUSALEM ARTICHOKE. Sometimes referred to as sunchokes, Jerusalem artichokes are not true artichokes; rather, they are a member of the sunflower family. These small, round, elongated tubers weigh from 3 to 4 ounces apiece. They are available most of the year. Look for firm brown ones for the best quality. Jerusalem artichokes are delicious raw or cooked. It is not necessary to peel them before slicing or baking.

JICAMA. Also known as yam bean root, jicama is a Mexican vegetable used often in California cooking. It is a large brown-skinned tuber that resembles a giant turnip or large rutabaga. A whole jicama weighs between 1 and 6 pounds. The larger ones tend to be woody. Jicama is white, mild, juicy, and crisp inside, but the peel is inedible. Choose jicama that is firm to the touch, blemish-free, and well formed. Fresh jicama is available from November to June.

Jicama can be prepared by boiling, steaming, or frying. It can be substituted raw in Asian dishes calling for water chestnuts, in which case the jicama should be added at the last minute. Overcooking this vegetable results in a mushy consistency.

LETTUCE

BOSTON LETTUCE. This is a green, delicate-flavored lettuce with tender loose leaves and a pale-colored heart. The center should be hard and full, the outside leaves a very dark green—not at all yellowish.

LIMESTONE LETTUCE. A type of butter lettuce, limestone is often called Bibb lettuce. The field variety is known as Kentucky limestone. Limestone is grown hydroponically in Southern California and has become nationally available year-round because of its successful adaptation to indoor agriculture. It is soft and fragile in texture and has spongy leaves with a delicate, sweet, buttery flavor. The heads never become solid, and there is no waste. Substitute butter lettuce if limestone is not available.

MUSHROOMS

There are many types of mushrooms now available in California other than the commonly cultivated white mushrooms (also known as button mushrooms). When selecting fresh mushrooms for a particular recipe, vary your usage according to season, availability, and personal preference. Choose those that are unblemished. A mushroom brush is useful for cleaning them. If substituting dry mushrooms, soak them in warm water, squeeze them dry, and proceed with the recipe.

Wild mushrooms have become increasingly available to the consumer. Make sure that the store you buy them from uses a reliable mycologist to ensure that none of their mushrooms are poisonous.

CÈPES, OR PORCINI. These are the French and Italian names for the same mushroom. The Latin name is Boletus edulis. Available fresh in the fall, they may also be dried and still hold their flavor well. The dried porcini imported from Italy are particularly good. Cèpes can replace cultivated mushrooms, with superior results, in almost every recipe that calls for sautéed mushrooms.

CHANTERELLES. These mushrooms are a wild, reddish-yellow French variety sometimes called vase-shaped mushrooms. They are available from October through the winter. These mushrooms are collected by mushroom harvesters and then sold to restaurants, markets, and distributors. When the season ends in California, the Pacific Northwest continues to supply them.

ENOKI. Japanese enoki mushrooms are also known as winter mushrooms. They are being cultivated locally with great success. They have long stems with a small, round cap at the end and are slightly sweet and spongy. When purchasing enoki, make sure there is no condensation in the package, as this indicates they are past their prime. They are used raw or sautéed quickly.

MORELS. Fresh morels are now available from Oregon in the spring months. These have brownish spongelike caps and an intense richness of flavor that is hard to equal. You may substitute dried morels when they are unavailable fresh. If you are using dried morels, soak them in warm water until hydrated, then cook with Madeira or port until tender.

OYSTER MUSHROOMS. Available year-round and cultivated commercially in California, the shimeji, or oyster tree mushroom, is sometimes referred to as "the shellfish of the forest" because of its taste and shape. It has a creamy white color and can be used in sautés, stews, or soups.

SHIITAKE. The dark brown shiitake mushroom, common to Japanese and Chinese cuisines, is an Oriental mushroom that has become important in California cooking. Formerly available only in dried form imported from Japan or China, shiitake mushrooms are now cultivated in California commercially and are available fresh almost year-round.

WHITE (BUTTON) MUSHROOMS. Try to buy mushrooms that are not packed in cellophane-covered boxes, so that you can verify that the tops are tightly closed around the stems. Avoid mushrooms with a spongy texture. Keep them in a brown paper bag in the refrigerator so they can breathe. Cultivated button mushrooms are used both raw and cooked.

PEAS. Two varieties of peas are most popular in California cooking.

SNOW PEAS. Also called sugar peas, snow peas have flat pods and are bright green. They are available year-round. As with sugar snap peas, the whole pod is edible. Remove the tips and string along their edge before cooking. The best way to cook them is by stir-frying. Cook briefly, or they will become mushy. Substitute sugar snap peas if snow peas are not available.

SUGAR SNAP PEAS. Fatter than the snow pea, the sugar snap pea is extremely sweet and crunchy and is about 3 inches long. When buying sugar snap peas, look for crisp, bright green pods; avoid any yellowish ones. It is necessary to remove the tips and string along their edge before cooking. This vegetable is either eaten raw or quickly steamed, sautéed, or blanched. Sugar snap peas are only sporadically available, and when they are not, snow peas may be substituted.

RADICCHIO This salad ingredient (pronounced ra-dée-kee-o) is shaped somewhat like a small cabbage, but it has tender red leaves (slightly firmer than those of Boston lettuce) with white stalks and veins. Although radicchio is very expensive, a little goes a long way. It is best when mixed with other greens. Radicchio can stand up to a very flavorful dressing because it has a slightly bitter taste. It is still being imported from Italy, but there are efforts under way to grow it in California and throughout the United States. This may lead to production on a commercial scale. Omit radicchio if it is unavailable.

SHALLOTS. The shallot is a cross between onion and garlic. Like garlic, it is divided into cloves, but unlike garlic, it is subtle and sweet in flavor. It is closer to the onion, although much stronger in flavor. Shallots are available year-round. Look for shallots that are firm; those that are slightly shriveled or soft and whose outside layer is coming apart should be discarded. Shallots are used often in salad dressings, sauces, and even as a vegetable.

SWEET PEPPERS. California sweet peppers are most sought after because of their highly desirable size, shape, and color. There are red, green, and golden bell peppers. The red bell pepper is simply a green bell pepper that has matured and changed color. The golden pepper is a different variety, although it is similar in shape and flavor. It is milder than the other types and more easily digested. These peppers add a distinct taste and bright color to many dishes. They are available during much of the year but are at their best in the fall.

The best-quality peppers are well shaped, thick-walled, and firm and have a uniform glossy color. Pale color and softness are signs of immaturity, while sunken spots on the surface indicate that the pepper may be too old.

Pimiento is a variety of sweet pepper available for a short period in the fall. It has a cone shape and is more elongated than the red bell pepper. If it is not available, substitute red bell pepper.

To peel and seed peppers, place them on broiler pan and broil approximately 6 inches from heat until blackened on all sides. Use tongs to turn. Put peppers in a plastic bag and close it tightly. Let peppers rest 10 minutes, remove from bag, and drain. Core and peel off skin using your fingertips. Make a slit in each pepper, open it up, and scrape off seeds and ribs.

wine glossary

These wine terms and descriptions are provided to aid in your understanding of the nature of California wines and their characteristics.

ACIDITY. The quality of natural fruit acids (mostly tartaric acid) in grapes, which make a wine state lively and fresh, or crisp. California wines, because of the warmer climate, are generally lower in acid than are French wines; the acidity is often adjusted upward in the winemaking, although it still does not attain levels as high as those in French wines.

BIG. Full-bodied (see Body).

BLANC DE BLANCS. Term applied to a white wine (usually sparkling) made entirely from white grapes.

BLANC DE NOIRS. Term applied to a pale pink wine (sometimes sparkling) made from red grapes crushed lightly so only a bit of the skin color remains in the wine.

BLANC DE PINOT NOIR. A pale, salmon pink wine made from the red Pinot Noir grapes by pressing the juice off the skins and fermenting the slightly colored juice in the manner of white wines. Blanc de Pinot Noirs, usually dry and light-bodied, have delicate flavors that are nonetheless unaffected by strongly spiced dishes; these wines go equally well with fish (especially salmon), poultry, and meats.

BODY. The sensation in the mouth of weightiness of alcohol and density of flavor. The degree of body generally corresponds to percentage of alcohol in the wine. Hence, a light or light-bodied wine usually contains less than 11.5 percent alcohol; a medium-bodied wine is usually of 11.5 to 13 percent alcohol; and a big, or full-bodied, wine is one of 13 to 14.5 percent alcohol.

BUTTERY. See Chardonnay.

CABERNET SAUVIGNON. The red wine grape that makes what are generally California's best red wines (and the red wines of the Médoc in Bordeaux). Tannic when young, medium- to full-bodied, this grape generally requires oak aging and about four years of age after the vintage year to soften into drinkability. Its aroma and flavors are often likened to those of black currants. In California versions, it has hints of olives, bell pepper, and eucalyptus. Sometimes blended with Merlot to soften the flavors, it is served with grilled beef, lamb, duck, squab, and cheeses.

CHARDONNAY. The grape of California's best white wines and of the white wines of Burgundy, in France. Ranging from medium to very full in body, they are often given oak aging to enhance their rich, elegant flavors. The creamy, oak-tinged flavor is often described as buttery. The biggest California versions have the depth and complexity of fine red wines. Chardonnay's usual place is with seafood, poultry of all sorts, and pork.

CHENIN BLANC. A soft, light- to medium-bodied gently fruity white wine, made in dry to slightly sweet versions. Their simple flavors are good for light meals and picnics.

CRISPY. See Acidity.

DRY. The opposite of sweet, a descriptive term for wines that have no perceptible sweetness, although a dry wine can nonetheless be fruity at the same time. (Also see Sweet.)

FRUITY. A descriptive term for wines with a prominent flavor of the fresh grapes from which they were made, a characteristic that is independent of the wine's sweetness or dryness. The fruitiness of California wines is accentuated by the cool fermentation techniques that enhance this quality in wine.

FUMÉ BLANC. The name often used for the lightest, crispest, and driest versions of wines made from the Sauvignon Blanc grape. Fumé Blancs are lively and refreshing, and their "grassy," or herbaceous, scent and flavor make them good accompaniments to delicate seafoods or simple grilled poultry when a crisp, rather dry wine is desired.

GAMAY. A grape that makes a soft, fairly fruity, gentle, and somewhat simple red wine. Originally from the Beaujolais region of France, the grape makes a coarser, heavier wine than in France, but it can be enjoyable slightly chilled with hearty casual meals.

GEWÜRZTRAMINER. A German-Alsatian grape that makes a very fruity, distinctively spicy-flavored white wine, usually semidry to sweet in California. Gewürztraminer accompanies few foods well—salmon and pork are notable exceptions—but it has a small, dedicated following among wine drinkers.

LIGHT. See Body.

MERLOT. The predominant red wine grape of the Saint-Emilion district of Bordeaux, it is grown in California primarily for blending with Cabernet Sauvignon, since it considerably softens that wine. Some Merlot is bottled by itself or with a bit of Cabernet added to it for firmness. Merlot has a softly grapy, somewhat herbaceous aroma and flavor. It is served with red meats and poultry.

OAKY. Descriptive term for wines that carry the noticeable aroma and flavor of the oak barrels they were aged in. The smoky vanilla flavor, to be found in red as well as white wines, works especially well with grilled dishes and butter sauces.

PETITE SIRAH. Red wine grape, actually a cousin of the Petit Syrah of the Rhône in France, which makes a darkly colored, solidly flavored but somewhat coarse red wine in California. Though they can accompany hearty country-style stews, their best use is in cooking, where their strength and color add much to sauces and marinades.

PINOT NOIR. A red wine grape that, because of its difficulties in growing, the fermenting is less frequently successful in California than in its home territory of Burgundy, in France. It is softer and more gentle in flavor than Cabernet Sauvignon. When Pinot Noir is good in California, it is lovely and velvety; when it is not good, it is thin and "weedy" in flavor. Perhaps the most susceptible grape in California to variations in weather from year to year, it tends to be completely successful only about three years out of every ten—but the successful wines can be marvelous. Pinot Noir is served with red meats and poultry.

RIESLING. The German name for what is often labeled White Riesling or Johannisberg Riesling in California, although the simpler name is coming into more frequent use. A grape that makes a delicately fruity floral wine, usually semidry to sweet. It can be served with seafood or pork dishes with fruit sauces; but it is usually best with simple fruit desserts. Some are made as very sweet "late harvest" dessert wines.

SAUVIGNON BLANC. A white wine grape that makes wines with two different names in California; also see Fumé Blanc. The versions labeled Sauvignon Blanc are generally made from grapes picked a bit more ripe than those for Fumé Blanc. Consequently, they are medium- rather than light-bodied and somewhat fruity, and lend themselves well to oak aging. The herbaceous quality of Fumé Blancs is still present, although less pronounced. They are increasingly being blended with the Sémillon grape, which evens out their otherwise awkward balance and aging patterns. The best Sauvignon Blancs can be very good and can be served with seafood with cream or butter sauces and with dishes strongly flavored by chiles and cilantro.

SWEET. Used to describe wines with perceptible residual sugar left after fermentation (not to be confused with fruity). Wines exist in all gradations, most from completely dry to very sweet. Most table wines are dry (less than 0.5 percent residual sugar). Semidry is a purposely vague term generally applied to wines that range from 0.5 percent to 2 percent residual sugar (although many people would even call these sweet). When the residual sugar is over 2 percent, most people would readily agree that the wine is sweet. "Late harvest" sweet wines usually list the residual sugar content on the label in fine print.

TANNIN. Tannic acid is the astringent flavor component (also found in tea) that comes from grape skins and thus is found in red wines. An antioxidant and preservative, its presence both enables and requires many red wines to be aged for several years, until the tannin softens and contributes its unique velvety flavor to the wines.

VIN GRIS. Literally "gray wine," an alternate name for Blanc de Pinot Noir.

VINTAGE. The year in which the grapes were picked and the wine was made from them. The particular balance of flavors in wines is a direct result of the weather during the growing season, and each year's wines are a bit different from those of any other; hence, vintage dates are often listed on wine labels. In general, hotter years yield full-flavored wines, and cooler years yield lighter, more delicate wines. However, every aspect of the weather patterns of a growing season contributes in some way to the overall characteristics of the wines of that year.

ZINFANDEL. A red wine grape that makes anything from a light, zesty, fruity wine to a big, powerful, densely flavored wine. A good version has a distinct berrylike aroma and flavor. Zinfandel is best with spicy foods, Italian foods in particular; it is ideal with dishes with plenty of cheese or tomatoes (or both). It works well with lamb, duck, and other poultry, less successfully with beef.

notes

notes

notes

notes

index

C

table of equivalents

The exact equivalents in the following tables have been rounded for convenience.

ABBREVIATIONS

US/UK	METRIC
oz=ounce	g=gram
lb=pound	kg=kilogram
in=inch	mm=millimeter
ft=foot	cm=centimeter
tbl=tablespoon	ml=milliliter
fl oz=fluid ounce	l=liter
qt=quart	

OVEN TEMPERATURES

FAHRENHEIT	CELSIUS	GAS
250	120	½
275	140	1
300	150	2
325	160	3
350	180	4
375	190	5
400	200	6
425	220	7
450	230	8
475	240	9
500	260	10

LIQUIDS

US	METRIC	UK
2 tbl	30 ml	1 fl oz
¼ cup	60 ml	2 fl oz
⅓ cup	80 ml	3 fl oz
½ cup	125 ml	4 fl oz
⅔ cup	160 ml	5 fl oz
¾ cup	180 ml	6 fl oz
1 cup	250 ml	8 fl oz
1½ cups	375 ml	12 fl oz
2 cups	500 ml	16 fl oz

WEIGHTS

US/UK	METRIC
1 oz	30 g
2 oz	60 g
3 oz	90 g
4 oz (¼ lb)	125g
5 oz (⅓ lb)	155 g
6 oz	185 g
7 oz	220 g
8 oz (½ lb)	250 g
10 oz	315 g
12 oz (¾ lb)	375 g
14 oz	440 g
16 oz (1 lb)	500 g
1½ lbs	750 g
2 lbs	1 kg
3 lbs	1.5 kg

LENGTH MEASURES

⅛ in	3 mm
¼ in	6 mm
½ in	12 mm
1 in	2.5 cm
2 in	5 cm
3 in	7.5 cm
4 in	10 cm
5 in	13 cm
6 in	15 cm
7 in	18 cm
8 in	20 cm
9 in	23 cm
10 in	25 cm
11 in	28 cm
12 in/1 ft	30 cm

EQUIVALENTS FOR COMMONLY USED INGREDIENTS

ALL-PURPOSE (PLAIN) FLOUR/DRIED BREAD CRUMBS/CHOPPED NUTS

¼ cup	1 oz	30 g
⅓ cup	1½ oz	45 g
½ cup	2 oz	60 g
¾ cup	3 oz	90 g
1 cup	4 oz	125 g
1½ cups	6 oz	185 g
2 cups	8 oz	250 g
3 tbl	1 oz	30 g

WHOLE-WHEAT (WHOLE MEAL) FLOUR

½ cup	2 oz	60 g
⅔ cup	3 oz	90 g
1 cup	4 oz	125 g
1¼ cups	5 oz	155 g
1⅔ cups	7 oz	210 g
1¾ cups	8 oz	250 g

BROWN SUGAR

¼ cup	1½ oz	45 g
½ cup	3 oz	90 g
¾ cup	4 oz	125 g
1 cup	5 ½ oz	170 g
1½ cups	8 oz	250 g
2 cups	10 oz	315 g

WHITE SUGAR

¼ cup	2 oz	60 g
⅓ cup	3 oz	90 g
½ cup	4 oz	125 g
¾ cup	6 oz	185 g
1 cup	8 oz	250 g
1½ cups	12 oz	375 g
2 cups	1 lb	500 g

RAISINS/CURRANTS/SEMOLINA

¼ cup	1 oz	30 g
⅓ cup	2 oz	60 g
½ cup	3 oz	90 g
¾ cup	4 oz	125 g
1 cup	5 oz	155 g

LONG-GRAIN RICE/CORNMEAL

⅓ cup	2 oz	60 g
½ cup	2½ oz	75 g
¾ cup	4 oz	125 g
1 cup	5 oz	155 g
1½ cups	8 oz	250 g

DRIED BEANS

¼ cup	1½ oz	45 g
⅓ cup	2 oz	60 g
½ cup	3 oz	90 g
¾ cup	5 oz	155 g
1 cup	6 oz	185 g
1¼ cups	8 oz	250 g
1½ cups	12 oz	375 g

ROLLED OATS

⅓ cup	1 oz	30 g
⅔ cup	2 oz	60 g
1 cup	3 oz	90 g
1½ cups	4 oz	125 g
2 cups	5 oz	155 g

JAM/HONEY

2 tbl	2 oz	60 g
¼ cup	3 oz	90 g
½ cup	5 oz	155 g
¾ cup	8 oz	250 g
1 cup	11 oz	345 g

GRATED PARMESAN/ROMANO CHEESE

¼ cup	1 oz	30 g
½ cup	2 oz	60 g
¾ cup	3 oz	90 g
1 cup	4 oz	125 g
1⅓ cups	5 oz	155 g
2 cups	7 oz	220 g